The Pearson
Custom Program for

Pearson Learning Solutions

New York   Boston   San Francisco
London   Toronto   Sydney   Tokyo   Singapore   Madrid
Mexico City   Munich   Paris   Cape Town   Hong Kong   Montreal

Senior Vice President, Editorial and Marketing: Patrick F. Boles
Editor: Ana Díaz-Caneja
Development Editor: Christina Martin
Operations Manager: Eric M. Kenney
Production Manager: Jennifer Berry
Art Director: Renée Sartell
Cover Designers: Blair Brown and Kristen Kiley

Cover Art: Jerry Driendl/Getty Images, Inc.; Steve Bloom/Getty Images, Inc.; "Cheetah" courtesy of Marvin Mattelson/Getty Images; "Tabs" courtesy of Andrey Prokhorov/iStockphoto; "Open Doors" courtesy of Spectral-Design/iStockphoto; "Compass" courtesy of Laurent Hamels/Getty Images; "Fortune Teller" courtesy of Ingvald Kaldhussaeter/iStockphoto; "Ladder of Success" courtesy of iStockphoto; "Global Communication in Blue" courtesy of iStockphoto.

This special edition published in cooperation with Pearson Learning Solutions.

Printed in the United States of America.

Please visit our web site at *www.pearsoncustom.com/custom-library/custom-phit*.

Attention bookstores: For permission to return any unsold stock, contact us at *pe-uscustomreturns@pearson.com*.

Pearson Learning Solutions, 501 Boylston Street, Suite 900, Boston, MA 02116
A Pearson Education Company
www.pearsoned.com

ISBN 10: 1-256-03930-6
ISBN 13: 978-1-256-03930-3

Contents

looking at computers:

understanding the parts

From Chapter 2 of *Technology in Action Complete,* Eighth Edition, Alan Evans, Kendall Martin, Mary Anne Poatsy.

looking at computers

understanding the parts

objectives

objectives

After reading this chapter, you should be able to answer the following questions:

1. What exactly is a computer, and what are its four main functions?
2. What is the difference between data and information?
3. What are bits and bytes, and how are they measured?
4. What devices do I use to get data into the computer?
5. What devices do I use to get information out of the computer?
6. What's on the motherboard?
7. Where are information and programs stored?
8. How are devices connected to the computer?
9. How do I set up my computer to avoid strain and injury?

multimedia resources

 Active Helpdesk

- Understanding Bits and Bytes
- Using Input Devices
- Using Output Devices
- Exploring Storage Devices and Ports

 Sound Bytes

- Binary Numbers Interactive
- Tablet and Notebook Tour
- Virtual Computer Tour
- Port Tour: How Do I Hook It Up?
- Healthy Computing

 Companion Website

The Companion Website includes a variety of additional materials to help you review and learn more about the topics in this chapter. Go to: *pearsonhighered.com/techinaction*

how cool is *this?*

If you have ever thought about **customizing** the layout of your **keyboard**, this Luxeed Dynamic Pixel LED Keyboard is the one for you. If you're a gamer, you can program specific keys to control your game and to **glow** with different colors that indicate each key **action**. If you're not a gamer but just would like to add a bit of fun to your otherwise dull keyboard, you can **animate** colored scenarios to "play" on the keys, or create an **illuminated** pattern or design. With 430 LEDs, the Luxeed is capable of individually lighting each key in your choice of color.

The keyboard comes in either black or white. The keys of the white keyboard light up more brightly and have a semitransparent look. The keys of the black keyboard can be set so just the letters light up.

Understanding Your Computer

You can see why becoming computer literate is very important. But where do you start? You've no doubt gleaned some knowledge about computers just from being a member of society. However, although you have undoubtedly used a computer before, do you really understand how it works, what all its parts are, and what these parts do? In this section, we discuss what a computer does and how its functions make it such a useful machine.

Computers Are Data Processing Devices

Strictly defined, a **computer** is a data processing device that performs four major functions:

1. It *gathers* data, or allows users to input data.

2. It *processes* that data into information.

3. It *outputs* data and information.

4. It *stores* data and information.

What is the difference between data and information? People often use the terms *data* and *information* interchangeably. Although they may mean the same thing in a simple conversation, the actual distinction between data and information is an important one.

In computer terms, **data** is a representation of a fact, a figure, or an idea. Data can be a number, a word, a picture, or even a recording of sound. For example, the number 7135553297 and the names Zoe and Richardson are pieces of data. Alone, these pieces of data probably mean little to you. **Information** is data that has been organized or presented in a meaningful fashion. When your computer provides you with a contact listing that indicates Zoe Richardson can be reached by phone at (713) 555-3297, then the previous data suddenly becomes useful—that is, it becomes information.

How do computers interact with data and information? Computers are excellent at **processing** (manipulating, calculating, or organizing) data into information. When you first arrived on campus, you probably were directed to a place where you could get an ID card. You most likely provided a clerk with personal data (such as your name and address) that was entered into a computer. The clerk then took your picture with a digital camera (collecting more data). This information was then processed appropriately so that it could be printed on your ID card (see Figure 1). This organized output of data on your ID card is useful information. Finally, the information was probably stored as digital data on the computer for later use.

Bits and Bytes: The Language of Computers

How do computers process data into information? Unlike humans, computers work exclusively with numbers (not words). To process data into information, computers need to work in a language they understand.

SOUND BYTE

Binary Numbers Interactive

This Sound Byte helps remove the mystery surrounding binary numbers. You'll learn about base conversion between decimal, binary, and hexadecimal numbers interactively using colors, sounds, and images.

Figure 1

Computers process data into information.

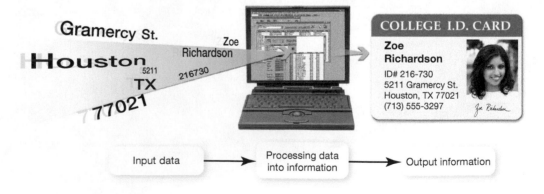

Input data → Processing data into information → Output information

Looking at Computers: Understanding the Parts

This language, called **binary language**, consists of just two digits: 0 and 1. Everything a computer does, such as processing data or printing a report, is broken down into a series of 0s and 1s. Each 0 and 1 is a **binary digit**, or **bit** for short. Eight binary digits (or bits) combine to create one **byte**. In computers, each letter of the alphabet, each number, and each special character (such as the @ sign) consists of a unique combination of eight bits, or a string of eight 0s and 1s. So, for example, in binary (computer) language, the letter K is represented as 01001011. This equals eight bits, or one byte.

What else can bits and bytes be used for? You've probably heard the terms *kilobyte (KB)*, *megabyte (MB)*, and *gigabyte (GB)*. Bits and bytes not only are used as the language that tells the computer what to do but also are what the computer uses to represent the data and information that it inputs and outputs. Word processing files, digital pictures, and even software are represented inside a computer as a series of bits and bytes. These files and applications can be quite large, containing thousands or millions of bytes.

To make it easier to measure the size of these files, we need units of measure larger than a byte. Kilobytes, megabytes, and

gigabytes are therefore simply amounts of bytes. As shown in Figure 2, a **kilobyte (KB)** is approximately 1,000 bytes, a **megabyte (MB)** is about 1 million bytes, a **gigabyte (GB)** is around 1 billion bytes, and a **terabyte (TB)** is around 1 trillion bytes. As our information-processing needs have grown, so too have our storage needs. Today, personal computers store terabytes of data, and many business computers can store up to a petabyte of data. The Google search engine processes more than 1 petabyte of user-generated data per *hour*—that's a lot of bytes!

How does your computer process bits and bytes? Your computer uses a combination of hardware and software to process data into information and enables you to complete tasks such as writing a letter or playing a game. An anonymous

Figure 2 | HOW MUCH IS A BYTE?

Name	Abbreviation	Number of Bytes	Relative Size
Byte	B	1 byte	Can hold one character of data.
Kilobyte	KB	1,024 bytes (2^{10})	Can hold 1,024 characters or about half of a double-spaced typewritten page.
Megabyte	MB	1,048,576 bytes (2^{20} bytes)	Can hold approximately 768 pages of typed text.
Gigabyte	GB	1,073,741,824 bytes (2^{30} bytes)	Approximately 786,432 pages of text; 500 sheets of paper is approximately 2 inches, so this represents a stack of paper 262 feet high.
Terabyte	TB	1,099,511,627,776 bytes (2^{40} bytes)	This represents a stack of typewritten pages almost 51 miles high.
Petabyte	PB	1,125,899,906,842,62 bytes (2^{50} bytes)	The stack of pages is now 52,000 miles high, or approximately one-fourth the distance from the Earth to the moon.
Exabyte	EB	1,152,921,504,606,846,976 bytes (2^{60} bytes)	The stack of pages is now 52 million miles high, or just about twice the distance between the Earth and Venus.
Zettabyte	ZB	1,180,591,620,717,411,303,424 bytes (2^{70} bytes)	The stack of pages is now 52 billion miles high. That's some 20 times the distance between the Earth and Pluto.

Looking at Computers: Understanding the Parts

person once said that hardware is any part of a computer that you can kick when it doesn't work properly. A more formal definition of **hardware** is "any part of the computer you can physically touch." However, a computer needs more than just hardware to work: It also needs some form of software (computer programs). Think of a book without words or a CD without music. Without words or music, these two common items are just shells that hold nothing.

Similarly, a computer without software is a shell full of hardware components that can't do anything. Software is the set of computer programs that enables the hardware to perform different tasks. There are two broad categories of software: application software and system software.

When you think of software, you are most likely thinking of application software. **Application software** is the set of programs you use on a computer to help you carry out tasks such as writing a research paper. If you've ever typed a document, created a spreadsheet, or edited a digital photo, for example, then you've used a form of application software.

System software is the set of programs that enables your computer's hardware devices and application software to work together. The most common type of system software is the **operating system (OS)**—the program that controls the way in which your computer system functions. It manages the hardware of the computer system, such as the monitor and the printer. The operating system also provides a means by which users can interact with the computer. For the rest of this chapter, we'll explore hardware.

Your Computer's Hardware

Are all computers the same?
Considering the amount of amazing things computers can do, they are really quite simple machines. You learned in the previous section that a basic computer system is made up of software and hardware. There are two basic designs of computers: portable and stationary. A **notebook computer** (or laptop computer) is a portable computer that is powered by batteries (or a handy electrical outlet) and has a keyboard, a monitor, and other devices integrated into a single compact case. A **netbook** is a small, lightweight notebook computer that is generally 7 to 10 inches wide and has a longer battery life than a notebook computer. A **tablet PC** is similar to a notebook but features a touch-sensitive screen that can swivel and fold flat (see Figure 14 later in this chapter). Users input data and commands on a tablet PC via a special pen called a *stylus* or with their fingers. A **desktop computer** is intended for use at a single location, and therefore, is stationary. Desktop computers consist of a separate case that houses the main components of the computer plus peripheral devices. A **peripheral device** is a component, such as a monitor or keyboard, that is connected to the computer. An **all-in-one computer** such as the Apple iMac (see Figure 3), the Dell Studio One 19″, or the Gateway One houses not just the computer's processor and memory but also its monitor.

Figure 3

The Apple iMac is an example of an all-in-one computer.

Are there other types of computers besides desktop and notebook computers? Desktop and notebook computers are the computers that you will most likely encounter. Although you may never come into direct contact with the following types of computers, they are still important to our society:

- A **mainframe** is a large, expensive computer that supports hundreds of users simultaneously. Mainframes are often used in insurance companies, for example, where many people are working on similar operations (such as claims processing) all at once. Your college also may use mainframe computers to handle the multitude of processing needs throughout the campus. Mainframes excel at executing many

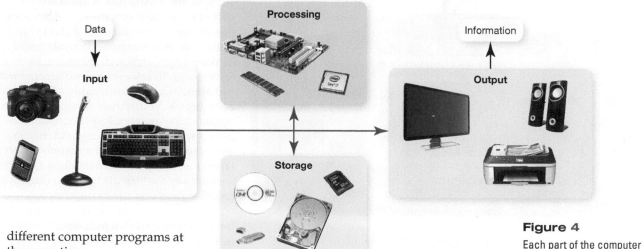

Data

Input

Processing

Storage

Information

Output

Figure 4

Each part of the computer serves a special function.

different computer programs at the same time.

- A **supercomputer** is a specially designed computer that can perform complex calculations extremely rapidly. Supercomputers are used in situations in which complex models requiring intensive mathematical calculations are needed (such as weather forecasting or atomic energy research). The main difference between a supercomputer and a mainframe is that supercomputers are designed to execute a few programs as quickly as possible, whereas mainframes are designed to handle many programs running at the same time but at a slower pace.
- An **embedded computer** is a specially designed computer chip that resides in another device, such as your car or the electronic thermostat in your home. Embedded computers are self-contained computer devices that have their own programming and typically do not receive input from you or interact with other systems.

In the following sections, we look more closely at your computer's hardware. Each part has a specific purpose that coordinates with one of the functions of the computer—input, processing, output, or storage (see Figure 4).

Additional devices, such as modems and routers, help a computer communicate with the Internet and other computers to facilitate the sharing of documents and other resources. We begin our exploration of hardware by looking at your computer's input devices.

Input Devices

An **input device** enables you to enter data (text, images, and sounds) and instructions (user responses and commands) into the computer. The most common input devices are the keyboard and the mouse. A **keyboard** is used to enter typed data and commands, and a **mouse** is used to enter user responses and commands.

There are other input devices as well. Microphones input sounds, and scanners and digital cameras input nondigital text and digital images, respectively. A **stylus** is an input device that looks like a skinny pen but has no ink. You use it like a mouse or pen to tap commands or draw on a screen. Electronic pens are also becoming quite popular and are often used in conjunction with graphics tablets that can translate a user's handwriting into digital input (see Figure 5).

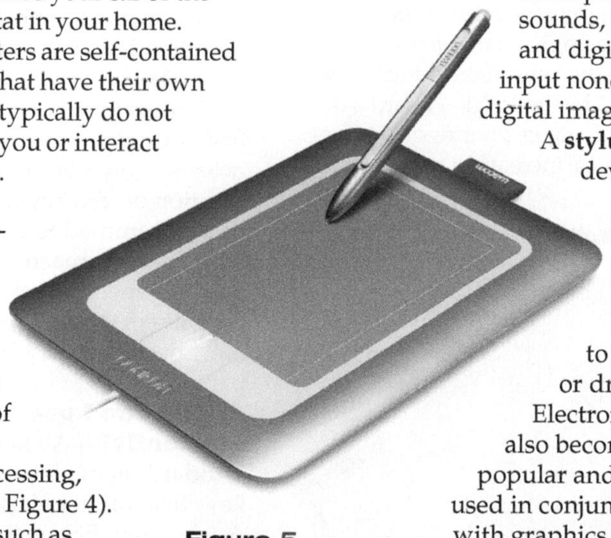

Figure 5

An electronic pen is a type of input device that is used with graphics tablets.

Figure 6
QWERTY keyboard layout.

Keyboards

Aren't all keyboards the same? Most desktop and notebook computers come with a standard **QWERTY keyboard** (see Figure 6). This keyboard layout gets its name from the first six letters in the top-left row of alphabetic keys on the keyboard and is the standard English-language keyboard layout. Over the years, there has been some debate over what is the best keyboard layout. The QWERTY layout was originally designed for typewriters and was meant to slow typists down and prevent typewriter keys from jamming. Although the QWERTY layout is considered inefficient because it slows typing speeds, efforts to change to more efficient layouts, such as that of the Dvorak keyboard, have not been met with much public interest. The Dvorak keyboard is an alternative keyboard layout that puts the most commonly used letters in the English language on "home keys," which are the keys in the middle row of the keyboard. The Dvorak keyboard's design reduces the distance your fingers travel for most keystrokes, increasing typing speed.

How do notebook keyboards differ? To save space and weight, some of the smaller notebook keyboards (14" and under) are more compact than standard desktop keyboards and, therefore, have fewer keys. To retain the same functionality as a standard keyboard, many of the notebook keys have alternate functions. For example, many notebook keyboards do not have a separate numeric keypad. Instead, some letter keys function as number keys when they are pressed in combination with another key such as the function (Fn) key. The keys you use as numeric keys on notebooks have number notations on them so you can tell which keys to use (see Figure 7).

What if the standard keyboard doesn't work for me? Because recent development efforts have focused on reducing the size and weight of notebook computers, the keyboards have had to shrink accordingly. Flexible keyboards are a terrific alternative if you want a full-sized keyboard for your notebook. You can roll one up, fit it in your backpack, and plug it into the USB port when you need to use it. The virtual laser keyboard (see Figure 8a) is about the size of a cellular phone. It projects the image of a keyboard on any surface, and sensors detect the motion of your fingers as you "type" on a desk or other flat surface. Data is transmitted via **Bluetooth** technology, which is a wireless transmission standard that facilitates the connection of electronic computing devices such as cell phones, smartphones, and computers to peripheral devices such as keyboards and headsets.

Gamers love keyboards such as the DX1 from Ergodex (see Figure 8b). These keyboards allow placement of the keys in any position on the keyboard pad. The keys can be programmed to execute individual keystrokes or macros (a series of tasks) to perform specific tasks. This makes it easy for gamers to configure a keyboard in the most desirable way for each game they play.

How can I use my keyboard most efficiently? All keyboards have the standard set of alphabetic and numeric keys that you regularly use when typing. As shown in Figure 9, many keyboards for notebook and desktop computers have additional keys that perform special functions.

Figure 7
On many notebooks, certain letter keys can function as number keys.

Figure 8

(a) The virtual laser keyboard projects the image of a QWERTY keyboard on any surface. Sensors detect typing motions, and data is transmitted to a computing device via Bluetooth technology. (b) The Ergodex DX1 allows keys to be relocated anywhere on the pad and reprogrammed easily, making the keyboard popular with gamers.

Knowing how to use these special keys will help you improve your efficiency:

- The numeric keypad allows you to enter numbers quickly.
- Function keys act as shortcut keys you press to perform special tasks. They are sometimes referred to as the "F" keys because they start with the letter F followed by a number. Each software application has its own set of tasks assigned to various function keys. For example, the F2 key moves text or graphics in Microsoft Word but allows editing of the active cell in Microsoft Excel. Many keys are universal: the F1 key is the Help key in most applications.
- The Control (Ctrl) key is used in combination with other keys to perform shortcuts and special tasks. For example, holding down the Control (Ctrl) key while pressing the B key adds bold formatting to selected text. The Alt key works with other keys to execute additional shortcuts and special tasks. (On Macs, the Control function is the Apple key or Command key, and the Alt function is the Option key.)

Figure 9

Keyboards have a variety of keys that help you work more efficiently.

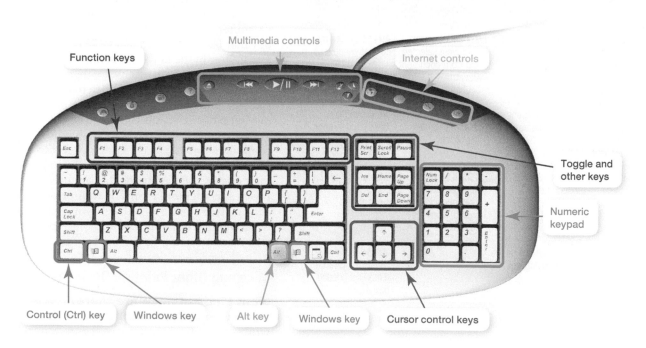

Multimedia controls

Function keys

Internet controls

Toggle and other keys

Numeric keypad

Control (Ctrl) key   Windows key   Alt key   Windows key   Cursor control keys

Looking at Computers: Understanding the Parts

- The Windows key is specific to the Windows operating system. Used alone, it opens the Start menu, although you use it most often in combination with other keys to perform shortcuts. For example, in Windows 7 and Vista, pressing the Windows key plus the M key minimizes all windows, and the Windows key plus the L key locks a computer (a good habit to get into when you use a computer in a group setting such as a business office).

What are some other features on keyboards? Some keyboards (such as the one shown in Figure 9) also include multimedia and Internet keys or buttons that enable you to open a Web browser, view e-mail, access Help features, or control your CD/DVD player. These buttons are not always in the same position on every keyboard, but the symbols on top of the buttons generally help you determine their function. Some desktop keyboards include USB ports

BITS AND BYTES

Keystroke Shortcuts

Did you know that you can combine certain keystrokes to take shortcuts within an application, such as Microsoft Word, or within the operating system itself? The following are a few of the most helpful Windows shortcuts. Use them to make more efficient use of your time. For more shortcuts for Windows-based PCs, visit **support. microsoft.com**. For a list of shortcuts for Macs, see **apple.com/support**.

Text Formatting	File Management	Cut/Copy/ Paste	Windows Controls
CTRL+B Applies (or removes) **bold** formatting to selected text	**CTRL+O** Opens the Open dialog box	**CTRL+X** Cuts (removes) selected text from document and stores in Clipboard	**Alt+F4** Closes the current window
CTRL+I Applies (or removes) *italic* formatting to selected text	**CTRL+N** Opens a new document	**CTRL+C** Copies selected text to Clipboard	**Windows Key+ Tab** Cycles through open programs using Flip 3-D
CTRL+U Applies (or removes) underlining to selected text	**CTRL+S** Saves a document	**CTRL+V** Pastes selected text (previously cut or copied) from Clipboard	**Windows Key+L** Locks the computer
	CTRL+P Opens the Print dialog box		**Windows Key+F** Opens the Search (Find Files) dialog box

to facilitate attaching other devices, such as a mouse or a keyboard.

Another set of controls on standard keyboards are the cursor control keys that move your *cursor* (the flashing I symbol on the monitor that indicates where the next character will be inserted). A **cursor control key** is also known as an *arrow key* because each one is represented by an arrow on standard keyboards. The arrow keys move the cursor one space at a time in a document: up, down, left, or right.

Above the arrow keys, you'll usually find Page Up (PGUP) and Page Down (PGDN) keys that move the cursor up or down one full page or even to the document's beginning (Home), or to the end of a line of text or document (End). The Delete (Del) key allows you to delete characters, and the Insert key allows you to insert or overwrite characters within a document. The Insert key is a *toggle key* because its function changes between one of two options each time you press it: When toggled on, the Insert key inserts new text within a line of existing text. When toggled off, the Insert key replaces (or overwrites) existing characters with new characters as you type. Other toggle keys that switch between an on state and an off state include the Num Lock key and the Caps Lock key.

Are all conventional keyboards connected to the computer via wires? Although most desktop PCs ship with wired keyboards, wireless keyboards are available. Wireless keyboards are powered by batteries. They send data to the computer using a form of wireless technology that uses radio frequency (RF). A radio transmitter in the keyboard sends out radio wave signals that are received either through a small receiving device that is plugged into a USB port or a Bluetooth receiving device that is contained in the system unit. RF keyboards used on home computers can be placed as far as 6 feet to 30 feet from the computer, depending on their quality. RF keyboards that are used in business conference rooms or auditoriums can be placed as far as 100 feet away from the computer, but they are far more expensive than traditional wired keyboards.

Mice and Other Pointing Devices

What kinds of mice are there? The mouse type you're probably most familiar with is the **optical mouse** (see Figure 10a).

An optical mouse uses an internal sensor or laser to detect the mouse's movement. The sensor sends signals to the computer, telling it where to move the pointer on the screen. Optical mice are often preferable to other types of mice because they have fewer moving parts, which lessens the chances that dirt will interfere with the mechanisms or that parts will break down. Optical mice also do not require a mouse pad, though you can still use one to protect your work surface from being scratched. You may still find a mouse at home or in school that has a rollerball on the bottom, which moves when you drag the mouse across a mouse pad. The movement of the rollerball controls the movement of the cursor that appears on the screen.

A **trackball mouse** (see Figure 10b) has the rollerball on top or on the side of the mouse, and you move the ball with your fingers, allowing the mouse to remain stationary. A trackball mouse doesn't demand much wrist motion, so it's considered better for the wrist than an optical mouse. Mice also have two or three buttons that enable you to execute commands and open shortcut menus. (Mice for Macs sometimes have only one button.) Many mice have additional programmable buttons and wheels that let you quickly scroll through documents or Web pages.

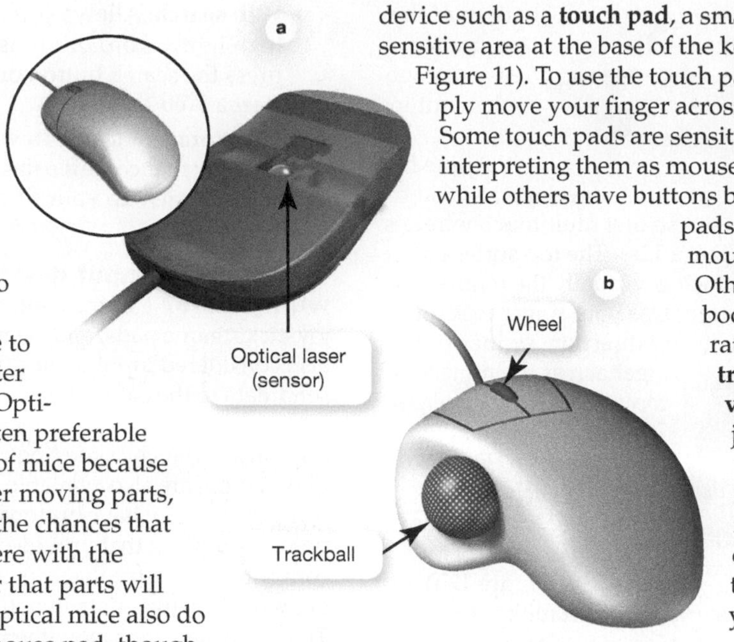

Do notebook computers include a mouse? Most notebooks do not have a mouse. Instead, they have an integrated pointing

a

Optical laser (sensor)

b

Wheel

Trackball

Figure 10

(a) An optical mouse has an optical laser (or sensor) on the bottom that detects its movement. (b) A trackball mouse turns the traditional mouse on its back, allowing you to control the rollerball with your fingers.

device such as a **touch pad**, a small, touch-sensitive area at the base of the keyboard (see Figure 11). To use the touch pad, you simply move your finger across the pad. Some touch pads are sensitive to taps, interpreting them as mouse clicks, while others have buttons beneath the pads to record mouse clicks. Other notebooks incorporate a **trackpoint device**, a small, joystick-like nub that allows you to move the cursor with the tip of your finger.

Are there wireless mice? Just as there are wireless keyboards, there are wireless mice, both optical and trackball. Wireless mice are similar to wireless keyboards in that they use batteries and send data to the computer by radio frequency or Bluetooth technologies. If you have an RF wireless keyboard, then your RF wireless mouse and keyboard usually can share the same RF receiver. Wireless mice for notebooks have their own receivers that often clip into the

Figure 11

Touch pads and trackpoint devices take the place of a mouse on notebook computers.

Trackpoint

Touch pad

Figure 12

(a) The Magic Mouse by Apple has multitouch technology. (b) The MoGo Mouse is a portable mouse that stores and charges in a PC Card slot.

Figure 13

The magnifier is a mouse feature that provides instant magnification of images or text.

bottom of the mouse for easy storage when not in use.

Apple has developed Magic Mouse, the first multitouch wireless mouse (see Figure 12a). The top surface of the mouse, which is virtually the mouse itself, is the button. Use your finger to scroll in any direction, swipe your finger across the mouse to move through Web pages and photos, and tap on the mouse to click and double-click.

Small, compact devices like the MoGo Mouse (see Figure 12b) are designed for portability. The MoGo Mouse fits into a peripheral slot on the side of a notebook; this slot serves to store the mouse, protect it, and charge its batteries all at the same time. The MoGo Mouse is wireless and uses Bluetooth technology to transmit data to the notebook.

What else can I do with my mouse? Manufacturers of mice are constantly releasing new models that allow you to perform useful tasks with a few clicks of the mouse. On some mouse models, Microsoft and Logitech now provide features such as the following:

- **Magnifier:** Pulls up a magnification box that you can drag around the screen to enhance viewing of hard-to-read images (see Figure 13). This feature is often used by people with visual disabilities.
- **Customizable buttons:** Provide extra buttons on the mouse that you can program to perform the functions that you use most often to help you speed through tasks.

- **Web search:** Allows you to quickly highlight a word or phrase and then press the search button on the mouse to start a Web search.
- **File storage:** Includes a wireless USB receiver that contains flash memory to store or back up your files (for example, a USB drive).

What other input devices are used with games? Game controllers such as joysticks, game pads, and steering wheels are also considered input devices because they send data to the computer. Game controllers, which are similar to the devices used on gaming consoles, such as the Xbox 360 and the PlayStation, are also available for use with computers. They have buttons and miniature pointing devices that provide input to the computer. Force-feedback joysticks and steering wheels deliver data in both directions. They translate your movements to the computer and translate its responses into forces on your hands, creating a richer simulated experience. Most game controllers, such as those for Rock Band and the Wii system, are wireless to provide extra mobility.

Touch Screens

How else can I input data and commands? You've seen and used touch-sensitive screens in fast food restaurants, airport check-in kiosks, and ATM machines for quite some time. A **touch screen** is a display screen that responds to commands initiated by a touch with a finger or a stylus. Touch screens are becoming increasingly popular on many computing devices, including desktops, notebooks, smartphones, and portable media players (PMPs). Tablet PCs were one of the first devices with touch-screen capabilities (see Figure 14). Although all tablet PCs have built-in keyboards that allow you to type text just as you would with a normal keyboard, the touch-screen functionality often makes it a better choice when inputting with a keyboard is impractical or

Window provides magnified view

SOUND BYTE
Tablet and Notebook Tour

In this Sound Byte, you'll take a tour of a Tablet PC and a notebook computer, learning about the unique features and ports available on each.

Looking at Computers: Understanding the Parts

Figure 14

Tablet PCs use the finger or a stylus to input data and commands on a touch-screen display that twists and folds flat.

unwieldy. The Apple iPod Touch, iPad, and iPhone all have touch capability, as do portable gaming devices such as the Nintendo DS. Dell and Hewlett Packard have released all-in-one desktop PCs with touch-screen displays.

Tablet PCs, which were developed primarily because many people find it easier to write than to type input into a computer, are expensive compared to conventional notebooks. An alternative is a digital pen like the Dane-Elec Digital Pen (see Figure 15). This pen works in conjunction with a flash drive

Figure 15

The Dane-Elec Digital Pen captures writing and stores it in a flash drive for later transfer to a computer. No typing is required!

(a portable electronic storage device that connects to a USB port on a computer). You can write with the pen on any conventional paper. The pen captures your writing and then wirelessly transmits and stores it in the flash drive. When the flash drive is connected to a computer, you can use software to translate your writing into digital text.

Image Input

How can I input digital images into my computer? Digital cameras, camcorders, and cell phones are common devices for capturing pictures and video, and all of them are considered input devices. Digital cameras and camcorders are usually used in remote settings (away from a computer) to capture images and video for later downloading to the computer. These devices either connect to a computer with a data cable or transmit data wirelessly. Windows automatically recognizes these devices when they are connected to a computer and makes the input of the digital data to the computer simple and easy. Scanners can also input images. They work similar to a photocopy machine, but instead of generating the image on paper, they create a digital image, which can then be printed, saved in storage, or e-mailed.

How do I capture live video from my computer? A **webcam** (see Figure 16) is a small camera that sits on top of a

Figure 16

A webcam is either built into a notebook monitor or placed on top of a monitor.

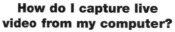

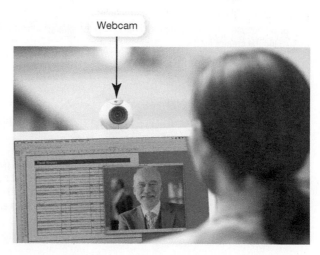

What Is Ethical Computing?

If you were asked to cite an example of unethical behavior while using a computer, you could easily provide an answer. You've probably heard news stories about people using computers to commit such crimes as unleashing viruses or committing identity theft. You may also have read about students who were prosecuted for illegally sharing copyrighted material such as videos. Or perhaps you heard about the case where the school district was monitoring students through notebook computer webcams without the students' knowledge. All of these are examples of unethical behavior while using a computer. However, if you were asked what constitutes *ethical* behavior while using a computer, could you provide an answer just as quickly?

Loosely defined, *ethics* is a system of moral principles, rules, and accepted standards of conduct. So what are the accepted standards of conduct when using computers (see Figure 17)? The Computer Ethics Institute developed the Ten Commandments of Computer Ethics, which is widely cited as a benchmark for companies that are developing computer usage and compliance policies for employees. These guidelines are applicable for schools and students as well. The ethical computing guidelines listed below are based on the Computer Ethics Institute's work.

Ethical Computing Guidelines

1. Avoid causing harm to others when using computers.
2. Do not interfere with other people's efforts at accomplishing work with computers.
3. Resist the temptation to snoop in other people's computer files.
4. Do not use computers to commit theft.
5. Agree not to use computers to promote lies.
6. Do not use software (or make illegal copies for others) without paying the creator for it.

7. Avoid using other people's computer resources without appropriate authorization or proper compensation.
8. Do not claim other people's intellectual output as your own.
9. Consider the social consequences of the products of your computer labor.
10. Only use computers in ways that show consideration and respect for others.

THE CHRISTIAN SCIENCE MONITOR Bennett

How important are ethics in today's society?

Figure 17

Make sure the work you claim as your intellectual output is the product of your intellect alone.

The United States has enacted laws that support some of these guidelines, such as Guideline 6, the breaking of which would violate copyright laws, and Guideline 4, which is enforceable under numerous federal and state larceny laws. Other guidelines, however, require more subtle interpretation as to what behavior is unethical because there are no laws designed to enforce them.

Consider Guideline 7, which covers unauthorized use of resources. The college you attend probably provides computer resources for you to use for coursework. But if the college gives you access to computers and the Internet, is it ethical for you to use those resources to run a business on eBay in between classes or on the weekends? Although it might not be technically illegal, you are tying up computer resources that could be used by other students for their intended purpose: learning and completing coursework. (This behavior also violates Guidelines 2 and 10.)

Using Input Devices

In this Active Helpdesk call, you'll play the role of a helpdesk staffer, fielding calls about different input devices, such as the different mice and keyboards on the market, what wireless input options are available, and how to best use these devices.

computer monitor (connected to the computer by a cable) or is built into a notebook computer. Although some webcams are able to capture still images, they are used mostly for transferring live video directly to a computer. Webcams make it possible to transmit live video over the Web. They are often used to facilitate videoconferencing or calls made with video phones. Videoconferencing technology allows a person sitting at a computer equipped with a web-cam and a microphone to transmit video and audio across the Internet.

Sound Input

Why would I want to input sound to my computer? Equipping your computer to accept sound input opens up a variety of possibilities. You can conduct audio conferences with work colleagues, chat with friends or family over the Internet instead of using a phone, record podcasts, and more. Inputting sound to your computer requires equipping it with a **microphone** or **mic**, a device that allows you to capture sound waves (such as your voice) and transfer them to digital format on your computer. Many notebook computers come with built-in microphones, and some desktop computers come with inexpensive microphones. If you don't have a microphone or you aren't getting the quality you need from your existing microphone, then you probably need to shop for one.

What types of microphones are available? There are several different types of microphones available for a variety of needs. Desktop microphones, which have an attached base that allows them to sit on a flat surface (see Figure 18), are convenient for recording podcasts or in other situations in which you might need your hands to be free. Unidirectional microphones pick up sound from only one direction. These are best used for recording podcasts with a single voice or making phone calls over the Internet with only one person on the sender's end of the call. Omnidirectional microphones pick up sounds from all directions at once. These mics are best for recording more than one

Figure 18

Professional-quality microphones such as the Snowball are essential for producing quality podcasts.

voice, such as during a conference call when you need to pick up the voices of multiple speakers.

Clip-on microphones (also called *lavalier microphones*) are useful in environments such as presentations, where you need to keep your hands free for other activities (such as writing on a white board) or move around the room. Many of these microphones are wireless.

Close-talk microphones, which are usually attached to a headset, facilitate using speech-recognition software, videoconferencing, or making telephone calls. With a microphone attached to a headset, your hands are free to perform other tasks while you speak (such as making notes or referring to paper documents), and the headset allows you to listen as well (such as when making Internet phone calls or playing games online).

What input devices are available for people with disabilities? Many people who have physical challenges use computers often, but they sometimes need special input devices to access them. For visually impaired users, voice recognition is an obvious option. For those users whose visual limitations are less severe, keyboards with larger keys are available. Keyboards that display on a touch screen can make input easier for some individuals. These keyboards are displayed as graphics on the computer monitor. The user presses the keys with a pointing device or simply presses on the touch-screen monitor. There are also keyboards designed for individuals who can only use one hand such as the Maltron keyboard (see Figure 19).

People with motor control issues may have difficulty with pointing devices. To aid such users, special trackballs are available that can easily be manipulated with one finger and can be attached to almost

Figure 19

For people who have physical disabilities, devices such as this keyboard adapt to accommodate special needs. This keyboard is shaped and designed for individuals who can only use one hand.

any surface, including a wheelchair. When arm motion is severely restrained, head-mounted pointing devices can be used. Generally, these involve a camera mounted on the computer monitor and a device attached to the head (often installed in a hat). When the user moves his or her head, the camera detects the movement, which controls the cursor on the screen. In this case, mouse clicks are controlled by a switch that can be manipulated by the user's hands or feet or even by using an instrument that fits into the mouth and senses the user blowing into it.

Output Devices

An **output device** enables you to send processed data out of your computer in the form of text, pictures (graphics), sounds (audio), or video. One common output device is a **monitor** (sometimes referred to as a **display screen**), which displays text, graphics, and video as soft copies (copies you can see only on screen). Another common output device is the **printer**, which creates hard copies (copies you can touch) of text and graphics. Speakers and earphones (or earbuds) are the output devices for sound.

Monitors

What are the different types of monitors? The most common type of monitor is a **liquid crystal display (LCD)** (see Figure 20). An LCD monitor, also called a **flat-panel monitor**, is light and energy efficient. Some newer LCD monitors use light-emitting diode (LED) technology, which is even more energy efficient, and may have better color accuracy and thinner panels than traditional LCD monitors. LCD monitors have replaced the cathode ray tube (CRT) monitor. CRT monitors are difficult to find or buy because they have become **legacy technology**, or computing devices or peripherals that use techniques, parts, and methods from an earlier time that are no longer popular. Although legacy technology may still be functional, it is quickly being replaced by newer technological advances. This doesn't mean that if you have a CRT monitor that is functioning well you should replace it with an LCD monitor. However, when your CRT monitor fails, you will most likely only be able to replace it with an LCD monitor.

How do monitors work? Monitor screens are grids made up of millions of tiny dots, each of which is called a **pixel**. Illuminated pixels create the images you see on your monitor. Each pixel is actually comprised of three subpixels of red, blue, and green, and some newer TVs on the market have added a fourth color: yellow. LCD monitors are made of two or more sheets of material filled with a liquid crystal solution (see Figure 21). A fluorescent panel at the back of the LCD monitor generates light waves. When electric current passes through the liquid crystal solution, the crystals move around and either block the fluorescent light or let the light shine through. This blocking or passing of light by the crystals causes images to form on the screen. The various combinations of red, blue, and green make up the components of color we see on our monitors.

Figure 20

LCDs (flat-panel monitors) save precious desktop space and weigh considerably less than older CRT monitors.

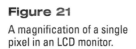

Figure 21

A magnification of a single pixel in an LCD monitor.

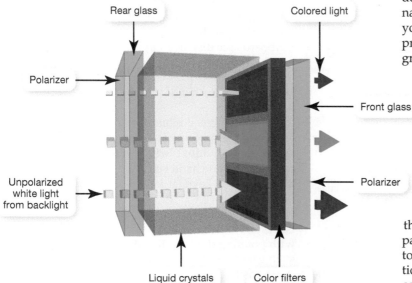

Rear glass

Colored light

Polarizer

Front glass

Unpolarized white light from backlight

Polarizer

Liquid crystals

Color filters

What factors affect the quality of an LCD monitor? When choosing an LCD monitor, there are several factors to consider, such as aspect ratio and resolution. The **aspect ratio** is the width-to-height proportion of a monitor. Traditionally, aspect ratios have been 4:3, but newer monitors are available with an aspect ratio of 16:9 or 16:10. The screen **resolution**, or the clearness or sharpness of the image, reflects the number of pixels on the screen. An LCD monitor may have a native (or maximum) resolution of 1,600 × 1,200, meaning it contains 1,600 vertical columns with 1,200 pixels in each column. The higher the resolution, the sharper and clearer the image will be, but generally the resolution of an LCD monitor is dictated by the screen size and aspect ratio. Although you can change the resolution of an LCD monitor beyond its native resolution, the images will become distorted. Generally, you should select a monitor with the highest resolution available for the screen size (measured in inches).

Other factors to consider when judging the quality of an LCD monitor include the following:

- **Contrast ratio**: This is a measure of the difference in light intensity between the brightest white and the darkest black that the monitor can produce. If the contrast ratio is too low, colors tend to fade when you adjust the brightness to a high or low setting. A contrast ratio between 400:1 and 1,000:1 is preferable. Some monitors may sport a dynamic contrast ratio that may be 10,000:1 or 50,000:1. This measurement is taken when the backlight is turned off completely; normal contrast ratio measurements have the backlight dimmed to its lowest setting but not completely off. Unfortunately, in normal use, the backlight is not turned off, so the dynamic contrast ratio is not a relevant measure, unless you are using an LED monitor.
- **Viewing angle**: An LCD's viewing angle, which is measured in degrees, tells how far you can move to the side of (or above or below) the monitor before the image quality degrades to unacceptable levels. For monitors that measure 17 inches or more, a viewing angle of at least 150 degrees is usually recommended.

- **Brightness**: Measured as candelas per square meter (cd/m^2) or *nits*, brightness is a measure of the greatest amount of light showing when the monitor is displaying pure white. A brightness level of $300 cd/m^2$ or greater is recommended.
- **Response time**: This is the measurement (in milliseconds) of the time it takes for a pixel to change color. A lower response time value means faster transitions; therefore, moving images will appear less jerky on the monitor.

Is a bigger screen size always better? The bigger the monitor, the more you can display, and depending on what you want to display, size may matter. In general, the larger the panel, the larger number of pixels it can display. For example, a 21-inch monitor will typically be able to display 1680 × 1050 pixels, while a 19-inch monitor may only be able to display 1440 × 900 or 1280 × 1024. If you watch many high-definition movies on your monitor, you will need a monitor with at least the 1920 × 1080 resolution required to display HD-DVDs and Blu-ray movies. Larger screens can also allow you to view multiple documents or Web pages at the same time, creating the effect of using two separate monitors side by side. Again, be mindful of cost. Buying two smaller monitors might be cheaper than buying one large monitor. For either option—a big screen or two screens—you should check that your computer has a special adapter card to support these video display devices.

 BITS AND BYTES | Cleaning Your Monitor

Have you ever noticed how quickly your monitor attracts dust? It's important to keep your monitor clean because dust buildup can act like insulation, keeping heat in and causing the electronic components to wear out much faster. To clean your LCD monitor, follow these steps:

1. Turn off the monitor (or your notebook computer) and make sure it is unplugged from the electrical power outlet.
2. Use a 50/50 solution of rubbing alcohol and water on a soft cloth and wipe the screen surface gently. Never spray anything directly onto the monitor. (Check your monitor's user manual to see if there are cleaning products you should avoid using.)
3. In addition to wiping the screen, wipe away the dust from around the case.

Also, don't place anything on top of the monitor or pack anything closely around it. This may block air from cooling it. Finally, avoid placing magnets (including your speaker system's subwoofer) anywhere near the monitor because they can interfere with the mechanisms inside the monitor.

What other features should I look for in an LCD monitor? Some monitors, especially those on notebook computers, come with convenient built-in features such as speakers, webcams, and microphones. A built-in multiformat card reader is convenient to display images directly on the monitor or to download pictures quickly from a camera memory card to the PC. Another nice feature to look for in a desktop LCD monitor is a built-in USB port. This will enable you to connect extra peripherals easily without reaching around the back of the PC.

If these features are important to you, then look for a monitor that has them, but be careful that the price of buying a monitor with these additional features isn't more than what it would cost you to buy the monitor and extra peripherals separately.

How do I show output to a large group of people? Crowding large groups of people around your computer isn't practical. However, it is possible to use a **projector**, a device that can project images from your computer onto a wall or viewing screen (see Figure 22). Projectors are commonly used in business and education settings such as conference rooms and classrooms. These projectors are small and lightweight, and some, like the 3M MPro 150, are small enough to fit into the palm of your hand! These portable projectors are ideal for businesspeople that have to make presentations at client locations. *Entertainment projectors,* such as the Wonderwall, include stereo speakers and an array of multimedia connectors, making them a good option for use in the home to display TV programs, DVDs, digital images, or video games in a large format.

Printers

What are the different types of printers? There are two primary categories of printers: inkjet and laser, both of which are considered nonimpact printers. A **nonimpact printer** sprays ink or uses laser

beams to transfer marks onto the paper. Today, nonimpact printers have replaced impact printers almost entirely. An **impact printer** has tiny hammerlike keys that strike the paper through an inked ribbon, making marks on the paper. The most common impact printer is the dot-matrix printer. The only place you may see a dot-matrix printer is at a company that still uses them to print multipart forms. For most users, dot-matrix printers are truly legacy technology.

What are the advantages of inkjet printers? An **inkjet printer** (see Figure 23) is the standard type of printer found in most homes. Inkjet printers are popular because they are affordable and produce high-quality color printouts quickly and quietly. Inkjet printers work by spraying tiny drops of ink onto paper and are great for printing black-and-white text as well as color images. In fact, when loaded with the right paper, higher-end inkjet printers can print images that look like professional-quality photos. One thing to consider when buying an inkjet printer is the type and cost of the ink cartridges the printer needs. Some printers use two cartridges: black and color. Other printers use four or more cartridges, typically black, magenta, cyan, and yellow. Often the cost of buying replacement cartridges is more than that of a brand-new printer! Depending on how frequently you

Figure 22

Inexpensive projectors are showing up more frequently in business and the home to provide large images for movie viewing and gaming.

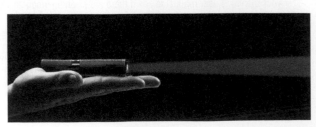

print, you might want to consider a laser printer.

Why would I want a laser printer? Laser printers (see Figure 24) are most often used in office or classroom settings because they have a faster printing speed than inkjet printers and produce higher-quality printouts. A **laser printer** uses laser beams and static electricity to deliver toner (similar to ink) onto the correct areas of the page. Heat is used to fuse the toner to the page, making the image permanent. In the past, laser printers generally were not found in the home because of their high purchase price and because they did not produce great color images. Recently, however, the quality has improved and the price of color laser printers has fallen dramatically, making them highly price competitive with high-end inkjet printers. When you include the price of ink or toner in the overall cost, laser printers can be more economical than inkjets.

What kind of printer can I take with me? Although some inkjet printers are small enough to carry with you, you may want to consider a printer designed for portability for added mobility and flexibility (see Figure 25). Portable printers are often compact enough to fit in a briefcase, are

Figure 23

Inkjet printers are popular among home users, especially with the rise of digital photography. Many inkjet printers are optimized for printing photos from digital cameras.

lightweight, and sometimes run on battery power instead of AC power.

Are there wireless printers? One reason you may have bought a notebook was to be able to use a computer without the restriction of wires. Wireless printing offers you the same freedom. In addition, wireless printers allow several people to print to the same printer from different places. There are two different types of wireless printers: WiFi and Bluetooth. Both WiFi and Bluetooth printers have a range of up to approximately 300 feet. WiFi, however, sends data more quickly than Bluetooth. If your printer is not Bluetooth enabled, you can add Bluetooth by plugging a Bluetooth adapter into a USB port. This lets you take advantage of a great printing solution for photos stored on your cell phone or any other Bluetooth-enabled portable device.

Are there any other types of specialty printers? An **all-in-one printer** is a device that combines the functions of a printer, scanner, copier, and fax into one machine. Popular for their space-saving convenience, all-in-one printers can use either inkjet or laser technology. A **plotter** is another type of printer. Plotters produce oversize pictures that require the drawing of

Figure 25

Modern portable printers feature Bluetooth connectivity, allowing them to be used with mobile devices.

Figure 24

Laser printers print quickly and offer high-quality printouts.

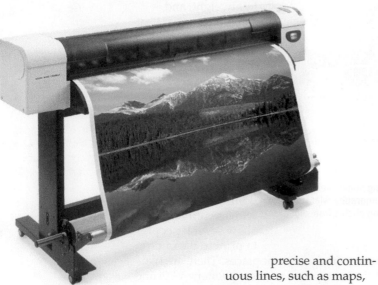

Figure 26

Plotters are large printers used to print oversize images, maps, and architectural plans.

Figure 27

Thermal printers are used in many restaurants to print receipts.

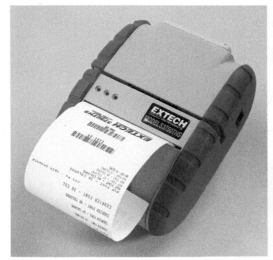

precise and continuous lines, such as maps, detailed images (see Figure 26), and architectural plans. Plotters use a computer-controlled pen that provides a greater level of precision than the series of dots that laser or inkjet printers are capable of making.

A **thermal printer**, such as the one shown in Figure 27, is another kind of specialty printer. These printers work either by melting wax-based ink onto ordinary paper (a process called *thermal wax transfer printing*), or by burning dots onto specially coated paper (a process called *direct thermal printing*). They are used in stores to print receipts and in airports for electronic ticketing, among other places. Thermal printers are also emerging as a popular technology for mobile and portable printing in conjunction with smartphones and similar devices. Many models, such as the printers that car rental agencies use to give you an instant receipt when you drop off your rental car, feature wireless infrared technology for complete portability.

How do I select the best printer? There is a printer for every printing need. First, you need to decide what your primary printing need is. If you will use your printer mostly to print digital images, then you will want to select a photo printer. If not, then a general-purpose printer will be a better choice. General-purpose printers have a finer, faster text output, whereas photo printers have a more distinctive color output. It's also important to determine whether you want just a printer or a device that prints and scans, copies, or faxes (an all-in-one). In addition, you should decide whether you want an inkjet or laser printer, and whether or not you want to print wirelessly. Once you have narrowed down the type of printer you want, the following criteria will help you determine the best model to meet your needs.

- **Speed:** A printer's speed determines how many pages it can print per minute. Print speed is expressed as *pages per minute* or *ppm*. The speed of inkjet printers has improved over the years, and many inkjet printers now print as fast as laser printers. Printing speeds vary by model and range from 8 ppm to 38 ppm for both laser and inkjet printers. Text documents printed in black and white print faster than documents printed in color.

- **Resolution:** A printer's resolution (printed image clarity) is measured in dots per inch (dpi), which is the number of dots of ink in a one-inch line. The higher the dpi, the greater the level of detail and quality of the image. You'll sometimes see dpi represented as a horizontal number multiplied by a vertical number, such as 600×600, but you may also see the same resolution simply stated as 600 dpi. For general-purpose printing, 1,200 dpi is sufficient. For printing photos, 4,800 dpi is better. The dpi for professional photo-quality printers is twice that.

- **Color output:** If you're using an inkjet printer to print color images, buy a four-color printer (cyan, magenta, yellow, and black) or a six-color one (four-color plus light cyan and light magenta) for the highest-quality output. Although some printers come with a single ink cartridge for all colors and others have two ink cartridges (one for black and one for color), the best setup is to have an individual ink cartridge for each color so you can replace only the specific color cartridge that is empty. Color

Ever wonder how a printer knows what to print and how it puts ink in just the right places? Most inkjet printers use drop-on-demand technology in which the ink is "demanded" and then "dropped" onto the paper. Two different processes use drop-on-demand technology: Thermal bubble is used by Hewlett-Packard and Canon, and piezoelectric is used by Epson. The difference between the two processes is how the ink is heated within the print cartridge reservoir (the chamber inside the printer that holds the ink).

In the thermal bubble process, the ink is heated in such a way that it expands (like a bubble) and leaves the cartridge reservoir through a small nozzle. Figure 28 shows the general process for thermal bubble.

In the piezoelectric process, each ink nozzle contains a crystal at the back of the ink reservoir that receives an electrical charge, causing the ink to vibrate and drop out of the nozzle.

Laser printers use a completely different process. Inside a laser printer is a big metal cylinder (also called a *drum*) that is charged with static electricity. When asked to print something, the printer sends signals to the laser in the laser printer, telling it to "uncharge" selected spots on the charged cylinder. These spots correspond to characters and images in the document you wish to print. Toner, a fine powder that is used in place of liquid ink, is only attracted to those areas on the drum that are not charged (the areas where the desired characters and images are to be printed). The toner is transferred to the paper as it feeds through the printer. Finally, the toner is melted onto the paper. All unused toner is swept back to the toner hopper before the next job starts the process all over again.

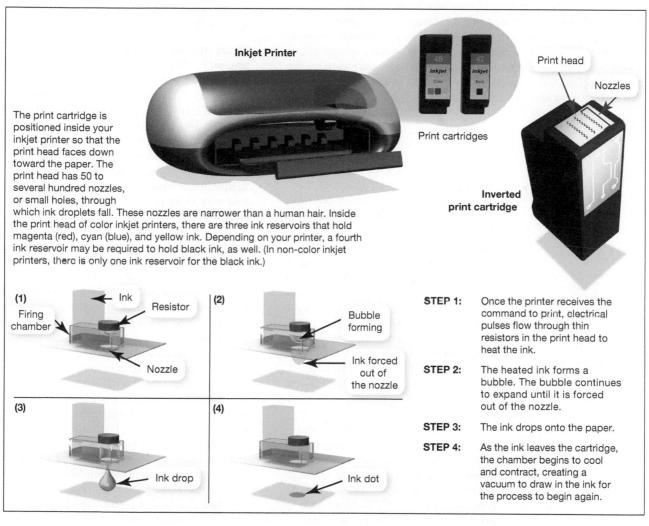

The print cartridge is positioned inside your inkjet printer so that the print head faces down toward the paper. The print head has 50 to several hundred nozzles, or small holes, through which ink droplets fall. These nozzles are narrower than a human hair. Inside the print head of color inkjet printers, there are three ink reservoirs that hold magenta (red), cyan (blue), and yellow ink. Depending on your printer, a fourth ink reservoir may be required to hold black ink, as well. (In non-color inkjet printers, there is only one ink reservoir for the black ink.)

STEP 1: Once the printer receives the command to print, electrical pulses flow through thin resistors in the print head to heat the ink.

STEP 2: The heated ink forms a bubble. The bubble continues to expand until it is forced out of the nozzle.

STEP 3: The ink drops onto the paper.

STEP 4: As the ink leaves the cartridge, the chamber begins to cool and contract, creating a vacuum to draw in the ink for the process to begin again.

Figure 28

How a thermal bubble inkjet printer works.

Does It Matter What Paper I Print On?

The quality of your printer is only part of what controls the quality of a printed image. The paper you use and the printer settings that control the amount of ink used are equally important. If you're printing text-only documents for personal use, then using low-cost paper is fine. You also may want to consider selecting draft mode in your printer settings to conserve ink. However, if you're printing more formal documents such as résumés, you may want to choose a higher-quality paper (determined by the paper's weight, whiteness, and brightness) and adjust your print setting to "normal" or "best."

The weight of paper is measured in pounds, with 20 pounds being standard. A heavier paper may be best for projects such as brochures, but be sure to check that your printer can handle the added thickness. The degree of paper whiteness is a matter of personal preference. Generally, the whiter the paper, the brighter the printed color. However, for more formal documents, such as résumés, you may want to use a creamier color. The brightness of paper usually varies from 85 to 94. The higher the number, the brighter the paper, and the easier it is to read printed text. Opacity is especially important if you're printing on both sides of the paper because it determines the amount of ink that shows through from the opposite side of the paper.

If you're printing photos, then paper quality can have a big impact on the results. Photo paper is more expensive than regular paper and comes in a variety of textures ranging from matte to high gloss. For a photo-lab look, high-gloss paper is the best choice. Semigloss (often referred to as *satin*) is good for portraits, while a matte surface is often used for black-and-white printing.

laser printers have four separate toner cartridges (black, cyan, magenta, and yellow), and the toner is blended in various quantities to produce the entire color spectrum.

- **Use and cost of the printer:** If you will be printing mostly black-and-white, text-based documents or will be sharing your printer with others, then a black-and-white laser printer is best because of its printing speed and overall economy for volume printing. If you're planning to print color photos and graphics, then an inkjet printer or color laser printer is a must, even though the cost per page will be higher. Keep in mind a printer's reported duty cycle. A duty cycle is a manufacturer's figure that refers to how long a machine can keep operating before it needs a rest, or what percentage of the time it's designed to be in use. For a printer, the duty cycle generally refers to the number of printed pages the printer can reliably produce on a monthly basis. If you buy a printer with a duty cycle of 1,000 copies per month, and you generally only print 100 copies a month, then you will have overpurchased. Alternatively, exceeding the duty cycle estimates might lead to printer malfunctions.

- **Cost of consumables:** You should carefully investigate the cost of consumables (such as printer cartridges and paper) for any printer you are considering purchasing because the cost of inkjet cartridges often can exceed the cost of the actual printer when purchased on sale. Reviews in consumer magazines such as *PC World* and *Consumer Reports* can help you evaluate the overall cost of producing documents with a particular printer.

Sound Output

What are the output devices for sound? Most computers include inexpensive speakers. A **speaker** is an output device for sound. These speakers are sufficient to play the standard audio clips you find on the Web and usually enable you to participate in videoconferencing or phone calls made over the Internet. However, if you plan to digitally edit audio files or are particular about how your music sounds, then you may want to upgrade to a more sophisticated speaker system, such as one that includes subwoofers (special speakers that produce only low bass sounds) and surround-sound speakers. A **surround-sound speaker** is a system of speakers and audio processing that envelops the listener in a full 360-degree field of sound. Wireless speaker systems are available now to help you avoid cluttering up your rooms with speaker wire.

If you work in close proximity to other employees or travel with a notebook, then you may need to use headphones or earbuds for your sound output to avoid distracting other people. Both devices will plug into the same jack on the computer that speakers connect to, so using them with a computer is easy. Studies of users of portable media players have shown that hearing might be damaged by excessive volume, especially when using earbuds, because they fit into the ear canals. Exercise caution when using these devices.

Processing and Memory on the Motherboard

We just looked at the components of your computer that you use to input and output data. But where does the processing take place, and where is the data stored? The **motherboard** is the main circuit board that contains the central electronic components of the computer, including the computer's processor (its brain), its memory, and the many circuit boards that help the computer function. On a desktop, the motherboard is located inside the **system unit**, the metal or plastic case that also houses the power source and all the storage devices (CD/DVD drive and hard drive). With a notebook computer, the system unit is combined with the monitor and the keyboard into a single package.

What's on the motherboard? Recall that the motherboard is the main circuit board that contains the set of chips that powers the system, including the central processing unit (CPU). The motherboard also houses ROM, RAM, and cache, the chips that provide the short-term memory for the computer. The motherboard also includes slots for **expansion cards** (or **adapter cards**), which are circuit boards that provide additional functionality (see Figure 29). Typical expansion cards found in the system unit are the sound and video cards. A **sound card** provides a connection for the speakers and microphone, whereas a **video card** provides a connection for the monitor. Many low-end computer models have video and sound capabilities integrated into their motherboards. High-end models use expansion cards to provide video and sound capabilities. Other expansion cards provide a means for network and Internet connections. These include the **modem card**, which provides the computer with a connection to the Internet via a traditional phone line, and a **network interface card (NIC)**, which enables your computer to connect with other computers or to a cable modem to facilitate a high-speed Internet connection. Lastly, some expansion cards provide additional USB and FireWire ports.

Memory

What exactly is RAM? **Random access memory (RAM)** is the place in a computer where the programs and data the computer is currently using are stored. RAM is much faster to read from and write to than the hard drive and other forms of storage. The processor can request the RAM's contents, which can be located, opened, and delivered to the CPU for processing in a few nanoseconds (billionths of a second). If you look at a motherboard, you'll see RAM as a series of small cards (called *memory cards* or *memory modules*) plugged into slots on the motherboard.

Because the entire contents of RAM are erased when you turn off the computer, RAM is a temporary or **volatile storage** location. To save data permanently, you need to save it to the hard drive or to another permanent storage device such as a CD or flash drive. You can think of RAM as

Figure 29

A motherboard contains the CPU, the memory (RAM) modules, and slots for expansion cards.

Expansion slot

Memory modules (RAM)

CPU

Expansion cards

Looking at Computers: Understanding the Parts

23

Maintaining Your Inkjet Printer

In general, printers require minimal maintenance. Occasionally, it's a good idea to wipe the case of the printer with a damp cloth to free it from accumulated dust. However, do not wipe away any ink residue that has accumulated inside the printer. If you are experiencing streaking or blank areas on your printed paper, then your print head nozzles may be clogged. To fix this, run the printer's cleaning cycle. (Check your printer's manual for instructions, because every printer is different.) If this doesn't work, you may want to use a cleaning sheet to brush the print head clean. These sheets often come with printers or with reams of photo paper. If you still have a problem, try a cleaning cartridge. Cleaning cartridges contain a special fluid that scrubs the print head. These cartridges can be found where most ink cartridges are sold. As with ink cartridges, make sure you buy one that is compatible with your printer.

Virtual Computer Tour

In this Sound Byte, you'll take a video tour of the inside of a system unit. From opening the cover to locating the power supply, CPU, and memory, you'll become more familiar with what's inside your computer.

the computer's temporary memory and the hard drive as permanent memory.

Does the motherboard contain any other kinds of memory besides RAM? In addition to RAM, the motherboard also contains a form of memory called **read-only memory (ROM)**. ROM holds all the instructions the computer needs to start up when the computer is powered on. Unlike data stored in RAM, which is volatile storage, the instructions stored in ROM are permanent, making ROM a nonvolatile storage location, which means the data is not erased when the power is turned off.

Processing

What is the CPU? The **central processing unit** (**CPU**, or **processor**) is sometimes referred to as the "brains" of the computer because it controls all the functions performed by the computer's other components and processes all the commands issued to it by software instructions. Modern CPUs can perform as many as 45 billion tasks per

second without error, making them extremely powerful components.

How is processor speed measured? Processor speed is measured in units of hertz (Hz). Hertz means "machine cycles per second." A machine cycle is the process of the CPU getting the data or instructions from RAM and decoding the instructions into something the computer can understand. Once the CPU has decoded the instructions, it executes them and stores the result back into system memory. Older machines ran at speeds measured in **megahertz (MHz)**, or millions of machine cycles per second, whereas current systems run at speeds measured in **gigahertz (GHz)**, or billions of machine cycles per second. Therefore, a 3.8 GHz processor performs work at a rate of 3.8 billion machine cycles per second. It's important to realize, however, that CPU clock speed alone doesn't determine the performance of the CPU.

What else determines processor performance? Although speed is an important consideration when determining processor performance, CPU performance also is affected by other factors. One factor is the number of *cores*, or processing paths, a processor has. Until just a few years ago, processors only could handle one instruction at a time. Now, processors have been designed so that they can have two, four, and even eight different paths, allowing them to process more than one instruction at a time (see Figure 30). Applications such as virus protection software and the operating system, which are always running behind the scenes, can have their own processors, freeing up the other processor to run other applications such as a Web browser, Word, or iTunes more efficiently.

Besides the number of cores, are there other factors that determine processing power? In addition to the number of cores in a processor, you should consider other factors such as cache memory

Figure 30

Two are faster than one! With their dual core processors, Intel CPUs can work in parallel, processing two separate programs at the same time instead of switching back and forth between them.

Single path vs. dual path processors for data

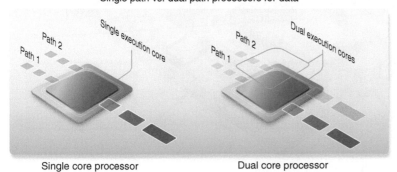

Single core processor   Dual core processor

and front side bus (FSB). (FSB determines how fast data is exchanged between the CPU and RAM.) The "best" processor will depend on your particular needs and is not always the processor with the highest GHz and the greatest number of cores. Intel, one of the leading manufacturers of computer processor chips, has created a pictorial rating system for CPU chips. Intel uses one to five stars to illustrate the relative computing power of each type of CPU within the Intel line of processors. It also provides an overall ranking of "smart," "smarter," and "genius" and an overview of each processor's key benefits.

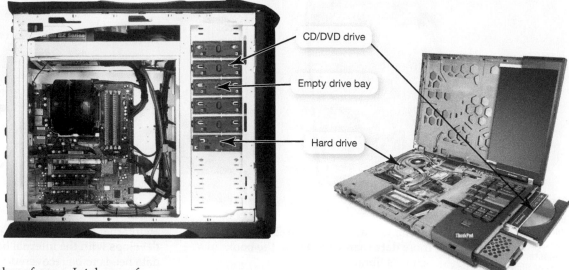

Figure 31
Storage devices in desktop and notebook computers.

Storing Data and Information

Earlier we characterized RAM as temporary or volatile memory because the entire contents of RAM are erased when you turn off the computer. Thus, if you permanently want to save the files you're working on, as well as your music, digital images, and any software applications you use, you need to store them in a different location than RAM. To save data permanently, you need to save it to the hard drive or to another permanent storage device such as a CD, DVD, or flash drive. Each of these permanent storage devices is located in your desktop or notebook computer in a space called a **drive bay** (see Figure 31). There are two kinds of drive bays—internal and external—as described below:

- Internal drive bays cannot be seen or accessed from outside the system unit. Generally, internal drive bays are reserved for internal hard drives. An **internal hard drive** usually holds all permanently stored programs and data.

- External drive bays can be seen and accessed from outside the system unit. External drive bays house CD and DVD drives, for example. On desktop computers, sometimes there are empty external drive bays that can be used to install additional drives. These extra spaces are covered by a faceplate on the front panel. Notebook computers generally do not give you the ability to add additional drives. Such expansion is done by attaching an external drive to the computer through a USB port.

You may occasionally see a PC that still has a bay for a *floppy disk drive*, which reads and writes to easily transportable floppy disks that hold a limited amount of data (1.44 MB). Some computers also feature what's called a *Zip disk drive*, which resembles a floppy disk drive but has a slightly wider opening. Zip disks work just like standard floppy disks but can carry much more data (up to 750 MB). These storage devices are legacy technologies and are not found on new computers.

Hard Drives

Which storage device holds the most data? The **hard drive** (see Figure 32a) is your computer's primary device for permanent storage of software and documents. The hard drive is a **nonvolatile storage** device, meaning it holds the data and instructions your computer needs permanently, even after the computer is turned off. Today's internal hard drives, with capacities

Figure 32

(a) Internal hard drives hold the data and instructions that the computer needs and are inaccessible from outside the system unit. (b) High-capacity external hard drives are often used to back up data on internal hard drives. (c) Smaller external hard drives enable you to take a significant amount of data and programs on the road with you.

of as much as 3.5 terabyte (TB), can hold more data than would fit in the books in a school's library.

Are all hard drives located inside the system? Because the hard drive stores all of the computer's data and programs, special measures are taken to protect the hard drive from any possible damage. Unlike other storage devices on the computer, the hard drive is enclosed in a case and is not accessible from the outside of the system unit. If you need a more portable solution, external hard drives are readily available. An **external hard drive** (see Figures 32b and 32c) is essentially like an internal hard drive. However, it has been made portable by making it small and lightweight and enclosing it in a protective case. Some external hard drives, which are small enough to fit into your pocket, have storage capacities of 1 or 2 TB (or larger). An external hard drive is often used to back up (make a copy of) data that is contained on

an internal hard drive in case a problem develops with the internal hard drive and data needs to be recovered.

Optical Storage

What other kinds of storage devices are available? Internal hard drives are used to store your data, files, and installed software programs. Hard drives store their data on magnetized platters. Also included on most desktop and notebook computers is at least one **optical drive** that can read from and maybe even write to CDs, DVDs, or Blu-ray discs. Data is saved to a **compact disc (CD)**, **digital video** (or **versatile**) **disc (DVD)**, or **Blu-ray disc (BD)** as tiny pits that are burned into the disc by a high-speed laser. CDs were initially created to store audio files. DVDs are the same size and shape as CDs but can hold more data. DVDs that store data on just one side and in one layer can store about seven times more data. If you're looking for more storage capacity, a double-sided/single-layer DVD is the next step. These discs have up to 8.5 GB of storage, and a double-sided/double-layer DVD can store nearly 16 GB of data. What if you want even more storage capacity? Blu-ray is the latest incarnation of optical storage to hit the market. Blu-ray discs, which are similar in size and shape to CDs and DVDs, can hold as much as 50 GB of data— enough to hold approximately 4.5 hours of movies in the

Figure 33

Flash drives are a convenient means of portable storage, and come in many different shapes and sizes.

Looking at Computers: Understanding the Parts

high-definition (HD) digital format that has become so popular. Many systems are now available with BD-ROM drives and even Blu-ray burners. External BD drives are another inexpensive way to add HD storage capacity to your system.

Flash Storage

A **flash drive**, sometimes referred to as a **jump drive**, **USB drive**, or **thumb drive**, is a way of storing portable data. Flash drives plug into USB ports. These devices originally were more or less the size of a thumb, but now they vary in size and are often combined with other devices such as pens or pocketknives (see Figure 33). Despite their diminutive size, flash drives have significant storage capacity—currently as much as 256 GB.

Several manufacturers now also include slots on the front of the system unit in which you can insert a portable **flash memory card** such as a Memory Stick or CompactFlash card. Many notebooks also include slots for flash memory cards in the sides. Flash memory cards let you transfer digital data between your computer and devices such as digital cameras, PDAs, smartphones, video cameras, and printers. Although incredibly small—some are just the size of a postage stamp—these memory cards have capacities that exceed the capacity of a DVD.

Some hard drives are also based on flash memory. A **solid state drive (SSD)** does not have any spinning platters or motors, so they are more efficient, run with no noise, emit very little heat, and require very little power.

Figure 34 shows the storage capacities of the various portable storage media used in your computer's drive bays.

Connecting Peripherals to the Computer

Throughout this chapter, we have discussed peripheral devices that input, store, and output data and information. A **port** is a place through which a peripheral device attaches to the computer so that data can be exchanged between it and the operating system. Many ports are located on the back

Figure 34 | STORAGE MEDIA CAPACITIES

Medium	Image	Capacity
Mechanical hard drive		As much as 3.5 TB
Solid state drive (SSD)		5 TB or more
External portable hard drive		4 TB or more
Flash drive		256 GB or more
Blu-ray (dual layer)		50 GB
Flash memory card		Up to 128 GB
Blu-ray (BD)		25 GB
DVD DL (dual layer)		88.5 GB
DVD		4.7 GB
CD		700 MB

Memory card slots

USB ports

Audio/video ports

FireWire ports

Ethernet port

S-video

Figure 35

Many of the same ports appear on both (a) notebook and (b) desktop computers.

of a notebook computer and the system unit of a desktop computer. However, some commonly used ports are placed on the front and sides of many desktop and notebook computers (see Figure 35) for easier access when connecting devices such as flash drives or digital and video cameras.

High-Speed and Data Transfer Ports

What is the most common way to connect devices to a computer? A **universal serial bus (USB) port** is now the most common port type used to connect input and output devices to the computer. This is mainly because of a USB port's ability to transfer data quickly. USB 2.0 ports (see Figure 36) are the current standard and transfer data at 480 megabits per second (Mbps), approximately 40 times faster than the original USB ports. USB ports can connect a wide variety of peripherals to the computer, including keyboards, printers, mice, smartphones, external hard drives, flash drives, and digital cameras. The new USB 3.0 standard provides transfer speeds of 4.8 Gbps, which is 10 times the

ACTIVE HELP-DESK

Exploring Storage Devices and Ports

In this Active Helpdesk call, you'll play the role of a helpdesk staffer, fielding calls about the computer's main storage devices and how to connect various peripheral devices to the computer.

SOUND BYTE

Port Tour: How Do I Hook It Up?

In this Sound Byte, you'll take a tour of both a desktop system and a notebook system to compare the number and variety of available ports. You'll also learn about the different types of ports and compare their speed and expandability.

speed of USB 2.0. USB 3.0 should quickly become the port of choice.

A traditional serial port sends data one bit (piece of data) at a time. Serial ports were often used to connect modems (devices used to transmit data over telecommunications lines) to the computer. Sending data one bit at a time was a slow way to communicate. A parallel port could send data between devices in groups of bits at speeds of 500 Kbps and was much faster than traditional serial ports. Parallel ports were often used to connect printers to computers. The speed advantage offered by USB ports has made serial and parallel ports legacy technology.

What are other types of ports? You may also see other ports, such as **FireWire 400** and **FireWire 800**. The FireWire 400 interface moves data at 400 Mbps, while the FireWire 800 doubles the rate to 800 Mbps. Devices such as external hard drives, digital video cameras, portable music players, and digital media

Figure 36

A USB port and a USB connector.

To transfer data between the two devices, a special cable that has an appropriate connector at each end is needed. The faster FireWire 800 requires a nine-pin connection and is found on storage devices such as external and portable hard drives.

Connectivity and Multimedia Ports

Which ports help me connect with other computers and the Internet? Another set of ports on your computer helps you communicate with other computers. A **connectivity port** can give you access to networks and the Internet or enable your computer to function as a fax machine. To find a connectivity port, look for a port that resembles a standard phone jack but is slightly larger. This port is called an **Ethernet port** (see Figure 38). Ethernet ports transfer data at speeds up to 1,000 Mbps. You can use an Ethernet port to connect your computer to a digital subscriber line (DSL) or cable modem, or a network. Many computers still feature a second connectivity port that will accept a standard phone line connector. This jack is the **modem port**. It uses a traditional telephone signal to connect to the Internet over a phone line.

players all benefit from the speedy data transfer capabilities of FireWire. The FireWire 3200 standard, with data transfer rates of 3.2 Gbps, has been ratified but has yet to reach the market. FireWire 400 ports and connectors have two different configurations, as shown in Figure 37. FireWire 400 ports on computers generally have six pins, while FireWire ports on digital cameras have four pins.

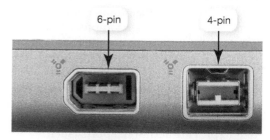

Figure 37

FireWire ports come in different configurations, some of which are illustrated here.

How do I connect monitors and multimedia devices? Other ports on the back of the computer include the audio and video ports (see Figure 39). Video ports are necessary to hook up monitors. Whether you are attaching a monitor to a desktop computer, or adding a second, larger display to a notebook computer, you will use video ports. The **video graphics array (VGA)** port is the port to which CRT monitors connect.

Figure 38

An Ethernet port and an Ethernet connector.

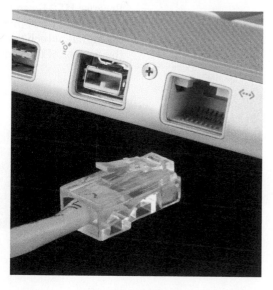

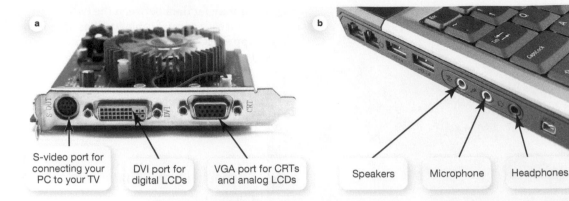

S-video port for connecting your PC to your TV

DVI port for digital LCDs

VGA port for CRTs and analog LCDs

Speakers   Microphone   Headphones

Figure 39

DVI, VGA, and S-video ports connect your monitors and multimedia devices to the computer.

Many older LCD monitors also connect with a VGA port. The newer LCD monitors, as well as other multimedia devices such as televisions, DVD players, and projectors, connect to **digital video interface (DVI)** and **S-video (super video)** ports. Audio ports are where you connect headphones, microphones, and speakers to the computer.

How can I connect my computer to TVs and gaming consoles? The latest digital connector designed for use in high-definition home theater environments is **high-definition multimedia interface (HDMI)**, a compact audio–video interface that carries both high-definition video and uncompressed digital audio on one cable. (DVI can only carry video signals.) Because HDMI can transmit uncompressed audio and video, there is no need to convert the signal, which could ultimately reduce the quality of the sound or picture. Most

Figure 40

HDMI is the latest digital connector type for HD home theater equipment.

devices such as DVD players, TVs, and game consoles have at least one HDMI port (see Figure 40).

Adding Ports: Expansion Cards and Hubs

What if I don't have all the ports I need? Because almost everything connects to your computer using USB ports, your desktop computer should have at least six USB ports, and a notebook computer should have at least three USB ports. Therefore, if you are looking to add the newest ports to an older computer or to expand the number of ports on your computer, you can use special expansion cards. For example, your computer may have only USB 2.0 ports, but you would like to upgrade to the new USB 3.0 ports. You can install expansion cards in your system unit to provide additional ports (such as USB 3.0 and FireWire). Like other expansion cards, these cards clip into an open expansion slot on the motherboard. Figure 41 shows an example of such an expansion card.

What if there are no open slots on the motherboard where I can insert an expansion card? If there are no open slots on the motherboard and you

Figure 41

This expansion card provides your computer with additional ports.

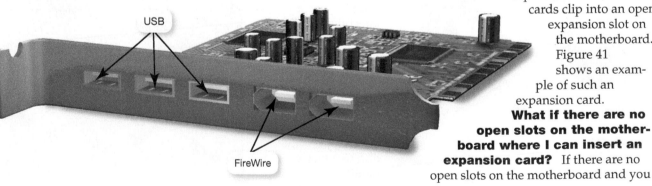

USB

FireWire

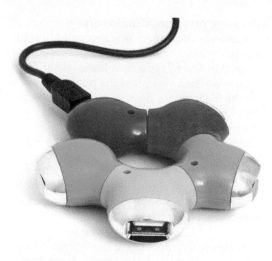

Figure 42

If you don't have enough USB ports to support your USB devices, consider getting an expansion hub, which can add four or more USB ports to your system.

still need extra ports, you can add an expansion hub (shown in Figure 42). An expansion hub is a device that connects to one port, such as a USB port, to provide additional new ports. It works like the multiplug extension cords used with electrical appliances.

You also can add ports to an empty drive bay, giving you easy-to-reach new ports. The Koutech 10-in-1, shown in Figure 43, fits into a regular drive bay and adds front-panel access to two USB 2.0 ports, two FireWire ports, three audio jacks, and a six-in-one digital media card reader.

Power Controls

What's the best way to turn my computer on and off? The **power supply**, which is housed inside the system unit, transforms the wall voltage to the voltages required by computer chips. A desktop system typically has a power-on button on the front panel of the system unit, though you may also find power-on buttons on some keyboards. On notebooks, the power-on button is generally located near the top of the keyboard. Powering on your computer from a completely turned off state, such as when you start your computer in the morning, is called a **cold boot**.

How do I power down a computer properly? Powering off your computer

properly helps to save energy, keeps your computer more secure, and ensures that your data is saved. You can turn your computer off by pressing the computer's power button or using the Shut Down button on the Start menu.

Should I turn off my computer every time I'm done using it? Some people say you should leave your computer on at all times. They argue that turning your computer on and off throughout the day subjects its components to stress because the heating and cooling process forces the components to expand and contract repeatedly. Other people say you should shut down your computer when you're not using it. They claim that it's not as environmentally friendly, and you'll end up wasting money on electricity to keep the computer running all the time. Modern operating systems include power-management settings that allow the most power-hungry components of the system (the hard drive and monitor) to shut down after a short idle period. With the power-management options of Windows 7, for example, you really need to shut down your computer completely only when you need to repair or install hardware in the system unit or move the system unit to another location. However, if you use your computer only for a little while each day, it would be best to power it off completely after each daily use.

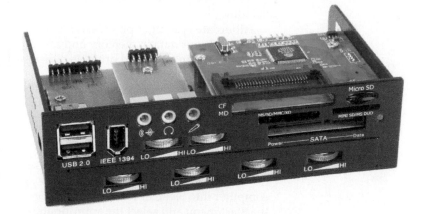

Figure 43

You can use an empty drive bay to add additional ports and even a flash card reader to the front panel of the system unit.

Figure 44

The Sleep and Hibernate settings are good for the environment and for your wallet.

>To open the Power Options dialog box, click the **Start** button, click **Control Panel**, and then click **Power Options**.

Can I "rest" my computer without turning it off completely? As mentioned earlier, your computer has power-management settings that help it conserve energy. In Windows 7, the two main methods of power management are Sleep and Hibernate. When your computer enters **Sleep mode**, all of the documents, applications, and data you were using remain in RAM (memory), where they are quickly accessible when you restart your computer. (In Windows XP, this mode is called Standby.)

Hibernate is another power-saving mode that stores your data in memory and saves it to your computer's hard drive. In either Sleep or Hibernate mode, the computer enters a state of greatly reduced power consumption, which saves energy. The big advantage to using Hibernate is that if there is a power failure while your computer is conserving power, your information is protected from loss, because it is saved on the hard drive. To put your computer into Sleep or Hibernate, open the Start menu and select the appropriate Sleep or Hibernate option. To wake up your computer, tap a key on the keyboard or move the mouse. In a few seconds, the computer will resume with exactly

the same programs running and documents displayed as when you put it to sleep.

In Windows 7, you can change what happens when you press the power button on the Start menu. By accessing the Power Options screen (see Figure 44), you can decide if you want your computer to Sleep or Hibernate when you click the power button.

What's the restart option in Windows for? If you're using Windows 7, you have the option to restart the computer when you click the right arrow button next to the Shut Down button on the Start menu (see Figure 45). Restarting the system while it's powered on is called a **warm boot**. You might need to perform a warm boot if the operating system or other software

Right arrow button

Figure 45

The Start menu in Windows 7 presents several power options. For a warm boot, choose **Restart**. To power down the computer completely, choose **Shut Down**. To put your computer into a lower power mode, select **Sleep** or **Hibernate**.

>To select a particular power option, click the **Start** menu button in the taskbar and then click the right arrow button.

application stops responding or if you have installed new programs. It takes less time to perform a warm boot than to power down completely and then restart all of your hardware.

Setting It All Up

It's important that you understand not only your computer's components and how they work together but also how to set up these components safely. *Merriam-Webster's Dictionary* defines **ergonomics** as "an applied science concerned with designing and arranging things people use so that the people and things interact most efficiently and

safely." In terms of computing, ergonomics refers to how you set up your computer and other equipment to minimize your risk of injury or discomfort.

Why is ergonomics important? You don't have to have a desk job to run the risk of becoming injured by working improperly on a computer. Studies suggest that teenagers, on average, spend 31 hours online each week. When you factor in other computer uses such as typing school reports and playing video games, there is great potential for injury. The repetitive nature of long-term computer activities can place too much stress on joints and pull at the tendons and muscles, causing repetitive stress injuries such as carpal tunnel syndrome and tendonitis. These injuries can take months or years to develop to a point where they becomes painful, and by the time you notice the symptoms, the damage has already taken place. If you take precautionary care now, you may prevent years of unnecessary pain later on.

How can I avoid injuries when I'm working at my computer? As Figure 46 illustrates, it is important to

Figure 46

Using proper equipment that is adjusted correctly helps prevent repetitive strain injuries while working at a computer.

Figure 47

Ergonomic keyboards that curve and contain built-in wrist rests help maintain proper hand position and minimize wrist strain.

arrange your monitor, chair, body, and keyboard in ways that will help you avoid injury, discomfort, and eyestrain as you work on your computer. The following additional guidelines can help keep you comfortable and productive:

- **Position your monitor correctly.** Studies suggest it's best to place your monitor at least 25 inches from your eyes. You may need to decrease the screen resolution to make text and images more readable at that distance. Experts recommend that the monitor be positioned either at eye level or so that it is at an angle 15 to 20 degrees below your line of sight.

- **Purchase an adjustable chair.** Adjust the height of your chair so that your feet touch the floor. (You may need to use a footrest to get the right position.) The back support needs to be adjustable so that you can position it to support your lumbar (lower back) region. You should also be able to move the seat or adjust the back so that you can sit without exerting pressure on your knees. If your chair doesn't adjust, placing a pillow behind your back can provide the same support.

- **Assume a proper position while typing.** A repetitive strain injury (RSI) is a painful condition caused by repetitive or awkward movements of a part of the body. Improperly positioned keyboards are one of the leading causes of RSIs in computer users. Your wrists should be flat (not bent) with respect to the keyboard, and your forearms should be parallel to the floor. Additionally, your wrists should not be resting on the keyboard while typing. You can either adjust the height of your chair or install a height-adjustable keyboard tray to ensure a proper position. Specially designed ergonomic keyboards such as the one shown in Figure 47 can help you achieve the proper wrist position.

- **Take breaks from computer tasks.** Remaining in the same position for long periods of time increases stress on your body. Shift your position in your chair and stretch your hands and fingers periodically. Likewise, staring at the screen for long periods of time can lead to eyestrain, so rest your eyes by periodically taking them off the screen and focusing them on an object at least 20 feet away.

- **Ensure the lighting is adequate.** Ensuring that you have proper lighting in your work area is a good way to minimize eyestrain. To do so, eliminate any sources of direct glare (light shining directly into your eyes) or reflected glare (light shining off the computer screen) and ensure there is enough light to read comfortably. If you still can't eliminate glare from your computer screen, you can purchase an antiglare screen to place over your monitor. Look for ones that are polarized or have a purplish optical coating. These will provide the greatest relief.

Is ergonomics important when using mobile devices? Working with mobile computing devices presents interesting challenges when it comes to injury prevention. For example, many users work with notebooks resting on their laps, placing the monitor outside of the optimal line of sight and thereby increasing neck strain. The table in Figure 48 provides guidelines on preventing injuries when computing on the go.

So whether you're computing at your desk or on the road, consider the ergonomics of your work environment. Doing so will help you avoid injury and discomfort.

Figure 48 | PREVENTING INJURIES WHILE ON THE GO

	PDA/Smartphone RSIs	PMP Hearing Damage	Small-Screen Vision Issues	Lap Injuries	Back, Neck, and Shoulder Injuries
			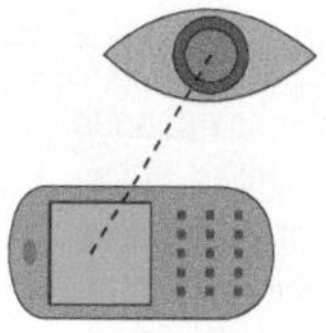		
Malady	Repetitive strain injuries (such as DeQuervain's tendonitis) from constant typing of instant messages.	Hearing loss from high decibel sound levels in earbuds or headphones.	Blurriness and dryness caused by squinting to view tiny screens on mobile devices.	Burns on legs from heat generated by notebook.	Pain caused from carrying notebook (messenger) bag hung over your shoulder.
Preventative measures	Restrict length and frequency of messages, take breaks often, and perform other motions with your thumbs and fingers during breaks to relieve tension.	Turn down volume (you should be able to hear external noises such as people talking), use software programs that limit sound levels (not over 60 decibels), and use external, over-ear style headphones instead of earbuds.	Blink frequently or use eye drops to maintain moisture level in eyes, after 10 minutes take a break and focus your eyes on something at least 8 feet away for 5 minutes, use an adequate amount of light, increase the size of fonts.	Place a book, magazine, or notebook cooling pad between your legs and your notebook.	Use a conventional backpack with two shoulder straps, lighten the load by only carrying essential equipment, and consider buying a lightweight notebook.

Today, LCD monitors dominate the desktop PC and notebook markets. Lighter and less bulky than previous monitors, they can be easily moved and take up less space on a desk. LCD technology has improved significantly over the past several years, and now monitors are sporting increased viewing angles, higher resolutions, and faster pixel response time, which makes full-motion video (critical for gamers) appear extremely smooth.

LCD technology has also infiltrated the television market and, along with plasma technology, has made the boxy TV as obsolete as the CRT monitor. However, as good as LCD technology is, some technology that is beginning to hit the market is even better.

OLED Displays

Organic light-emitting diode (OLED) displays use organic compounds that produce light when exposed to an electric current. Unlike LCDs, OLEDs do not require a backlight to function and therefore draw less power and have a much thinner display, sometimes as thin as 3 mm. They are also brighter, cheaper to manufacture, and more environmentally friendly than plasma displays or LCDs. Because of their lower power needs, OLED displays run longer on a single battery charge than do LEDs, which is why OLED technology is currently being used in small screens of mobile devices such as cell phones, portable media players, and digital cameras.

More recently, OLED technology has been incorporated in some high-end televisions. The benefits of OLED technology may make LCD flat-panel displays quickly obsolete (see Figure 49). The pixels in OLED screens illuminate quickly, like lightbulbs, and produce brighter images than does LCD technology. Because of the quick on/off illumination capacity of OLED pixels, the faster refresh rate enables these screens to display full-motion videos with lifelike motion. Sony and Toshiba have already produced OLED televisions. Eventually, you might not even need a separate display device; it could very well be built into the walls of your house!

Figure 49

Because they do not need a backlight, OLED displays are much thinner than LEDs, making LCD screens seem bulky!

Flexible Screens

An offshoot of OLED technology is the flexible OLED (FOLED). Unlike LCDs, which use rigid surfaces such as glass, FOLED screens use lightweight, inexpensive, flexible material such as transparent plastics or metal foils. As shown in Figure 50, these flexible screens can play a full-motion video while being completely bent.

Figure 50
This 2.5-inch screen is playing a full-motion video while being bent into a semicircle.

Figure 51
Personal media viewers allow you to have a big-screen experience with your mobile devices. The display is projected in front of your eyes, giving you an "in the action" experience.

FOLEDs would allow advertising to progress to a new dimension. Screens could be hung where posters hang now (such as on billboards). Wireless transmission of data to these screens would allow advertisers to display easily updatable full-motion images. Combining transparency and flexibility, these displays can be mounted on windshields and eyeglasses.

Wearable Screens
Who needs a computer screen when you can just wear one? With the rise of the iPod and other portable devices that play digital video, users are demanding larger viewing areas. Although a larger screen is often incompatible with the main design features of portable devices (light weight and long battery life), wearable virtual displays offer a solution. Personal media viewer displays such as the *myvu*, shown in Figure 51, are available now (**myvu.com**). Eventually, when the technology advances sufficiently, you might be able to purchase conventional eyeglasses with displays built right in. Wearable displays might eventually replace heavier screens on notebooks, desktops, and even PDAs.

"Bistable" Screens
Your computer screen constantly changes its images when you are surfing the Internet or playing a game. Because PDA and cell phone screens don't necessarily change that often, something called a "bistable" display, which is currently used in retail stores for pricing signs and in Amazon's Kindle (a wireless reading device), may one day be used in these devices. A bistable display has the ability to retain its image even when the power is turned off. In addition, bistable displays are lighter than LCD displays and reduce overall power consumption, resulting in longer battery life— perhaps as much as 600 times longer, according to Motorola. Because the market for portable devices such as smartphones continues to explode, you can expect to see bistable technologies emerging in mobile computer screens.

1. What exactly is a computer, and what are its four main functions?

Computers are devices that process data. They help organize, sort, and categorize data to turn it into information. The computer's four major functions are to (1) gather data (or allow users to input data), (2) process (manipulate, calculate, or organize) that data, (3) output data or information (display information in a form suitable for the user), and (4) store data and information for later use.

2. What is the difference between data and information?

Data is a representation of a fact or idea. The number 3 and the words *televisions* and *Sony* are pieces of data. Information is data that has been organized or presented in a meaningful fashion. An inventory list that indicates that "three Sony televisions" are in stock is processed information. It allows a retail clerk to answer a customer query about the availability of merchandise. Information is more powerful than raw data.

3. What are bits and bytes, and how are they measured?

To process data into information, computers need to work in a language they understand. This language, called *binary language*, consists of two numbers: 0 and 1. Each 0 and each 1 is a binary digit, or bit. Eight bits create one byte. In computers, each letter of the alphabet, each number, and each special character consists of a unique combination of eight bits (one byte)—a string of eight 0s and 1s. For describing large amounts of storage capacity, the terms *megabyte* (approximately 1 million bytes), *gigabyte* (approximately 1 billion bytes), and *terabyte* (approximately 1 trillion bytes) are used.

4. What devices do I use to get data into the computer?

An input device enables you to enter data (text, images, and sounds) and instructions (user responses and commands) into a computer. You use keyboards to enter typed data and commands, whereas you use the mouse to enter user responses and commands.

Keyboards and mice come in both wired and wireless versions, as well as other special layouts and designs to fit almost every need.

Touch screens are display screens that respond to commands initiated by a touch with a finger or a stylus. Images are input into the computer with scanners, digital cameras, camcorders, and cell phones. Live video is captured with webcams and digital video recorders. Microphones capture sounds. There are many different types of microphones, including desktop, headset, and clip-on models.

5. What devices do I use to get information out of the computer?

Output devices enable you to send processed data out of your computer. It can take the form of text, pictures, sounds, or video. Monitors display soft copies of text, graphics, and video, while printers create hard copies of text and graphics. LCDs are the most popular type of monitor.

There are two primary categories of printers used today: inkjet and laser. Specialty printers are also available. These include all-in-one printers, plotters, and thermal printers. When choosing a printer, you should be aware of factors such as speed, resolution, color output, and cost.

Speakers are the output devices for sound. Most computers include speakers, with more sophisticated systems including subwoofers and surround sound.

6. What's on the motherboard?

The motherboard, the main circuit board of the system, contains a computer's central processing unit (CPU), which coordinates the functions of all other devices on the computer. The performance of a CPU is affected by the speed of the processor (measured in gigahertz), the amount of cache memory, the speed of the front side bus (FSB), and the number of processing cores. RAM, the computer's volatile memory, is also located on the motherboard. RAM is where all the data and instructions are held while the computer is running. ROM, a permanent type of memory, is responsible for housing instructions to help start up a computer. The motherboard also

Looking at Computers: Understanding the Parts

houses a set of slots for expansion cards, which have specific functions that augment the computer's basic functions. Typical expansion cards found in the system unit are the sound and video cards.

7. Where are information and programs stored?

To save programs and information permanently, you need to save them to the hard drive or to another permanent storage device such as a CD, DVD, or flash drive. The hard drive is your computer's primary device for permanent storage of software and files. The hard drive is a nonvolatile storage device, meaning it holds the data and instructions your computer needs permanently, even after the computer is turned off. Mechanical hard drives have spinning platters on which data is saved, whereas newer solid state hard drives (SSD) use solid state memory, similar to that used with flash drives. External hard drives are essentially internal hard drives that have been made portable by enclosing them in a protective case and making them small and lightweight. Optical drives that can read from and maybe even write to CD, DVD, or Blu-ray discs are another means of permanent, portable storage. Data is saved to compact discs (CDs), digital video discs (DVDs), and Blu-ray discs (BDs) as tiny pits that are burned into the disc by a high-speed laser. Flash drives are another portable means of storing data. Flash drives plug into USB ports. Flash memory cards let you transfer digital data between your computer and devices such as digital cameras, smartphones, video cameras, and printers.

8. How are devices connected to the computer?

There are a wide variety of ports that allow you to hook up peripheral devices (such as your monitor and keyboard) to your system.

The most common type of port used to connect devices to a computer is the USB port. USB technology has replaced serial ports and parallel ports, which are now considered legacy technology. USB 2.0 is the current standard but will be quickly replaced by the newer, faster, USB 3.0 standard. FireWire ports provide additional options for data transfer.

Connectivity ports give you access to networks and the Internet and enable your computer to function as a fax machine. Connectivity ports include Ethernet ports and modem ports. Multimedia ports include VGA, DVI, and S-video ports. They connect the computer to monitors and other multimedia devices. Audio ports are where you connect headphones, microphones, and speakers to the computer. HDMI ports are used as a connection between monitors, TVs and gaming consoles and work with both audio and video content.

9. How do I set up my computer to avoid strain and injury?

Ergonomics refers to how you arrange your computer and equipment to minimize your risk of injury or discomfort. This includes positioning your monitor correctly, buying an adjustable chair that ensures you have good posture while using the computer, assuming a proper position while typing, making sure the lighting is adequate, and not looking at the screen for long periods of time. Other good practices include taking frequent breaks and using other specially designed equipment such as ergonomic keyboards. Ergonomics is also important to consider when using mobile devices.

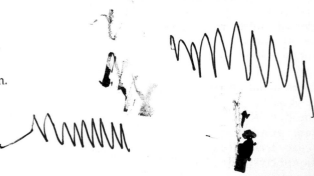

Looking at Computers: Understanding the Parts

key terms

all-in-one computer
all-in-one printer
application software
aspect ratio
binary digit (bit)
binary language
Blu-ray disc (BD)
Bluetooth
brightness
byte
compact disc (CD)
central processing unit
  (CPU or processor)
cold boot
computer
connectivity port
contrast ratio
cursor control key
data
desktop computer
digital video (or versatile) disc (DVD)
digital video interface (DVI)
drive bay
embedded computer
ergonomics
Ethernet port
expansion card (adapter card)
external hard drive
FireWire 400
FireWire 800
flash drive (jump drive, USB drive, or
  thumb drive)
flash memory card
flat-panel monitor
gigabyte (GB)
gigahertz (GHz)
hard drive
hardware
hibernate
high-definition multimedia interface
  (HDMI)
impact printer
information
inkjet printer
input device
internal hard drive
keyboard
kilobyte (KB)
laser printer
legacy technology
liquid crystal display (LCD)
mainframe
megabyte (MB)
megahertz (MHz)

microphone (mic)
modem card
modem port
monitor (display screen)
motherboard
mouse
netbook
network interface card (NIC)
nonimpact printer
nonvolatile storage
notebook computer
operating system (OS)
optical drive
optical mouse
organic light-emitting diode
  (OLED) displays
output device
peripheral device
pixel
plotter
port
power supply
printer
processing
projector
QWERTY keyboard
random access memory (RAM)
read-only memory (ROM)
resolution
response time
S-video (super video)
Sleep mode
solid state drive (SSD)
sound card
speaker
stylus
supercomputer
surround-sound speaker
system software
system unit
tablet PC
terabyte (TB)
thermal printer
touch screen
touch pad
trackball mouse
trackpoint device
universal serial bus (USB) port
video card
video graphics array (VGA)
viewing angle
volatile storage
warm boot
webcam

Looking at Computers: Understanding the Parts

buzzwords

Word Bank

- CPU
- DVI
- ergonomics
- external hard drive
- FireWire
- inkjet printer
- laser printer

- LCD
- microphone
- monitor
- mouse
- notebook
- optical mouse
- QWERTY

- RAM
- ROM
- speakers
- SSD
- system unit
- USB
- webcam

Instructions: Fill in the blanks using the words from the Word Bank above.

Austin had been getting a sore back and stiff arms when he sat at his desk, so he redesigned the (1) _____ of his notebook setup. He placed the notebook in a stand so the (2) _____ was elevated to eye level and was 25 inches from his eyes. He decided to improve his equipment in other ways. His (3) _____ was old, so he replaced it with a(n) (4) _____ that didn't need a mouse pad. To plug in the mouse, he used a(n) (5) _____ port on the side of his (6) _____. He considered buying a larger (7) _____ keyboard with a number pad because it's not convenient to input numeric data with his current keyboard. Because he often printed flyers for his band, Austin decided to buy a printer that could print text-based pages quickly. Although he decided to keep his (8) _____ to print photos, he decided to buy a new (9) _____ to print his flyers faster. While looking at printers, Austin also noticed widescreen (10) _____ monitors that would provide a larger display than that on his notebook, so he bought one on sale. He hooked up the monitor to the (11) _____ port on the back of the notebook. He also bought a(n) (12) _____ that was attached to a headset and a(n) (13) _____ so he could talk to his friends over the Internet. Austin also knew he had to buy a(n) (14) _____ to back up all his files. Finally, knowing his system could use more memory, Austin checked out prices for additional (15) _____.

becoming computer literate

Your grandparents live a day's drive from your school and have just called asking you for help in purchasing a new computer, but they don't know what type of computer to get.

Instructions: Because you can't help them in person, write a letter to your grandparents detailing the differences between desktop, notebook, tablet PC, and netbook computers. Include the pros and cons of each device, and explain why or why not each device may suit your grandparents. Because your grandparents are not as familiar about these devices as you are, you should also incorporate images for each device in the letter. You may use the Internet for information, device pictures, and illustrations, but remember to credit all sources.

Instructions: Answer the multiple-choice and true–false questions below for more practice with key terms and concepts from this chapter.

Multiple Choice

1. What controls the way in which your computer system functions?
   a. System software
   b. Operating system
   c. Application software
   d. Hardware

2. Which is the most common type of monitor?
   a. LCD monitor   c. LED monitor
   b. CRT monitor   d. HD monitor

3. What enables your computer to connect with other computers?
   a. Expansion card
   b. Adapter card
   c. Video card
   d. Network interface card

4. Which is NOT another name for a flash drive?
   a. Zip   c. Jump
   b. USB   d. Thumb

5. To add additional ports to your computer, what do you need?
   a. A digital media card reader
   b. An external hard drive
   c. An expansion card
   d. A flash memory card

6. Which holds the instructions the computer needs to start up?
   a. CPU   c. USB
   b. RAM   d. ROM

7. Which is TRUE about mainframe computers?
   a. They perform complex calculations rapidly.
   b. They support hundreds of users simultaneously.
   c. They execute many programs at a fast pace.
   d. They excel at running a few programs quickly.

8. Which is NOT important to consider when buying a printer?
   a. Paper
   b. Duty cycle
   c. Cost of consumables
   d. Resolution

9. Which is NOT a storage device?
   a. External hard drive
   b. DVD
   c. Flash memory card
   d. Touch screen

10. What lets you transfer digital data between your computer and devices such as digital cameras?
    a. Flash memory card
    b. Optical drive
    c. Connectivity port
    d. HDMI port

True-False

_____ 1. The CPU clock speed determines the performance of the CPU.

_____ 2. The hard drive is an example of a nonvolatile storage device.

_____ 3. Ergonomics is important only with desktop computers, not mobile devices.

_____ 4. For printing photos, printing at 1,200 dpi is sufficient.

_____ 5. Some mice include wireless USB receivers that contain flash memory to store your files.

1. **Choosing the Best Keyboard and Mouse**

   Once you become more familiar with software products such as Microsoft Office, you may want to migrate to customized keyboard and mouse designs. Although most keyboards and mice have similar setups, there are some devices that provide special features to support different users and their specific needs. For example, some keyboards are designed specifically for multimedia use, Internet use, or gaming use. Some mice have buttons for certain tasks. Which ones are best for you?

   a. Examine the various keyboard setups at the Microsoft Web site (**microsoft.com/hardware/mouseandkeyboard/default.mspx**). Which keyboard would best suit your needs and why? What features would be most useful to you?

   b. Look at the new cool mice at **laptopshop.co.uk/news/2009/05/coolest-computer-mice**. Would any of these mice or the multitouch Magic Mouse by Apple mentioned earlier in this chapter work for you? Why or why not?

2. **Watching Device Demos**

   YouTube is a great resource for product demonstrations. Open your browser, navigate to the YouTube Web site (**youtube.com**), and search on any type of computer peripheral discussed in this chapter to see if you can find a demonstration of a cool product.

   How helpful are these demonstrations? Make a demonstration of a computing device you have and upload it to YouTube.

3. **Communicating with the Computer**

   You want to start using Voice over Internet Protocol (VoIP) to chat over the Internet with your family and friends who live far away. On the Web, investigate the following:

   a. List the devices you need to start using VoIP.

   b. Research the prices and features of each required device and create a shopping list of the specific devices you would purchase.

4. **Turn Your Monitor into a TV**

   You've heard how easy it is to convert an LCD monitor into a TV. Your parents just bought a new computer and are giving you their old PC monitor. You need a new TV for your dorm room, so you decide to give it a try.

   a. What does your monitor need to retrofit it into a TV? What other devices do you need?

   b. How much will it cost?

   c. How much do new LCD TVs cost? Is this something you would consider doing? Why or why not?

   d. What would you do if your parents gave you their old LCD TV? Could you turn it into a monitor? If so, what would you need to do that?

5. **Green Computing**

   Reducing energy consumption and promoting the recycling of computer components are key aspects of many businesses' "green" (environmentally friendly) initiatives. Using the Web, research the following:

   a. What are the key attributes of the Energy Star and EPEAT Gold green PC certifications? Does your PC have these certifications?

   b. What toxic components are contained in computers and monitors? Where can you recycle computers and monitors in your area?

   c. Check out **goodcleantech.com** and find out which companies are currently working toward better green technology. If your school had to replace computers in a lab, which environmentally friendly company would you recommend? Why?

Looking at Computers: Understanding the Parts

1. **Backing up your Work**

   You have embarked on a position as a freelance editor. You will be using your own computer. Until now you have not worried too much about backing up your data. Now, however, it's extremely important that you back up all your work frequently.

   Research the various backup options that are available including online backup, external hard drives, and portable flash storage. What are the size limitations of each? What are the initial and ongoing costs of each? How frequently do the various options allow you to perform backups? Which would be the option you would choose, and why?

2. **What Hardware Will You Use?**

   When you arrive at a new position for a company, your employer will most likely provide you with a computer. Based on the career you are in now or are planning to pursue, answer the following questions:
   a. What kind of computer system would the company mostly likely provide to you—desktop, notebook, tablet PC, or something else? How does that compare with the type of system you would prefer to work with?
   b. If you were required to use a type of computer you had never used before (such as a Mac instead of a PC), how would you go about learning to use the new computer?
   c. What other devices might your employer provide? Consider such items as smartphones or printers. How important is it in for these devices to conform to the latest trends?
   d. Should you be able to use employer-provided equipment, such as a smartphone, for personal benefit? Does your answer differ if you have to pay for part or all of the device?

3. **Exploring Monitors**

   You have been asked to help edit video for a friend. You have a great notebook computer, which is powerful enough to handle this type of task, but you need to buy a separate LCD monitor to hook up to your computer and are not exactly sure what to buy. You know it should be larger than 15", capable of displaying HD, and can't cost more than $200.
   a. Research five different monitors that would fit your needs. Create a table that lists each monitor and its specifications, including display type, screen size, aspect ratio, native resolution, and response time. Also list the types of ports and connectors the monitor has.
   b. Note whether each monitor has HDMI. Why or why not would HDMI capability be important?
   c. Research two LED monitors. Would an LED monitor be a viable option? Explain.

   Explain which of the five monitors would best suit your needs and why.

4. **What's the Coolest Mouse?**

   The Luxeed Dynamic Pixel LED Keyboard is a very cool keyboard that was described in the "How Cool Is *This?*" feature at the beginning of the chapter. There are some equally cool and innovative mice on the market. For example, some mice have vertical orientations, are washable, and can be used without touching a surface. Investigate some of these new mice and come up with your list of the top five coolest ones. Which one would be your choice to be "The Coolest Mouse"?

5. **Choosing the Best Laser Printer**

   You are looking to replace your inkjet printer with a laser printer. You haven't decided whether a color laser printer is necessary.
   a. What are the cost considerations between getting a laser printer and a color laser printer (i.e., initial costs, costs of cartridges, and so on)?
   b. Investigate wireless and Bluetooth options. What are the considerations involved with regard to these features?
   c. Investigate all-in-one laser printers that have printer, scanner, and fax capabilities. How much more expensive are they than laser printers? Are there any drawbacks to these multipurpose machines? Do they perform each function as well as their stand-alone counterparts do? Can you print in color on these machines?

   Based on your research, which printer would be your choice, and why?

Looking at Computers: Understanding the Parts

Instructions: Albert Einstein used *Gedankenexperiments*, or critical thinking questions, to develop his theory of relativity. Some ideas are best understood by experimenting with them in our own minds. The following critical thinking questions are designed to demand your full attention but require only a comfortable chair—no technology.

1. Computer of the Future

Think about how mobile our computing devices have become and the convergence of different devices such as cameras, phones, computers, etc. What do you think the computer of the future will be like? What capabilities will it have that computers currently don't have? Do you see desktop computers becoming obsolete in the near future?

2. Table Monitors and Surface Monitors

Table monitors and surface monitors are tabletop devices that are designed to "grab" and manipulate objects on the display. Like an iPod touch or iPhone, the display is multitouch and can accept simultaneous input from multiple users, so the table monitor can be helpful with games or other products that require interactivity. Microsoft launched a product called "Surface" in 2007, and although it never really took off, you see similar devices featured on some TV crime-fighting shows as detectives manipulate crime evidence and photos. Why do you think this device never really captured the interest of the public? Would this be a useful object to have in your home, classroom, or office? Why or why not?

3. Storage on the Web

There are many options available to store your files in the "cloud" (i.e., on the Web). What do you think are the advantages of this type of storage versus storing your files on a physical device such as a hard drive or flash drive? What are the disadvantages?

4. Computers and Productivity

How have computers increased your productivity as a student? How have computers decreased your productivity? Would your answers be any different if you were working in an office? Why or why not? Would your parents answer any differently if you asked them how computers have increased or decreased their productivity levels?

5. "Smart" Cars

Cars are becoming more technically advanced every day. They are now able to parallel park by themselves, avoid collisions, alert you if you are falling asleep at the wheel, provide emergency response, and sense if you are going to back up over something inadvertently. What other technical advances do you see cars incorporating? Do you think that any of these current or potential advancements could result in unexpected negative consequences? If so, what?

6. iPad

The Apple iPad has been enthusiastically accepted because of its multitouch screen, useful applications, and small, light frame. But it is without certain features that might make it even better. If Steven Jobs, the CEO of Apple, were to ask you for your advice as to what to include in the next version of the iPad, what would you suggest?

Looking at Computers: Understanding the Parts

Notebook Versus Desktop: Which Is Best?

Problem

You have joined a small business that is beginning to evaluate its technology setup. Because of the addition of several new sales representatives and other administrative employees, many new computers need to be purchased. You are trying to decide which would be better to purchase: notebook computers, tablet PCs, or desktops or a combination.

Task

Split your class into small groups, divide each group into three teams, and assign the following tasks:

Member A explores the benefits and downfalls of desktop computers.
Member B explores the benefits and downfalls of notebook computers.
Member C explores the benefits and downfalls of tablet PCs.

Process

1. Form the teams. Think about what the technology goals are for the company and what information and resources you need to tackle this project.
2. Research and then discuss the components of each system you are recommending. Are any components better suited for the particular needs of the various employees (sales representatives versus administrative staff)? Consider all the input, output, processing, and storage devices. Are any special devices or peripherals required?
3. Consider the different types of employees in the company. Would a combination of devices be better than a single solution? If so, what kinds of employees would get which type of computer?
4. As a team, write a summary position paper. Support your system recommendation for the company. Each team member should include why his or her type of computer will be part of the solution or not.

Conclusion

Desktop, notebook, and tablet PC computers have their own merits as computing systems. Beyond portability, there are other things to think about. Being aware of the options in the marketplace, knowing how to analyze the trade-offs of different designs, and recognizing the different needs each type fulfills allows you to become a better consumer as well as a better computer user.

ethics project

Ethical conduct is a stream of decisions you make all day long. In this exercise, you will research and then role-play a complicated ethical situation. The role you play may or may not match your own personal beliefs but your research and use of logic will enable you to represent whichever view is assigned. An arbitrator will watch and comment on both sides of the arguments, and together the team will agree on an ethical solution.

Topic: Green Computing

Green computing—conducting computing needs with the least possible amount of power—is on everyone's minds. Although it's hard to argue with an environmentally conscious agenda, the pinch to our pocketbooks and the loss of some comforts sometimes makes green computing difficult. Businesses, including colleges, need to consider a variety of issues and concerns before jumping into a complete green overhaul.

Research Areas to Consider

- End-of-life management: E-waste and recycling
- Energy-efficient devices
- Costs of green computing
- Government funding and incentives

Process

Divide the class into teams.

1. Research the areas cited above and devise a scenario in which your college is considering modifying its current technology setup to a more green IT strategy.
2. Team members should write a summary that provides background information for their character—for example, environmentalist, college IT administrator, or arbitrator—and details their character's behaviors to set the stage for the role-playing event. Then, team members should create an outline to use during the role-playing event.
3. Team members should arrange a mutually convenient time to meet for the exchange, using the chat room feature of MyITLab, the discussion board feature of Blackboard, or meeting in person.
4. Team members should present their case to the class or submit a PowerPoint presentation for review by the rest of the class, along with the summary and resolution they developed.

Conclusion

As technology becomes ever more prevalent and integrated into our lives, more and more ethical dilemmas will present themselves. Being able to understand and evaluate both sides of the argument, while responding in a personally or socially ethical manner, will be an important skill.

all-in-one computer A desktop system unit that houses the computer's processor, memory, and monitor in a single unit.

all-in-one printer A device that combines the functions of a printer, scanner, fax machine, and copier into one machine.

application software The set of programs on a computer that helps a user carry out tasks such as word processing, sending e-mail, balancing a budget, creating presentations, editing photos, taking an online course, and playing games.

aspect ratio The width-to-height proportion of a monitor.

binary digit (bit) A digit that corresponds to the on and off states of a computer's switches. A bit contains a value of either 0 or 1.

binary language The language computers use to process data into information, consisting of only the values 0 and 1.

Blu-ray disc A method of optical storage for digital data, developed for storing high-definition media. It has the largest storage capacity of all optical storage options.

Bluetooth technology A type of wireless technology that uses radio waves to transmit data over short distances (approximately 30 feet for Bluetooth 1 and 60 feet for Bluetooth 2). Often used to connect peripherals such as printers and keyboards to computers or headsets to cell phones.

brightness A measure of the greatest amount of light showing when a monitor is displaying pure white; measured as candelas per square meter (cd/m²) or *nits*.

byte Eight binary digits (bits).

central processing unit (CPU or processor) The part of the system unit of a computer that is responsible for data processing (the "brains" of the computer); it is the largest and most important chip in the computer. The CPU controls all the functions performed by the computer's other components and processes all the commands issued to it by software instructions.

cold boot The process of starting a computer from a powered-down or off state.

compact disc (CD) A method of optical storage for digital data; originally developed for storing digital audio.

computer A data-processing device that gathers, processes, outputs, and stores data and information.

connectivity port A port that enables the computer (or other device) to be connected to other devices or systems such as networks, modems, and the Internet.

contrast ratio A measure of the difference in light intensity between the brightest white and the darkest black colors that a monitor can produce. If the contrast ratio is too low, colors tend to fade when the brightness is adjusted to a high or low setting.

cursor control key A set of controls on standard keyboards that moves the *cursor* (the flashing symbol on the monitor that indicates where the next character will be inserted); also known as an *arrow key*.

data Numbers, words, pictures, or sounds that represent facts, figures, or ideas.

desktop computer A computer that is intended for use at a single location. A desktop computer consists of a case that houses the main components of the computer, plus peripheral devices.

digital video disc (DVD) A method of optical storage for digital data that has greater storage capacity than compact discs.

digital video interface (DVI) Video interface technology that newer LCD monitors, as well as other multimedia devices such as televisions, DVD players, and projectors, use to connect to a PC.

drive bay A special shelf inside a computer that is designed to hold storage devices.

embedded computer A specially designed computer chip that resides inside another device, such as a car. These self-contained computer devices have their own programming and typically neither receive input from users nor interact with other systems.

ergonomics How a user sets up his or her computer and other equipment to minimize risk of injury or discomfort.

Ethernet port A port that is slightly larger than a standard phone jack and transfers data at speeds of up to 10,000 Mbps; used to connect a computer to a DSL or cable modem or a network.

expansion card (adapter card) A circuit board with specific functions that augment the computer's basic functions and provide connections to other devices; examples include the sound card and the video card.

external hard drive An internal hard drive that is enclosed in a protective case to make it portable; the drive is connected to the computer with a data transfer cable and is often used to back up data.

FireWire 400 (IEEE 1394) An interface port that transfers data at 400 Mbps.

FireWire 800 One of the fastest ports available, moving data at 800 Mbps.

flash drive A drive that plugs into a universal serial bus (USB) port on a computer and stores data digitally. Also called *USB drive*, *jump drive*, or *thumb drive*.

flash memory card A form of portable storage; this removable memory card is often used in digital cameras, portable media players, and personal digital assistants (PDAs).

flat-panel monitor A type of monitor that is lighter and more energy-efficient than a CRT monitor; often used with portable computers such as notebooks.

gigabyte (GB) About a billion bytes.

gigahertz (GHz) One billion hertz.

glossary

hard drive A device that holds all permanently stored programs and data; can be located inside the system unit or attached to the system unit via a USB port.

hardware Any part of the computer you can physically touch.

hibernate A power-management mode that saves the current state of the current system to the computer's hard drive.

high-definition multimedia interface (HDMI) A compact audio–video interface standard that carries both high-definition video and uncompressed digital audio.

impact printer A printer that has tiny hammer-like keys that strike the paper through an inked ribbon, thus making a mark on the paper. The most common impact printer is the dot-matrix printer.

information Data that has been organized or presented in a meaningful fashion.

inkjet printer A nonimpact printer that sprays tiny drops of ink onto paper.

input device A hardware device used to enter, or input, data (text, images, and sounds) and instructions (user responses and commands) into a computer. Some input devices are keyboards and mice.

internal hard drive A hard drive that is installed inside the system unit.

keyword (1) A specific word a user wishes to query (or look for) in an Internet search. (2) A specific word that has a predefined meaning in a particular programming language.

kilobyte (KB) A unit of computer storage equal to approximately one thousand bytes.

laser printer A nonimpact printer known for quick and quiet production and high-quality printouts.

legacy technology Comprises computing devices, software, or peripherals that use techniques, parts, and methods from an earlier time that are no longer popular.

liquid crystal display (LCD) The technology used in flat-panel computer monitors.

mainframe A large, expensive computer that supports hundreds or thousands of users simultaneously and executes many different programs at the same time.

megabyte (MB) A unit of computer storage equal to approximately 1 million bytes.

megahertz (MHz) A measure of processing speed equal to 1 million hertz.

microphone (mic) A device that allows you to capture sound waves, such as those created by your voice, and transfer them to digital format on your computer.

modem card An expansion card that provides the computer with a connection to the Internet via conventional phone lines.

modem port A port that uses a traditional telephone signal to connect a computer to the Internet.

monitor (display screen) A common output device that displays text, graphics, and video as soft copies (copies that can be seen only on screen).

motherboard A special circuit board in the system unit that contains the central processing unit (CPU), the memory (RAM) chips, and the slots available for expansion cards; all of the other boards (video cards, sound cards, and so on) connect to it to receive power and to communicate.

mouse A hardware device used to enter user responses and commands into a computer.

netbook A computing device that runs a full-featured operating system but weighs two pounds or less.

network interface card (NIC) An expansion card that enables a computer to connect other computers or to a cable modem to facilitate a high-speed Internet connection.

nonimpact printer A printer that sprays ink or uses laser beams to make marks on the paper. The most common nonimpact printers are inkjet and laser printers.

nonvolatile storage Permanent storage, as in read-only memory (ROM).

notebook computer A small, compact portable computer.

operating system (OS) The system software that controls the way in which a computer system functions, including the management of hardware, peripherals, and software.

optical drive A hardware device that uses lasers or light to read from, and maybe even write to, CDs, DVDs, or Blu-ray discs.

optical mouse A mouse that uses an internal sensor or laser to control the mouse's movement. The sensor sends signals to the computer, telling it where to move the pointer on the screen.

organic light-emitting diode (OLED) display A display that uses organic compounds to produce light when exposed to an electric current. Unlike LCDs, OLEDs do not require a backlight to function and therefore draw less power and have a much thinner display, sometimes as thin as 3 mm.

output device A device that sends processed data and information out of a computer in the form of text, pictures (graphics), sounds (audio), or video.

peripheral device A device such as a monitor, printer, or keyboard that connects to the system unit through ports.

pixel A single point that creates the images on a computer monitor. Pixels are illuminated by an electron beam that passes rapidly back and forth across the back of the screen so that the pixels appear to glow continuously.

plotter A large printer that uses a computer-controlled pen to produce oversize pictures that require precise continuous lines to be drawn, such as maps and architectural plans.

port An interface through which external devices are connected to the computer.

power supply A power supply regulates the wall voltage to the voltages required by computer chips; it is housed inside the system unit.

printer A common output device that creates tangible or hard copies of text and graphics.

processing Manipulating or organizing data into information.

projector A device that can project images from your computer onto a wall or viewing screen.

QWERTY keyboard A keyboard that gets its name from the first six letters on the top-left row of alphabetic keys on the keyboard.

random access memory (RAM) The computer's temporary storage space or short-term memory. It is located in a set of chips on the system unit's motherboard, and its capacity is measured in megabytes or gigabytes.

read-only memory (ROM) A set of memory chips, located on the motherboard, which stores data and instructions that cannot be changed or erased; it holds all the instructions the computer needs to start up.

resolution The clearness or sharpness of an image, which is controlled by the number of pixels displayed on the screen.

response time The measurement (in milliseconds) of the time it takes for a pixel to change color; the lower the response time, the smoother moving images will appear on the monitor.

S-video (super video) A type of technology used to transmit video signals; used on newer LCD monitors, as well as other multimedia devices such as televisions, DVD players, and projectors.

Sleep mode A low-power mode for electronic devices such as computers that saves electric power consumption and saves your computer settings where you left off. When the computer is "woken up," you can resume working more quickly than when cold booting the computer.

solid state drive (SSD) A drive that uses the same kind of memory that flash drives use, but can reach data in only a tenth of the time a flash drive requires.

sound card An expansion card that attaches to the motherboard inside the system unit and that enables the computer to produce sounds by providing a connection for the speakers and microphone.

speaker An output device for sound.

stylus A pen-shaped device used to tap or write on touch-sensitive screens.

supercomputer A specially designed computer that can perform complex calculations extremely rapidly; used in situations in which complex models requiring intensive mathematical calculations are needed (such as weather forecasting or atomic energy research).

surround-sound speakers Speaker systems set up in such a way that they surround an entire area (and the people in it) with sound.

system software The set of programs that enables a computer's hardware devices and application software to work together; it includes the operating system and utility programs.

system unit The metal or plastic case that holds all the physical parts of the computer together, including the computer's processor (its brains), its memory, and the many circuit boards that help the computer function.

Tablet PC A notebook computer designed specifically to work with handwriting recognition technology.

terabyte 1,099,511,627,776 bytes or 2^{40} bytes.

thermal printer A printer that works either by melting wax-based ink onto ordinary paper (in a process called *thermal wax transfer printing*) or by burning dots onto specially coated paper (in a process called *direct thermal printing*).

touch screen A type of monitor (or display in a notebook or PDA) that accepts input from a user touching the screen.

touchpad A small, touch-sensitive screen at the base of a notebook keyboard. To use the touchpad, you simply move your finger across the pad to direct the cursor.

trackball mouse A mouse with a rollerball on top instead of on the bottom. Because you move the trackball with your fingers, it doesn't require much wrist motion, so it's considered healthier for your wrists than a traditional mouse.

trackpoint device A small, joystick-like nub that enables you to move the cursor with the tip of your finger.

universal serial bus (USB) port A port that can connect a wide variety of peripheral devices to the computer, including keyboards, printers, mice, smartphones, PDAs, flash drives, and digital cameras.

video card (video adapter) An expansion card that is installed inside a system unit to translate binary data (the 1s and 0s the computer uses) into the images viewed on the monitor.

video graphics array (VGA) port A port to which a CRT monitor connects.

viewing angle Measured in degrees, this tells how far you can move to the side of (or above or below) the monitor before the image quality degrades to unacceptable levels.

volatile storage Temporary storage, such as in random access memory (RAM). When the power is off, the data in volatile storage is cleared out.

warm boot The process of restarting the system while it's powered on.

webcam A small camera that sits on top of a computer monitor (connected to the computer by a cable) or is built into a notebook computer and is usually used to transfer live video.

credits

Figure 3	Apple Computer, Inc.	**Figure 34a**	D. Hurst\Alamy Images Royalty Free
Figure 5	Wacom Technology Corporation	**Figure 34b**	Courtesy Western Digital Corporation
Figure 6	Logitech Inc.	**Figure 34c**	Christophe Testi\Shutterstock
Figure 7	Alan Ford\Alamy Images	**Figure 34d**	Sony Electronics, Inc.\ Newscom
Figure 8a	Martin Meissner\AP Wide World Photos	**Figure 34e**	Olaf Jansen\Alamy Images
Figure 8b	Ergodex	**Figure 34f**	Studio 101\Alamy Images Royalty Free
Figure 11	Lenovo, Inc.	**Figure 34g**	Studio 101\Alamy Images Royalty Free
Figure 12	Newton Peripherals, LLC		
Figure 14	Hewlett-Packard Company	**Figure 34h**	Samsung Electronics America, Inc.
Figure 15	EPOS	**Figure 34i**	Silicon Power Computer and Communications
Figure 16a	Courtesy of Sony Electronics Inc.		
Figure 16b	Fancy/Veer\Corbis RF	**Figure 35a**	David A. Tietz
Figure 17	Bennet\The Christian Science Publishing Society	**Figure 35b**	Hewlett Packard HP 1
Figure 18	Blue Microphones	**Figure 36**	Phil Burton\Alamy Images
Figure 19	© Owen Franken/Corbis	**Figure 37**	David A. Tietz
Figure 22b	PRNewsFoto/NEC Solutions (America) Inc.\AP Wide World Photos	**Figure 38**	Editorial Image, LLC\Alamy Images Royalty Free
		Figure 38a	Tim Arbaev\Shutterstock
Figure 23	Canon U.S.A., Inc.	**Figure 38b**	Szymon Apanowicz\ Shutterstock
Figure 24	Courtesy Xerox Corporation		
Figure 26	Photo courtesy of XEROX Corporate Public Relations.	**Figure 40**	Syd M Johnson\The Image Works
Figure 27	Extech Instruments Corporation	**Figure 42a**	Artur Synenko\Shutterstock
Figure 29	© 2008 XFXForce.com	**Figure 43**	Look Twice\Alamy Images
Figure 31	Hugh Threlfall\Alamy Images	**Figure 46**	ROBYN BECK/AFP/Getty Images\Newscom
Figure 31b	Lenovo, Inc.		
Figure 32b	Photo courtesy of Iomega Corporation	**Figure 47**	Courtesy of Sony Electronics Inc.
Figure 32c	Courtesy Western Digital Corporation	**Figure 48**	Tom Theobald\Alamy Images
Figure 33a	Rafael Angel Irusta Machin\Alamy Images Royalty Free		
Figure 33b	Handout/KRT\Newscom		
Figure 33c	Copyright 2008 Mimoco. COURTESY OF LUCASFILM LTD. TM & © Lucasfilm Ltd. All rights reserved. Used under authorization. Unauthorized duplication is a violation of applicable law.		

understanding and assessing hardware:

evaluating your system

From Chapter 6 of *Technology in Action Complete,* Eighth Edition, Alan Evans, Kendall Martin, Mary Anne Poatsy.

understanding and assessing hardware:

evaluating your system

how cool is *this?*

It used to be that the case for a desktop computer was just a boring rectangular box—but no longer! Consider some of the new designs on the market. On the **Phobos** computer system by BFG Technologies, the front of the case features a **touch-panel LCD** that reports system performance parameters, controls music content, and presents a summary of storage and memory usage. There is also an integrated iPod/iPhone **docking station** on the top of the case. Or consider Falcon NorthWest, which delivers **custom paint** jobs on its system cases—images from its library, your own image, or even a screen from your favorite game.

The Thermaltake Level 10 wins for pure **artistry**. It isolates all the major subsections—motherboard, power supply, hard drives, optical drives—in a separate physical space. Each section is hinged and can swing open for easy access. Made of aluminum, the entire case helps disperse heat . . . and looks cool doing it!

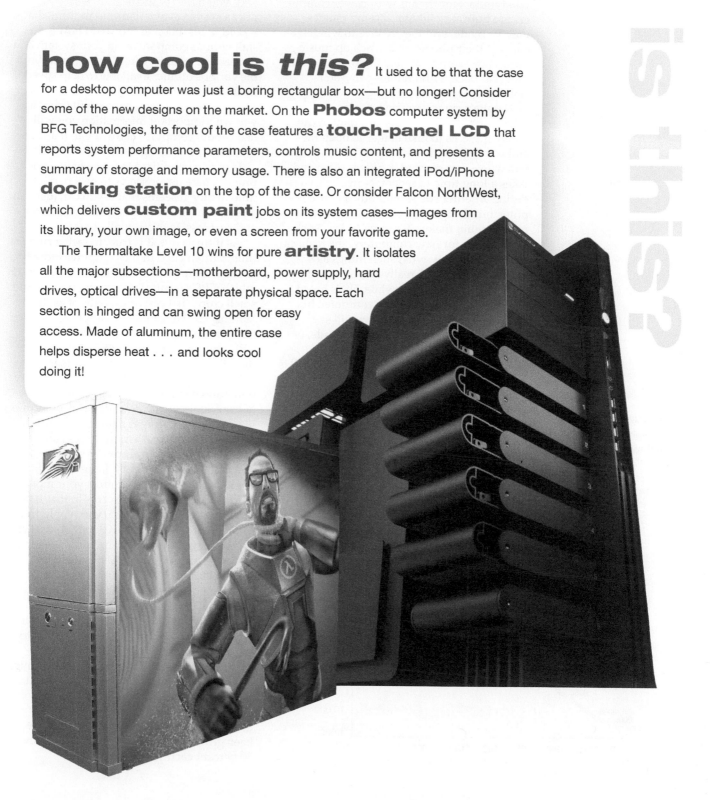

Is It the Computer or Me?

After saving up for a computer, Natalie took the leap a couple of years ago and bought a new desktop PC. Now she is wondering what to do. Her friends with newer computers are burning high-def Blu-ray movies they've made, and they're able to wirelessly connect their phones and synch up music files. They seem to be able to do a hundred things at once without their computers slowing down at all.

Natalie's computer can't do any of these things—or at least she doesn't think it can. Lately it seems to take longer to open files and scroll through Web pages. Making matters worse, her computer freezes often and takes a long time to reboot. Now she's wondering whether she should buy a new computer, but the thought of spending all that money again makes her think twice. As she looks at ads for new computers, she realizes she doesn't know what such things as "CPU" and "RAM" really are, or how they affect her system. Meanwhile, she's heard it's possible to upgrade her computer, but the task seems daunting. How will she know what she needs to do to upgrade, or whether it's even worth it?

Are you in the same situation? How well is your computer meeting your needs? Do you ever wonder whether your computer is fine and you just need more training to get it to work smoothly? Is that true, or do you really need a more sophisticated computer system? In this chapter, you'll learn how to evaluate your computer system to determine whether it is meeting your needs. You'll start by figuring out what you want your ideal computer to be able to do. You'll then learn more about important components of your computer— its CPU, memory, storage devices, audio and video devices, and ports—and how these components affect your system. Along the way, you'll find worksheets to help you conduct a system evaluation, and multimedia Sound Bytes that will show you how to install various components in your system and increase its reliability. You'll also learn about the various utilities available to help speed up and clean up your system. If you don't have a computer, this chapter will provide you with important information you will need about computer hardware to make an informed purchasing decision.

Is now a good time to buy a new computer? There never seems to be a perfect time to buy. It seems that if you can just wait a year, computers will inevitably be faster and cost less. Is this actually true?

As it turns out, it is true. In fact, a rule of thumb often cited in the computer industry, called **Moore's Law**, describes the pace at which CPUs (central processing units)—the small chips that can be thought of as the "brains" of the computer—improve. Named for Gordon Moore, the cofounder of the CPU chip manufacturer Intel, this rule predicts that the number of transistors inside a CPU will increase so fast that CPU capacity will double every 18 months. (The number of transistors on a CPU chip helps determine how fast it can process data.)

As you can see in Figure 1, this rule of thumb has held true since 1970, when Moore first published his theory. Imagine finding a bank that would agree to treat your money in this way. If you put 10 cents in that kind of savings account in 1965, you would have a balance of more than $100 million today! Moore himself, however, has predicted that around the year 2020 CPU chips will be manufactured in a different way, thus changing or eliminating the effects of Moore's Law altogether.

In addition to the CPU becoming faster, other system components also continue to improve dramatically. For example, the capacity of memory chips such as dynamic random access memory (DRAM)—the most common form of memory found in personal computers—increases about 60 percent every year. Meanwhile, hard drives have been growing in storage capacity by some 50 percent each year.

Figure 1

Moore's Law predicts that CPUs will continue to get faster.

Source: Adapted from the Moore's Law animated demo at Intel.com.

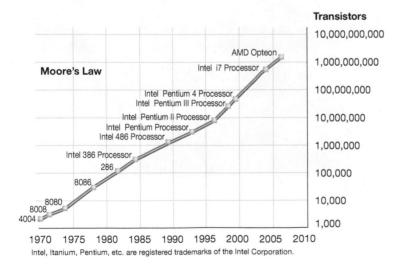

Intel, Itanium, Pentium, etc. are registered trademarks of the Intel Corporation.

So, with technology advancing so quickly, how do you make sure you have a computer that matches your needs? No one wants to buy a new computer every year just to keep up with technology. Even if money weren't a consideration, the time it would take to transfer all of your files and reinstall and reconfigure your software would make buying a new computer every year terribly inefficient. Extending the life of a computer also reduces or postpones the environmental and security concerns involved in the disposal of computers.

No one wants to keep doing costly upgrades that won't significantly extend the life of a system, either. How can you determine if your system is suitable or if it just needs to be upgraded? Moreover, how can you know which is the better option—upgrading or buying a new computer? The first step is figuring out what you want your computer to do for you.

What Is Your Ideal Computer?

As you decide whether your computer suits you, it's important to know exactly what you would want your ideal computer system to be able to do. Later, as you perform a system evaluation, you can compare your existing system to your ideal system. This will help you determine whether you should purchase hardware components to add to your system or buy a new system.

But what if I don't have a computer? Even if you're a new computer user and are looking to buy your first system, you will still need to evaluate what you want your system to do for you before you purchase a computer. Being able to understand and evaluate computer systems will make you a more informed buyer. You should be comfortable answering questions such as "What kinds of CPUs are there, and how does the CPU affect system performance?" and "How much RAM do I need, and what role will it play in my system?" It's important for you to be able to answer such questions before you buy a computer.

How do I know what my ideal system is? To determine your ideal system, consider what you want to be able to do with

"To determine your ideal system, consider what you want to be able to do with your computer."

your computer. For example, do you need to bring your computer to school or work with you? Do you want to be able to edit digital photos and video? Do you want to watch and record Blu-ray discs? Or do you mainly use your computer for word processing and Internet access? The worksheet in Figure 2 lists a number of ways in which you may want to use your computer. In the second column, place a check next to those computer uses that apply to you. Also, set a priority of high, medium, or low in the rightmost column so that you can determine which features are most important to you.

Next, look at the list of desired uses for your computer and determine whether your current system can perform these activities. If there are things it can't do, you may need to purchase additional hardware or a new computer. For example, if you want to play and burn CDs and DVDs, all you need is a DVD–RW drive. However, you need a Blu-ray burner if you want to burn (record) the higher capacity Blu-ray discs. Likewise, if you plan to edit digital video files or play games that require high video frame rates for smooth in-game motion and have amazing soundtracks, you may want to add more memory, upgrade your video card, and buy a better set of speakers. Depending on the costs of the individual upgrade components, you may be better off buying a new system.

BITS AND BYTES

Moving to a New Computer Doesn't Have to Be Painful

Are you ready to buy a new computer but dread the prospect of transferring all your files and redoing all of your Windows settings? You could transfer all those files and settings manually, but Windows stores much information in the registry files, which can be tricky to update. So what do you do? Windows 7 incorporates Windows Easy Transfer, which lets you migrate files and settings from a Windows Vista system to a Windows 7 system via a network connection by using a flash drive or external hard drive or using optical media such as a CD or DVD.

Alternatively, other PC migration software is available, such as LapLink's PCmover, which is designed to make the transition to a new computer easier. For the latest information on such utilities, search on migration software at PCmag (**pcmag.com**). You'll be ready to upgrade painlessly in no time. If you prefer to avoid the do-it-yourself option, support technicians at retail stores (such as the Geek Squad at Best Buy) will often perform the migration for a small charge.

Figure 2 | WHAT SHOULD YOUR IDEAL COMPUTER SYSTEM BE ABLE TO DO?

Computer Uses	Do You Want Your System to Do This?	Can Your System Do This Now?	Priority (High, Medium, Low)
Portability Uses			
Be light enough to carry easily			
Access the Internet wirelessly			
Entertainment Uses			
Access the Internet			
Play and record CDs and DVDs			
Play and record Blu-ray discs			
Record and edit digital videos			
Record and edit digital music			
Edit digital photos			
Play graphics-intensive games			
Transfer files wirelessly to mobile devices and other computers			
Transfer files using flash memory cards			
Upload media to social networking sites			
Have your peripheral devices work easily and speedily with your computer			
Purchase/rent music and videos from the Internet			
Talk with friends and family with live video and audio			
Use the computer to stream television and movies			
Other			
Educational Uses			
Perform word processing tasks			
Use educational software			
Access library and newspaper archives			
Create multimedia presentations			
Create backups of all your files			
Record notes with synchronized audio recordings			
Other			
Business Uses			
Create spreadsheets and databases			
Work on multiple software applications quickly and simultaneously			
Conduct online banking, pay bills online, or prepare your taxes			
Conduct online job searches or post résumés			
Synchronize your mobile device (smartphone or portable media player) with your computer			
Conduct online meetings with video and audio			
Organize business contacts and manage scheduling			
Other			

Understanding and Assessing Hardware: Evaluating Your System

Note that you also may need new software and training to use new system components. Many computer users forget to consider the training they'll need when they upgrade their computer. Missing any one of these pieces might make the difference between your computer enriching your life and its becoming another source of stress.

Where do I get the training I need? Of course, colleges offer a number of training options from full semester classes, to online modules, to weekend courses. In addition many online tutorials are available for most software products. For specific questions or skills, be sure to check YouTube and podcast directories. Many valuable series exist that answer your questions in step-by-step video demonstrations, such as MrExcel or Photoshop Quicktips. Some manufacturers, like Apple, offer classes at their stores for a yearly fee. Training shouldn't be an afterthought. Consider the time and effort involved in learning about what you want your computer to do before you buy hardware or software. If you don't, you may have a wonderful computer system but lack the skills necessary to take full advantage of it.

Choosing Either a Desktop or Notebook System

The first step in evaluating your system needs is determining whether you want a desktop or a notebook. In this discussion, we'll only be considering full-size desktops and notebooks. If your main need is Internet connectivity, not processing power, and a small screen and small keyboard are acceptable, a netbook may be a workable option.

To make the best decision, it's important to evaluate how and where you will use the computer. The main distinction between desktops and notebooks is portability. If you indicated in the chart in Figure 2 that you need to take your computer with you to work or school, or even want the flexibility to move from room to room in your house, a notebook is the best choice. If portability is not an absolute requirement, you should consider a desktop.

How does a notebook compare to a desktop for value? Desktop systems are invariably a better value than notebooks in terms of computing power gained for your dollar. Because of the notebook's small footprint (the amount of space it takes up on the desk), you pay more for each component. Each piece has had extra engineering time invested to make sure it fits in the smallest space. In addition, a desktop system offers more expandability options. It's easier to add new ports and devices because of the amount of room available in the desktop computer's design.

If a large monitor is important, desktops have an edge. Although 18-inch screens are now available on some notebooks, the weight of these systems (often more than 10 pounds) makes them really more of a "desktop replacement" than a portable computing solution. Light notebooks typically have 17-inch screens or smaller, while inexpensive 23-inch monitors are readily available for desktop solutions. If you need a large screen and portability, you may end up buying a notebook and a fixed desk monitor to connect to when you are at home, an extra cost.

Desktop systems also are more reliable. Because of the amount of vibration that a notebook experiences and the added exposure to dust, water, and temperature fluctuations that portability brings, notebooks often have a shorter lifespan than desktop computers. Manufacturers offer extended warranty plans that cover accidental damage and unexpected drops; however, such plans may be costly.

 **Taking Your System Out of the Box**

You just brought your brand-new machine home, and it's loaded up with all kinds of bloat! Here are two steps you can take right away to have that truly fresh beginning you were hoping for.

1. Remove the preinstalled trial programs and advertisements installed by most vendors. A quick way to do this is with the free program PC DeCrapifier. Its wizard walks you through uninstalling the most common annoyances that came preloaded on your new system.

2. Grab the really valuable free software you *will* want to use. Consider loading OpenOffice.org, Firefox, iTunes, Picasa, and Gimp. (These packages are discussed in more detail in the Technology in Focus section titled "Computing Alternatives.")

Now go enjoy your new machine!

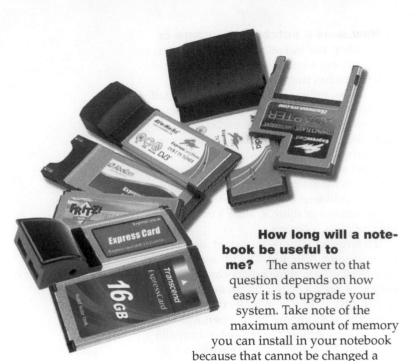

Figure 3

ExpressCards add functionality to your notebook.

How long will a notebook be useful to me? The answer to that question depends on how easy it is to upgrade your system. Take note of the maximum amount of memory you can install in your notebook because that cannot be changed a few years down the road. Internal hard drives are not easy for novices to install in a notebook, but if you have a fast transfer port like an **external SATA (eSATA)** or USB 3.0 on your notebook, you can easily add an external hard drive for more storage space.

Notebooks are often equipped with an ExpressCard slot. **ExpressCard** (shown in Figure 3) can add a solid state drive (SSD), eSATA and FireWire ports, and other capabilities to your system. You can add an ExpressCard that allows you to read flash memory cards such as CompactFlash, Memory Sticks, and Secure Digital cards. As new types of ports and devices are introduced, like those for the new USB 3.0 standard, they will be manufactured in ExpressCard formats so you can make sure your notebook does not become obsolete before its time. Figure 4 summarizes the advantages and disadvantages of each style of computer.

Assessing Your Hardware: Evaluating Your System

With a better picture of your ideal computer system in mind, you can make a more informed assessment of your current computer. To determine whether your computer system has the right hardware components to do what you ultimately want it to do, you need to conduct a **system evaluation**. To do this, you look at your computer's subsystems, see what they do, and check how they perform. These subsystems include the following:

- CPU subsystem
- Memory subsystem (the computer's random access memory, or RAM)
- Storage subsystem (hard drive and other drives)
- Video subsystem (video card and monitor)
- Audio subsystem (sound card and speakers)
- Ports

In the rest of this chapter, we will examine each subsystem. At the end of each section, you'll find a small worksheet you can use to evaluate each subsystem on your computer. *Note:* This chapter discusses tools you can use to assess a Windows-based PC.

Evaluating the CPU Subsystem

Early in the process of determining whether your computer system adequately meets your needs, you'll want to consider the type

Figure 4 | DESKTOP VERSUS NOTEBOOK COMPUTERS—WHICH FITS YOU?

Notebooks	Desktops
Portable—lightweight, thin	Best value: more processing power, memory, and storage capacity for lower price
Take up less physical space	More difficult to steal, less susceptible to damage from dropping or mishandling
Easier to ship or transport if the system needs repair	Easier to expand and upgrade
Smaller video display (17 inches or smaller)	Large monitors available (19 inches or larger)

of processor in your system. Your computer's central processing unit (CPU or processor) is critically important because it processes instructions, performs calculations, manages the flow of information through a computer system, and is responsible for turning raw data into valuable information through processing operations. The CPU is located on the motherboard, the primary circuit board of the computer system. There are several types of processors on the market including Intel processors (such as the Core family with the i7, i5, i3, and the Centrino line) and AMD processors (such as the Athlon and Phenom). The Intel Core i7 is the most advanced desktop CPU ever made by Intel. Figure 5 shows the i7 as well as the three-core PowerPC processor used in the Microsoft Xbox 360 gaming console, the Xenon.

Figure 5

(a) The Intel i7 is the most advanced desktop CPU ever made by Intel. (b) The Microsoft Xbox 360 gaming console uses a custom PowerPC–based CPU to perform 115 billion calculations per second.

How does the CPU work? The CPU is comprised of two units: the control unit and the arithmetic logic unit (ALU). The control unit coordinates the activities of all the other computer components. The ALU is responsible for performing all the arithmetic calculations (addition, subtraction, multiplication, and division). The ALU also makes logic and comparison decisions such as comparing items to determine if one is greater than, less than, equal to, or not equal to another.

Every time the CPU performs a program instruction, it goes through the same series of steps. First, it fetches the required piece of data or instruction from RAM, the temporary storage location for all the data and instructions the computer needs while it is running. Next, it decodes the instruction into something the computer can understand. Once the CPU has decoded the instruction, it executes the instruction and stores the result to RAM before fetching the next instruction. This process is called a machine cycle.

What makes one CPU different from another? The primary distinction between CPUs is processing power, which is determined by a number of factors. One such factor is the design of the CPU in terms of the number of cores. A **core** is a complete processing section from a CPU embedded into one physical chip. In addition to core design, other factors differentiate CPUs, including how quickly the processor can work (called its **clock speed**) and the amount of immediate access memory the CPU has (called its cache memory).

How will a multiple-core CPU help me? CPUs began to execute more than one instruction at a time quite a while ago, when hyperthreading was introduced. **Hyperthreading** provides quicker processing of information by enabling a new set of instructions to start executing before the previous set has finished. The most recent design innovation for PC processors, an improvement upon hyperthreading, is the use of multiple cores on one CPU chip. With core technology, two or more processors reside on the same chip, enabling the execution of two sets of instructions at the same time. Now applications that are always running behind the scenes, such as virus protection software and your operating system, can have their own processor, freeing the other processor to run other applications such as a Web browser, Word, or iTunes more efficiently. Figure 6 shows these different approaches.

In Figure 6c, hyperthreading allows two different programs to be processed at one time, but they are sharing the computing resources of the chip. With multiple cores, each program has the full attention of its own processing core (see Figure 6a and Figure 6b). This results in faster processing

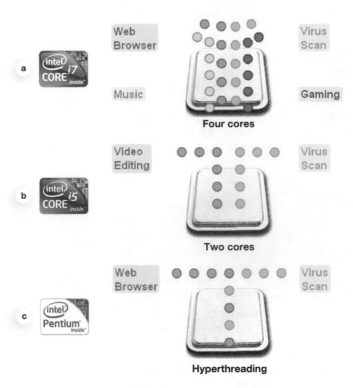

Web Browser | Music — Four cores — Virus Scan | Gaming

Video Editing — Two cores — Virus Scan

Web Browser — Hyperthreading — Virus Scan

Figure 6

(a) Some Intel processors have four cores able to run four programs simultaneously. (b) Some Intel processors have two cores. (c) The Intel Pentium 4 Hyperthreading operates with only one core but it hyperthreads (working on two processes at once).

and smoother multitasking. It is possible to design a CPU to have multiple cores *and* hyperthreading. The Intel i7-980x has six cores, each one using hyperthreading, so it simulates having twelve processors!

How do I pick the fastest processor? While clock speed is an important consideration when determining processor performance, CPU performance also is affected by the amount of cache memory and the speed of the front side bus (FSB). **Cache memory** is a form of random access memory that is more accessible to the CPU than regular RAM. Because of its ready access to the CPU, cache memory gets data to the CPU for processing much faster than bringing the data in from RAM.

There are several levels of cache memory. These levels are defined by a chip's proximity to the CPU. Level 1 cache is a block of memory that is built onto the CPU chip for the storage of data or commands that have just been used. Level 2 cache is located on the CPU chip but is slightly farther away from the CPU, or it's on a separate chip next to the CPU and therefore takes somewhat longer to access. Level 2 cache contains more storage area than does level 1 cache. In the same way, some chips continue on to have a third cache, Level 3. Again, this level of cache is slower for the CPU to reach but larger in size.

Another factor that impacts overall performance is the FSB speed. The **front side bus (FSB)** connects the processor (CPU) in your computer to the system memory. Think of the front side bus as the highway on which data travels between the CPU and RAM. With a wider highway, traffic can move faster because more cars can travel at the same time. Consequently, the faster the FSB is, the faster you can get data to your processor. The faster you get data to the processor, the faster your processor can work on it. FSB speed is measured in megahertz (MHz). The speed of the front side bus is an important consideration that determines CPU performance.

Modern processors are defined by the combination of processor speed, front side bus speed, and the amount of cache memory. For example, Intel has several processor families, in a range of clock speeds, cache memory sizes, and FSB speeds, as shown in Figure 7. Even within one processor family, there is a variety of choices. For example, the i7-980X processor has six cores, and a 12 MB cache, whereas the i7-860S processor has four cores and an 8 MB L3 cache.

Figure 7 | PROCESSOR SPECIFICATIONS

		Number of Cores	Max Clock Speed	Max FSB	Max L3 Cache
Desktop Processors	i3-530	2	2.93 GHz	1333 MHz	4 MB
	i5-750	4	2.66 GHz	1333 MHz	8 MB
	i7-980X	6	3.30 GHz	1600 MHz	12 MB
Notebook Processors	Celeron 585	1	2.16 GHz	666 MHz	1 MB
	i5 mobile 520	2	1.07 GHz	1066 MHz	3 MB
	i7 mobile 820	4	1.73 GHz	1333 MHz	8 MB

There are many factors that influence CPU design, so picking the fastest CPU for the kind of work you do often involves researching some performance benchmarks. **Benchmarks** are measurements used to compare CPU performance between processors. Benchmarks are generated by running software programs specifically designed to push the limits of CPU performance. Articles are often published comparing a number of chips, or complete systems, based on their benchmark performance. Investigate a few, like **cpubenchmark.net**, before you select the chip that is best for you.

Why are there different CPU choices for notebooks and desktops? Both Intel and AMD make processors that are specifically designed for notebook computers. Notebook processors not only need to perform quickly and efficiently, like their desktop counterparts, but also need better power savings to improve battery life. Processors used in notebooks work to combine low power consumption, to support long battery life, and more flexible wireless connectivity options. AMD features notebook processors like the Turion X2 Mobile and the Mobile AMD Sempron, while Intel has mobile versions of the i5 and i7 series.

What CPU does my current computer have? You can easily identify the type of CPU in your current system by accessing the System Properties. As shown in Figure 8, you can view basic information about your computer, including which CPU is installed in your system as well as its speed. More detailed information, like the FSB speed and the amount of cache memory, is not shown in this screen. You can find those values by checking the manufacturer's Web site for the specific model number of

CPU shown. For example, the CPU illustrated here is the Intel i7, version 960.

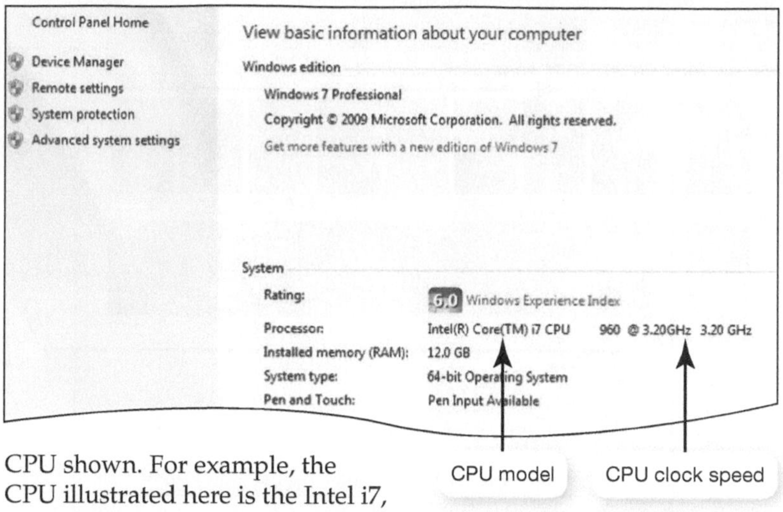

How can I tell whether my CPU is meeting my needs? As shown in Figure 9, several factors determine whether your CPU is meeting your needs. Even if your CPU meets the minimum requirements specified for a particular software application, if you're running other software at the same time (in addition to the operating system, which is always running), you'll need to check to see how well the CPU is handling the entire load. You can tell whether your CPU speed is limiting your system performance if you periodically watch how busy it is as you work on your computer. Keep in mind that the workload your CPU experiences will vary considerably depending on what you're doing. Even though it might run Word just fine, it may not be able to handle running Word, Photoshop, iTunes, and IM at the same time. The percentage of time that your CPU is working is referred to as **CPU usage**.

A utility that measures information such as CPU usage and RAM usage is incredibly

CPU model   CPU clock speed

Figure 8

The System Properties window identifies which CPU you have, as well as its speed.

>Click the **Start** button and then click **Computer** on the right panel of the **Start** menu. On the top toolbar, click **System Properties**.

Figure 9	HOW IS YOUR CPU PERFORMING?		
		Current System	My Ideal System
What is my computer's CPU speed?			
How much cache memory is on the CPU*?			
What is the FSB speed*?			
What kind of multilevel processing does the CPU have—multiple cores, hyperthreaded, etc.?			
Is the CPU usage value below 90% during most of my daily tasks?			

*You can find these by checking the manufacturer's specifications for your model of CPU.

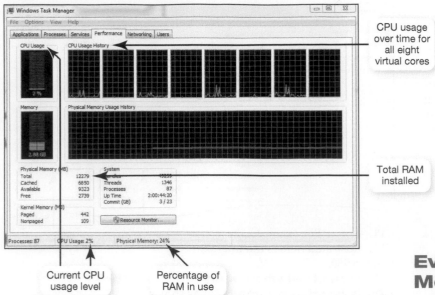

CPU usage over time for all eight virtual cores

Total RAM installed

Current CPU usage level

Percentage of RAM in use

Figure 10

The Performance tab of the Windows Task Manager utility shows you how busy your CPU actually is.

>In an empty area of the taskbar, right-click, select **Start Task Manager**, and click the **Performance** tab.

useful, both for considering whether you should upgrade and for investigating if your computer's performance suddenly seems to drop off for no apparent reason. On Windows systems, a program called Task Manager gives you easy access to all this data. Mac OS X has a utility similar to Task Manager called Activity Monitor, which is located in the Utilities folder in your Applications folder.

To view information on CPU usage, right-click an empty area of the taskbar, select Start Task Manager, and click the Performance tab, as shown in Figure 10. The CPU Usage graph records your CPU usage for the past several seconds. (Note: If you have multiple cores and hyperthreading, you will see several CPUs listed.) Of course, there will be periodic peaks of high CPU usage, but if you see that your CPU usage levels are greater than 90 percent during most of your work session, a faster CPU will contribute a great deal to your system's performance. If you are using the Windows Sidebar, there is a CPU Meter gadget you can add to track both CPU and RAM usage. To see exactly how to use the Task Manager and the Sidebar gadget, watch the Sound Byte "Using Windows 7 to Evaluate CPU Performance."

Will improving the performance of the CPU be enough to improve my computer's performance? You may think that if you have the best processor, you will have a system with the best

performance. However, upgrading your CPU will affect only the processing portion of the system performance, not how quickly data can move to or from the CPU. Your system's overall performance depends on many factors, including the amount of RAM installed as well as hard drive speed. Therefore, your selection of a CPU may not offer significant improvements to your system's performance if there is a bottleneck in processing because of insufficient RAM or hard drive capacity.

Evaluating RAM: The Memory Subsystem

Random access memory (RAM) is your computer's temporary storage space. Although we refer to RAM as a form of storage, it really is the computer's short-term memory. As such, it remembers everything that the computer needs to process the data into information, such as data that has been entered and software instructions, but only when the computer is on. RAM is an example of **volatile storage**. When the power is off, the data stored in RAM is cleared out. This is why, in addition to RAM, systems always include **nonvolatile storage** devices for permanent storage of instructions and data when the computer is powered off. ROM memory, for example, holds the critical startup instructions. Hard drives provide the greatest nonvolatile storage capacity in the computer system.

Why not use a hard drive to store the data and instructions? It's about one million times faster for the CPU to retrieve a piece of data from RAM than from a hard drive. The time it takes the CPU to retrieve data from RAM is measured in

  Using Windows 7 to Evaluate CPU Performance

In this Sound Byte, you'll learn how to use the utilities provided by Windows 7 to evaluate your CPU's performance. You'll also learn about shareware utilities (software that you can install and try before you purchase it) that expand on the capabilities the Task Manager utility provides.

nanoseconds (billionths of seconds), whereas retrieving data from a fast hard drive takes an average of 10 milliseconds (ms), or thousandths of seconds. Figure 11 shows the various types of memory and storage that are distributed throughout your system: CPU registers, cache, RAM, and hard drive. Each of these has its own tradeoff of speed vs. price. Because the fastest memory is so much more expensive, systems are designed with much less of it. This principle is influential in the design of a balanced computer system and can have a tremendous impact on system performance.

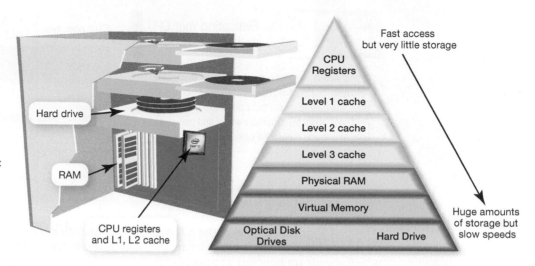

Are there different types of RAM? Like most computer components, RAM has gone through a series of transitions. In current systems, the RAM used most often comes in the form of double data rate 2 (DDR2) memory modules. Double data rate 3 memory (DDR3), which has an even faster data transfer rate, is seen in high-performance systems. In older systems, other types of RAM may have been used, including dynamic RAM (DRAM), static RAM (SRAM), and synchronous DRAM (SDRAM). RAM appears in the system on **memory modules** (or **memory cards**), small circuit boards that hold a series of RAM chips and fit into special slots on the motherboard (see Figure 12). Most memory modules in today's systems are called *dual inline memory modules* (DIMMs).

Types of RAM are slightly different from each other in how they function and in the speed at which they access memory. On high-end systems, manufacturers may offer an option to purchase Corsair Dominator DDR3 modules. These are tested to high levels to guarantee optimum performance. A special heat exchanger is designed into the RAM module to help it operate at a lower temperature, making it more stable and more reliable. All of these factors boost the performance of the memory and make it popular with demanding video gamers.

If you're adding RAM to any system, you must determine what type your system needs. Consult your user's manual or the manufacturer's Web site. In addition, many online RAM resellers, such as Crucial (**crucial.com**), can help you determine the type of RAM that is compatible with your system by running an automated system scan program on your computer.

How can I tell how much RAM is installed in my computer and how it's being used? The amount of RAM that is actually sitting on memory modules in your computer is your computer's **physical memory**. The easiest way to see how much RAM you have is to look in the System Properties window. (On the Mac, choose the Apple menu and then About This Mac.) This is the same tab you looked in to determine your system's CPU type and speed, and is shown in Figure 8. RAM capacity is measured in gigabytes (GB), and most machines sold today, especially those running Windows, have at least 2 GB of RAM. The computer in Figure 10 has 12 GB of RAM installed.

Windows 7 uses a memory-management technique known as SuperFetch. SuperFetch monitors which applications you use the

Figure 11

A computer system's memory has many different levels, ranging from the small amounts in the CPU to the much slower but more plentiful storage of a hard drive.

Figure 12

(a) Memory modules hold a series of RAM chips. (b) This Corsair memory module has an aluminum plate called a heat sink to cool the chips beneath it.

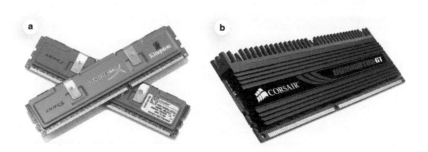

Figure 14 SAMPLE RAM ALLOCATION

Application	RAM Recommended
Windows 7	2,000 MB (or 2 GB)
Microsoft Office Professional 2010	512 MB
Internet Explorer 8	512 MB
iTunes 9	512 MB to 1,000 MB (1 GB)
Adobe Photoshop Elements 8	1,000 MB (1 GB)
Total RAM required to run all programs simultaneously	4,536 MB to 5,024 MB (or 4.5 GB to 5.0 GB)

most and preloads them into your system memory so that they'll be ready to go. For example, if you have Word running, Windows 7 stores as much of the information related to Word in RAM as it can, which speeds up how fast your application responds, because pulling information from RAM is so much faster than pulling it from the hard drive. This idea of caching the data you need in RAM, having it ready to use quickly when it is asked for, is different from how memory was used in earlier operating systems. You can watch this work using the Resource Monitor, which shows in Figure 13 how the 12 GB of installed RAM is being used: 3 GB is running programs, 6 GB is holding cached data and files ready to be quickly accessed, and 3 GB is currently unused.

How much memory does the operating system need to run? The memory that your operating system uses is referred to as **kernel memory**. This memory is listed in a separate Kernel Memory table in the Performance tab. In Figure 10, the Kernel Memory table tells you that approximately 555 MB (total kernel memory) of the total 12 GB of RAM is being used to run the operating system.

The operating system is the main software application that runs the computer. Without it, the computer does not work. At a minimum, the system needs enough RAM to run the operating system. However, because you run additional applications, you need to have more RAM than the minimum.

How much RAM do I need? Because RAM is the temporary holding space for all the data and instructions that the computer uses while it's on, most computer users need quite a bit of RAM. In fact, systems running all the new features of Windows 7 should have a minimum of 1 GB of RAM, but for peak performance, systems are recommended to have at least 2 GB of RAM.

To determine how much RAM you need, list all the software applications you might be running at one time. Figure 14 shows an example of RAM requirements. In this example, if you are running your operating system, word processing and spreadsheet programs, a Web browser, a music player, and photo editing software simultaneously, then you will need a minimum of 4.5 GB of RAM. It's always best to check the system requirements of any software program

Figure 13

The Resource Monitor's Memory tab shows a detailed breakdown of how the computer is using memory.

>In the **Resource Monitor**, click the **Memory** tab.

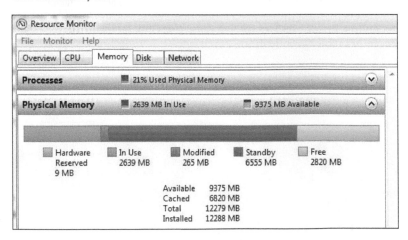

before you buy it to make sure your system can handle it. System requirements can be found on the software packaging or on the manufacturer's Web site.

It's a good idea to have more than the minimum amount of RAM you need now, so you can use more programs in the future. Remember, too, that "required" means these are the minimum values recommended by the manufacturers, and having more RAM often helps programs run more efficiently. When upgrading RAM, the rule of thumb is to buy as much as you can afford but no more than your system will handle.

Adding RAM

Is there a limit to how much RAM I can add to my computer? Every computer has a maximum limit on the amount of RAM it can support. A motherboard is designed with a specific number of slots into which the memory cards fit, and each slot has a limit on the amount of RAM it can hold. To determine your specific system limits, check your owner's manual or the manufacturer's Web site.

In addition, the operating system running on your machine imposes its own limit. For example, the maximum amount of RAM for the 32-bit version of Windows 7 is 4 GB, while the 64-bit version of Windows 7 Ultimate can address up to 192 GB.

Once you know how much RAM your computer can support, you can determine the best configuration of memory modules to achieve the greatest amount of RAM. For example, say you have a total of four memory card slots: two are already filled with 512 MB RAM cards and the other two are empty. The maximum RAM allowed for your system is 4 GB. This means you can buy two more 512 MB RAM modules for the two empty slots, for a total of 2 GB (4 × 512 MB) of RAM. Alternatively, you could

Figure 15 | DO YOU NEED TO UPGRADE YOUR RAM?

	Application	Current System	Ideal System
How much RAM does my system have?			
What is the maximum amount of RAM I need for the applications I currently run?			
What is the maximum amount of RAM the system can hold*?			
Would I be willing to upgrade to a 64-bit operating system and 64-bit CPU to support having 4 GB or more of RAM?			

*Check the manufacturer's specifications for your system.

throw away the 512 MB cards you have and purchase four new 1 GB cards, filling the system up to its capacity of 4 GB.

Review the considerations presented in Figure 15 to see if your system could benefit from an upgrade of additional RAM.

Is it difficult or expensive to add RAM? Adding RAM to a computer is fairly easy (see Figure 16). RAM comes with installation instructions, which you should follow carefully. RAM is also relatively inexpensive compared with other system upgrade options. Still, the cost of RAM fluctuates in the marketplace as much as 400 percent over time, so if you're considering adding RAM, you should watch the prices of memory in online and print advertisements.

Adding RAM to a personal computer is quite simple and relatively inexpensive. You simply line up the notches and push in the memory module. Just be sure that you're adding a memory module that's compatible with your computer. For a video demonstration and more details, watch the Sound Byte, "Installing RAM."

Evaluating the Storage Subsystem

As you've learned, there are two ways data is stored on your computer: temporary storage and permanent storage. RAM is a form of temporary (or volatile) storage. Thus, anything that resides in RAM is not stored permanently. It's critical to have the means to store data and software applications permanently.

SOUND BYTE Installing RAM

In this Sound Byte, you'll learn how to select the appropriate type of memory to purchase, how to order memory online, and how to install it yourself. As you'll discover, the procedure is a simple one and can add great performance benefits to your system.

Figure 16

Adding RAM to a computer is quite simple and relatively inexpensive.

Fortunately, several storage options exist within every computer system. Storage devices for a typical personal computer include the hard drive, USB flash drives, optical drives, and external hard drives. When you turn off your computer, the data that has been written to these devices will be available the next time the machine is powered on. These devices are therefore referred to as *nonvolatile* storage devices.

The Hard Drive

What makes the hard drive the most popular storage device? With storage capacities exceeding 2 terabytes (TB), a **hard drive** has the largest storage capacity of any storage device. The hard drive is also a much more economical device than other storage options, because it offers the most gigabytes of storage per dollar. Most system units are designed to support more than one internal hard drive. The Apple Mac Pro, shown in Figure 17, has room for four hard drives. Each one simply slides into place when you want to upgrade.

Another reason the hard drive is so useful for storage is that the hard drive's **access time**, the time it takes a storage device to locate its stored data and make it available for processing, is faster than that of other permanent storage devices, like optical drives. Hard drive access times are measured in milliseconds (ms), meaning thousandths of seconds. For large-capacity drives, access times of approximately 12–13

milliseconds—that's less than one-hundredth of a second—are typical. A DVD drive can take over 150 milliseconds to access data.

Solid state drives offer even faster access times. A **solid state drive (SSD)** uses the same kind of memory that flash drives use, but whereas flash drives have access times of about 1 ms, SSD drives can reach data in only a tenth of that time (around 0.1 ms). Because there are no spinning platters or motors needed, SSDs run with no noise, very little heat, and require very little power. As the storage capacities for SSDs continue to increase and the prices for SSDs continue to drop, you'll start to see them in a wide range of systems.

Figure 18 provides a listing of the various storage options and compares their access times.

Another key performance specification for a hard drive is the speed at which it can transfer data to other computer components (such as RAM). This speed of transfer is referred to as **data transfer rate**. Depending on the manufacturer, the rate is expressed in either megabits or megabytes per second.

How is data stored on a hard drive? A hard drive is composed of several coated round, thin plates of metal stacked on a spindle. Each plate is called a **platter**. When data is saved to a hard drive platter, a pattern of magnetized spots is created on the iron oxide coating of each platter. When the spots are aligned in one

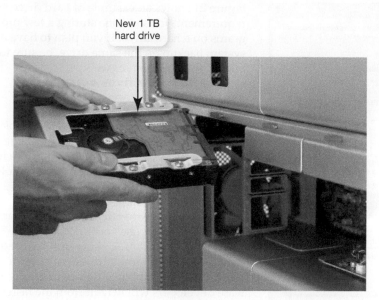

New 1 TB
hard drive

Figure 17

The Mac Pro allows you to slide a new hard drive into place easily. In all, the Mac Pro can hold up to 4 hard drives.

direction, they represent a 1; when aligned in the other direction, the represent a 0. These 0s and 1s are bits (or binary digits) and are the smallest pieces of data that computers can understand. When data stored on the hard drive platter is retrieved (or read), your computer translates these patterns of magnetized spots into the data you have saved.

How do I know how much storage capacity I need? Typically, hard drive capacity is measured in gigabytes (GB), although hard drives with capacity in the terabytes (TB) are now available. To check how much total capacity your hard drive has, as well as how much is being used, click the Start button and select Computer from the right side of the Start menu. Windows displays the hard drives, their capacity, and usage information, as seen in Figure 19. To get a slightly more detailed view, select a drive; then right-click and choose Properties.

To determine the storage capacity your system needs, calculate the amount of storage required by all the types of files you will be keeping on your system. If you have a large digital music library, that alone could require 30 to 50 GB. Do you keep all of your photographs on your hard drive? You may need another 40 GB or more for them. If you store digital video of television shows and movies, that could easily be 100 to 200 GB more, even higher if the videos are all high definition. Of course, the operating system also requires storage space. The demands on system requirements have grown with new versions of operating systems. Windows 7, the latest Microsoft operating system, can require up to 20 GB of available hard drive capacity, depending on the configuration.

In addition to having space for the operating system, you need enough space to store the software applications you use, such as Microsoft Office, music, and games.

Device

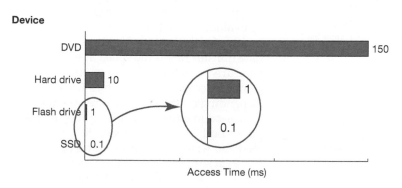

Access Time (ms)

Figure 18

Access times for non-volatile storage options.

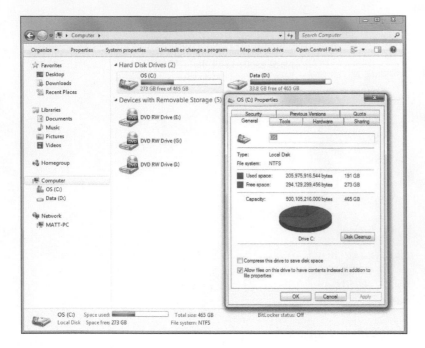

Figure 19

In Windows, the free and used capacity of each device in the computer system are shown in the Computer window. The General tab of the Properties dialog box gives you information that is more detailed.

>To view the Computer window, click **Start**, and click **Computer**. To view the pie chart, right-click the C drive, and select **Properties**.

HDTV on Your Notebook

If you are moving through your day with a notebook in tow, why not use it to pull up your favorite television shows? There are now several USB devices that allow your notebook or desktop to receive the high-definition television (HDTV) signals whizzing by in the airwaves.

Devices like the Hauppauge HDTV stick (see Figure 20) are USB digital TV tuners. One end plugs into any available USB port. The other end connects to the provided digital antenna. Software is included that allows you to schedule shows to record onto your hard drive, so your notebook essentially becomes a time-shifting digital video recorder. If you are at home, you can remove the antenna and connect to your home cable television signal. It's enough to make you think about buying a larger hard drive on your next computer!

Figure 20

The Hauppauge HDTV stick allows you to watch and record high-definition television shows on your computer.

Figure 21 shows an example of hard drive requirements for someone storing a few programs on a hard drive. If you plan to have a system backup on the same drive, be sure to budget for that room as well.

How do hard drives compare for speed? There are several types of hard drives. Integrated Drive Electronics (IDE), which is also called *parallel advanced technology attachment (PATA)*, is an older style that uses wide cables to connect the hard drive to the motherboard. **Serial Advanced Technology Attachment (Serial ATA)** hard drives use much thinner cables, and can transfer data more quickly than IDE drives. A slower drive is fine if you use your computer primarily for word processing, spreadsheets, e-mail, and the Internet. However, "power users" such as graphic designers and software developers will benefit from the faster Serial ATA hard drive.

Another factor that affects a hard drive's performance is access time (the speed with which it locates data for processing). As noted earlier, access time is measured in milliseconds. The faster the access time the better, although many hard drives have similar access times.

The latest and fastest hard drive option is the solid state drive (SSD). These are popular in the netbook market because they require so little power to run and are so cool and quiet. With access times of merely a tenth of a millisecond, SSDs can deliver data many times more quickly than mechanical hard drives. SSD drives as large as 1 TB are available, but right now, all SSD drives are still much more expensive than mechanical drives. Currently, some machines compromise by using an SSD just to hold the operating system. This takes advantage of their great speed, making the boot-up time for the system very quick. Watch for further integration of SSD drives into systems as the cost of SSDs continues to drop.

Evaluate hard drive transfer rate when looking for the best performing drive. The data transfer rate is the speed at which a hard drive can transfer data to other computer components (such as RAM). Depending on the manufacturer, the rate is expressed in either megabits or megabytes per second. You can compare the average read and write data transfer rates of hard drives at sites that do performance benchmarking, like Tom's Hardware (**tomshardware.com**).

If you are adding an external hard drive to your system, there are two popular ports to use. Many hard drives use a USB 2.0 port to connect, which limits the transfer rate of data to 400 Mbps. The USB 3.0 standard has raised that limit to 5 Gbps (5,000 Mbps). In addition, some computer systems now offer an eSATA port, shown in Figure 22. This is an external SATA port that will connect to some external hard drive models. It allows a data transfer rate of up to 3 Gbps.

Do I want one huge drive or several smaller drives? It depends on what is important to you: speed or security. If you purchase two smaller drives, you can combine them using RAID technology. RAID (redundant array of independent disks) is a set of strategies for using more than one drive in a system. RAID 0 and RAID 1 are the most popular for consumer machines.

In RAID 0 configuration, every time data is written to a hard drive, it is actually spread across two physical drives (see Figure 23a). The write begins on the first drive, and while the system is waiting for that write to be completed, the system jumps ahead and begins to write the next block of data to the second drive. This makes writing information to disk almost twice as fast as using just one hard drive. The downside is that if either of these disks fail, you lose all your data, because part of each file is on each drive. So RAID 0 is for those most concerned with performance.

In RAID 1 configuration, all the data written to one drive is perfectly mirrored and written to a second drive (see Figure 23b). This provides you a perfect, instant by instant backup of all your work. It also means that if you buy two 1 TB drives, you only have room to store 1TB of data because the second 1 TB drive is being used as the "mirror."

RAID 0 and RAID 1 systems are available on many consumer systems and are even beginning to appear on notebook computers. The Sony Vaio Z is a notebook available with two 256 GB SSDs, connected

| Figure 21 | SAMPLE HARD DRIVE SPACE REQUIREMENTS |

Application	Hard Drive Space Required
Windows 7	16–20 GB
MS Office 2007 Professional	3.5 GB
Adobe Photoshop Elements 8	2 GB
Roxio Easy Media Creator 2010	3 GB installation space and up to several 10's of GB to copy BDs or DVDs
Total required	At least 24.5 GB

in RAID 0. This gives you access to 500 GB of storage and incredibly quick access speeds, with very little power consumption or noise.

Optical Storage

Optical drives are disc drives that use a laser to store and read data. Data is saved to a compact disc (CD), digital video disc (DVD), or **Blu-ray disc (BDs)** within established tracks and sectors, just like on a hard drive. However, unlike hard drives, which store their data on magnetized platters, optical discs store data as tiny pits that are burned into the disc by a high-speed laser. These pits are extremely small. For CDs and DVDs, they are less than 1 micron in diameter, so nearly 1,500 pits fit across the top of a pinhead. The pits on a Blu-ray disc are only 0.15 microns in diameter, more than twice as small as the pits on a DVD. As

Figure 22

An eSATA port allows you to connect an external hard drive that can transfer data at speeds faster than USB 2.0 but slower than USB 3.0.

SOUND BYTE

CD, DVD, and Blu-ray Reading and Writing Interactive

In this Sound Byte, you'll learn about the process of storing and retrieving data from CD-RW, DVD, and Blu-ray discs. You'll be amazed to see how much precision engineering is required to burn MP3 files onto a disc.

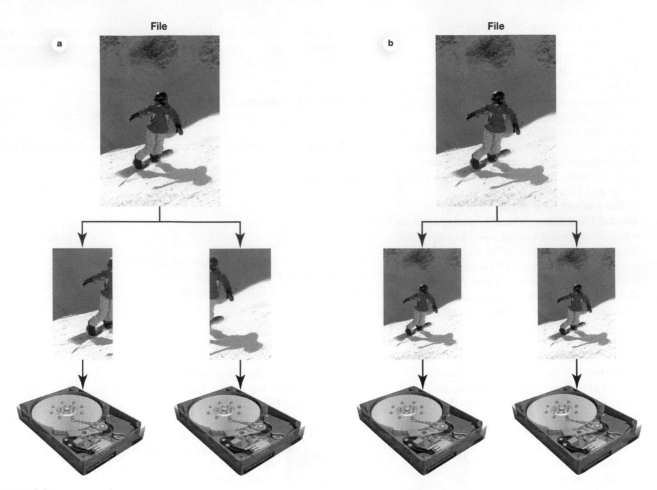

Figure 23

(a) RAID 0 speeds up file read/write time. (b) RAID 1 gives you an instant backup.

you can see in Figure 24, data is read from a disc by a laser beam, with the pits and nonpits (called *lands*) translating into the 1s and 0s of the binary code computers understand. CDs and DVDs use a red laser to read and write data. Blu-ray discs get their name because they are read with a blue laser light. All of them collectively are referred to as **optical media**.

Why can I store data on some discs but not others? All forms of optical media come in prerecorded, recordable, and rewritable formats. The prerecorded discs—known as CD-ROM, **DVD-ROM**, and **BD-ROM discs**—are read-only optical discs, meaning you can't save any data onto them. Pre-recorded CDs usually contain audio content, software programs, or games, whereas DVD-ROMs and BD-ROMs typically contain movies or prerecorded TV shows in regular or high definition, respectively. Recordable formats such as CD-R, DVD-R, and BD-R allow data to be written (saved or burned) to them. If

you want to be able to use a form of optical media repetitively, writing and rewriting data to it many times, read/writeable formats such as CD-RW, DVD-RW, and BD-RE are available.

Do I need separate players and burners for CD, DVD, and now BD formats? Although CDs and DVDs are based on the same optical technology, CD drives cannot read DVDs. If your system has only a CD drive, you will need to add a DVD drive to view DVDs. However, if your system has a DVD drive, that is all you need, even just to listen to CDs, because DVD drives can read them. Although Blu-ray discs are read with a different type of laser than CDs and DVDs, most Blu-ray players are backward compatible and can play DVDs and CDs. There are different types of optical drives for playing or recording to discs. If you want to record to CDs, DVDs, or Blu-ray discs, you need to make sure your drive is capable of recording (or burning) and not just playing.

Because recording drives are also backward compatible, you do not need separate burners for each form of media. A DVD burner will also record CDs, and a Blu-ray burner will most likely record both CDs and DVDs (although there may be some compatibility issues).

Are there different standards of optical media? Unfortunately, technology experts have not agreed on a standard DVD format. Currently, there are multiple recognized formats, **DVD-R/RW** (pronounced "DVD dash") and **DVD+R/RW** (pronounced "DVD plus"). **DVD-RAM** is a third format. You can record, erase, and rewrite on DVD-RAM, as you can with the plus and minus formats, but DVD-RAM discs are generally encased in a plastic cartridge. Web sites such as Video Help (**videohelp.com**) list the compatibility of various DVD players with the various DVD formats. However, you must make sure you purchase blank DVD discs that match the type of drive you own. Most new systems come equipped with a DVD +/– RW drive that supports both the plus and minus formats.

There were "format wars" like this for high-definition discs as well. Blu-ray competed against another storage format called HD-DVD (high-definition DVD). Some movie companies would only provide their films on HD discs, while other films were exclusive to Blu-ray. Different players were required to view each kind of disc. In 2008, HD-DVDs were retired, and HD discs and players are no longer in production.

Are some CD and DVD drives faster than others? When you buy an optical drive, knowing the drive speed is important. Speeds are listed on the device's packaging. Record (write) speed is always listed first, rewrite speed is listed second (except for CD-R drives and DVD-R, which cannot rewrite data), and playback speed is listed last. For example, a CD-RW drive may have speeds of 52X32X52X, meaning that the device can record data at 52X speed, rewrite data at 32X speed, and play back data at 52X speed. For CDs, the X after each number represents the transfer of 150 KB of data per second. For example, a CD-RW drive with a 52X32X52X rating records data at 52 times 150 KB per second, or 7,800 KB per second.

DVD drives are much faster than CD drives. For example, a 1X DVD-ROM

To read information stored on a disc, a laser inside the disk drive sends a beam of light through the spinning disc.

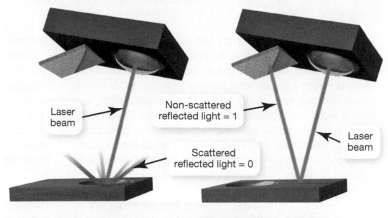

If the light reflected back is scattered in all directions (which happens when the laser hits a pit), the laser translates this into the binary digit 0.

If non-scattered light is reflected back to the laser (which happens when the laser hits an area in which there is no pit), the laser translates this into the binary digit 1.

In this way, the laser reads the pits and non-pits as a series of bits (0s and 1s), which the computer can then process.

Figure 24
Data is read from a disc using focused laser light.

drive provides a data transfer rate of approximately 1.3 MB of data per second, which is roughly equivalent to a CD-ROM speed of 9X. CD and DVD drives are constantly getting faster. If you're in the market for a new CD or DVD burner, then you'll want to investigate the drive speeds on the market and make sure you get the fastest one you can afford.

Blu-ray drives are the fastest optical devices on the market. Blu-ray technology defines 1X speed as 36 MB per second.

SOUND BYTE

Installing a Blu-ray Drive

In this Sound Byte, you'll learn how to install a Blu-ray drive in your computer.

The thin metal platters that make up a hard drive are covered with a special magnetic coating that enables the data to be recorded onto one or both sides of the platter. Hard drive manufacturers prepare the disks to hold data through a process called *low-level formatting*. In this process, concentric circles, each called a **track**, and pie-shaped wedges, each called a **sector**, are created in the magnetized surface of each platter, setting up a gridlike pattern that identifies file locations on the hard drive. A separate process called *high-level formatting* establishes the catalog that the computer uses to keep track of where each file is located on the hard drive.

Hard drive platters spin at a high rate of speed, some as fast as 15,000 revolutions per minute (rpm). Sitting between the platters are special "arms" that contain read/write heads (see Figure 25). A **read/write head** moves from the outer edge of the spinning platter to the center, as frequently as 50 times per second, to retrieve (read) and record (write) the magnetic data to and from the hard drive platter. As noted earlier, the average total time it takes for the read/write head to locate the data on the platter and return it to the CPU for processing is called its access time. A new hard drive should have an average access time of approximately 12 ms.

Access time is mostly the sum of two factors: seek time and latency. The time it takes for the read/write heads to move over the surface of the disk, moving to the correct track, is called the **seek time**. (Sometimes people incorrectly refer to this as access time.) Once the read/write head locates the correct track, it may need to wait for the correct sector to spin to the read/write head. This waiting time is called **latency** (or *rotational delay*). The faster the platters spin (or the faster the rpm), the less time you'll have to wait for your data to be accessed. Currently, most hard drives for home systems spin at 7,200 rpm. Some people design their systems to have a faster hard drive run the operating system, such as the Western Digital Velociraptor, which spins at 10,000 rpm. They then add a slower drive with greater capacity for storage.

The read/write heads do not touch the platters of the hard drive; rather, they float above them on a thin cushion of air at a height of 0.5 microinches. As a matter of comparison, a human hair is 2,000 microinches thick and a particle of dust is larger than a human hair. Therefore, it's critical to keep your hard drive free from all dust and dirt, because even the smallest particle could find its way between the read/write head and the disk platter, causing a **head crash**—a stoppage of the hard drive that often results in data loss.

Capacities for hard drives in personal computers can exceed 2000 GB (2 TB). Increasing the amount of data stored in a hard drive is achieved either by adding more platters or by increasing the amount of data stored on each platter. How tightly the tracks are placed next to each other, how tightly spaced the sectors are, and how closely the bits of data are placed affect the measurement of the amount of data that can be stored in a specific area of a hard drive platter. Modern technology continues to increase the standards on all three levels, enabling massive quantities of data to be stored in small places.

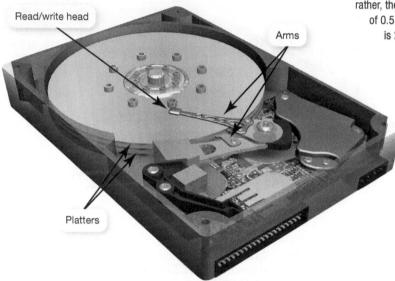

Figure 25

The hard drive is a stack of platters enclosed in a sealed case. Special arms fit in between each platter. The read/write heads at the end of each arm read from and save data to the platters.

Because BD movies require data transfer rates of at least 54 MB per second, most Blu-ray disc players have a minimum of 2X speeds (72 MB per second). Many units are available with 12X speeds.

So how do my storage devices measure up? The table in Figure 26 will help you determine if your computer's storage subsystem needs upgrading.

Evaluating the Video Subsystem

How video is displayed depends on two components: your video card and your monitor. It's important that your system have the correct monitor and video card to meet your needs. If you are considering loading Windows 7 on your system, or

Figure 26 | DO YOU WANT TO UPGRADE YOUR STORAGE SUBSYSTEM?

	Current System	Ideal System
What is my current hard drive capacity?		
Do I want to have a very fast startup time (i.e., use an SSD drive for my operating system)?		
Do I want to implement multiple drives in RAID 0 for performance?		
Do I want to implement multiple drives in RAID 1 for instant backup?		
Do I have a DVD-ROM drive?		
Can I burn DVDs (i.e., do I have a DVD-/+RW drive)?		
Can I play Blu-ray discs (i.e., do I have a Blu-ray drive)?		
Can I burn my own Blu-ray discs (i.e., do I have a Blu-ray burner installed)?		
Do I have a working data backup solution such as external backup drives or remote data storage?		
Do I use any portable storage devices such as flash drives or external hard drives?		

using your computer system to display files that have complex graphics, such as videos on Blu-ray or from your camcorder, or even playing graphics-rich games with a lot of fast action, you may want to consider upgrading your video subsystem.

Video Cards

What is a video card? A video card (or **video adapter**) is an expansion card that is installed inside your system unit to translate binary data into the images you view on your monitor. Modern video cards like the ones shown in Figure 27 and

ACTIVE HELP-DESK

Evaluating Computer System Components

In this Active Helpdesk call, you'll play the role of a helpdesk staffer, fielding calls about the computer's storage, video, and audio devices and how to evaluate whether they match your needs, as well as how to improve the reliability of your system.

Figure 27

Video cards have grown to be highly specialized subsystems.

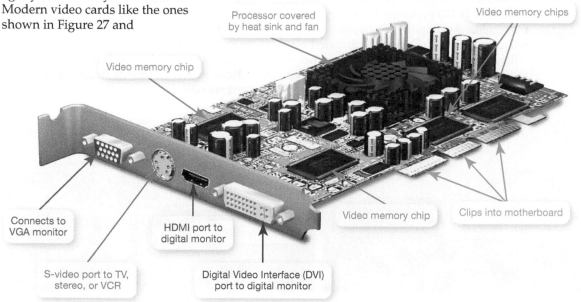

Processor covered by heat sink and fan

Video memory chips

Video memory chip

Video memory chip

Clips into motherboard

Connects to VGA monitor

HDMI port to digital monitor

S-video port to TV, stereo, or VCR

Digital Video Interface (DVI) port to digital monitor

Fan built into graphics card

Figure 28

Because of the large amount of graphics memory and the fast graphics processing units on modern video cards, they have their own fan to remove heat.

Figure 29

The graphics processing unit (GPU) is specialized to handle processing of photos, videos, and video game images. It frees the CPU to work on other system demands.

Figure 28 are extremely sophisticated. They include ports that allow you to connect to different video equipment such as the DVI ports for digital LCDs, HDMI ports to connect to high-definition TVs or gaming consoles, lower-resolution S-video ports for connecting your computer to a TV, and Super VGA ports for CRT and analog LCD monitors. In addition, video cards include their own RAM, called **video memory**. Several standards of video memory are available, including graphics double data rate 3 (GDDR3) memory and the newer graphics double data rate 5 (GDDR5) memory. Because displaying graphics demands a lot of the CPU, video cards also come with their own graphics processing units (GPUs). When the CPU is asked to process graphics, those tasks are redirected to the GPU, significantly speeding up graphics processing.

Is a GPU different from a CPU?
The **graphics processing unit (GPU)** performs the same kind of computational work that a CPU performs. However, a GPU is specialized to handle 3-D graphics and image and video processing with incredible efficiency and speed. Figure 29 shows that the CPU can run much more efficiently when a GPU does all of the graphics computation.

Special lighting effects can be achieved with a modern GPU. Designers can now change the type of light, the texture, and the color of objects based on complex interactions. Some GPU designs incorporate dedicated hardware to allow high-definition movies to be decoded.

Does the GPU live on the motherboard or on the video card? Basic video processing is sometimes integrated into the motherboard. However, high-end video cards that have their own GPUs are separate from the motherboard. These sophisticated video cards connect through the ultrafast PCI Express bus. The ATI Radeon HD 5970, a top-end card, is a multi-GPU card with two GPUs that work together to add even more processing punch. Cards like this one carry their own processing RAM space, which can range between 512 MB and 2 GB, depending on the model. Together they provide an unprecedented level of realism and detail in gaming environments.

How can I tell how much memory my video card has? Information about your system's video card can be found in the Advanced Settings of the Screen resolution dialog box. To get to the Screen resolution dialog box, right-click on your desktop and select Screen resolution. In the Screen resolution dialog box, click the Advanced Settings link. A window will appear that shows you the type of graphics card installed in your system, as well as memory information including total available graphics memory, dedicated video memory, system video memory, and shared system memory. The documentation that came with your computer should also contain specifications for the video card, including the amount of video memory it has installed.

How much memory does my video card need? The amount of memory your

Without a GPU

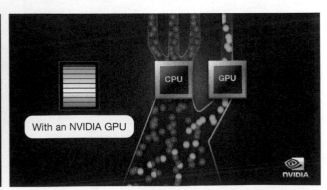

With a GPU

video card needs depends on what you want to display on your monitor. If you work primarily in Microsoft Word and conduct general Web searches, 128 MB is a realistic minimum. For the serious gamer, a 512 MB or greater video card is essential, although cards with as much as 1 or 2 GB are available in the market and are preferred. These high-end video cards, which have greater amounts of memory, allow games to generate smoother animations and more sophisticated shading and texture. Before purchasing new software, check the specifications to ensure your video card has enough video memory to handle the load.

How many video cards can I add to a system? For users who are primarily doing text processing or spreadsheet work, one video card is certainly enough. However, computer gamers and users of high-end visualization software often take advantage of the ability to install more than one video card at a time. Two or even three video cards can be used in one system. The two major video card manufacturers, Nvidia and ATI, have each developed their own standards supporting the combining of multiple video cards. For Nvidia this standard is named SLI and for ATI it is called CrossFire. When the system is running at very high video resolutions, such as 1920 × 1200 or higher, multiple video cards working together provide the ultimate in performance. If you are buying a new system and might be interested in employing multiple video cards, be sure to check whether the motherboard supports SLI or CrossFire.

What else does the video card do? The video card also controls the number of colors your monitor can display. The number of bits the video card uses to represent each pixel (or dot) on the monitor, referred to as **bit depth**, defines the color quality of the image displayed. The more bits, the better an image's color detail. A 4-bit

Figure 30 | BIT DEPTH AND COLOR QUALITY

Bit Depth	Color Quality Description	Number of Colors Displayed
4-bit	Standard VGA	16
8-bit	256-color mode	256
16-bit	High color	65,536
24-bit	True color	16,777,216
32-bit	True color	16,777,216 plus 8 bits to help with transparency

video card displays 16 colors, the minimum number of colors your system works with (referred to as Standard VGA). Most video cards today are 24-bit cards, displaying more than 16 million colors. This mode is called *true color mode* (see Figure 30).

The most recent generation of video cards can add some great features to your computer if you are a TV fan. Multimedia cards such as the ATI All-In-Wonder Radeon HD 3650 can open a live TV window on your screen, including features such as picture-in-picture. Using this video card, you can record programs to your hard drive or pause a live TV broadcast. The card even comes with a wireless remote control.

When is it time to get a new video card? If your monitor takes a while to refresh when you are editing photos, surfing the Web, or playing a graphics-rich game, then the video card could be short on memory or the GPU is being taxed to beyond its capacity.

You also may want to upgrade if added features such as television viewing or importing analog video are important to you. If you want to use multiple monitors at the same time, you also may need to upgrade your video card. Working with multiple monitors is a great advantage if you often have more than one application running at a time (see Figure 31). ATI has introduced a

Figure 31

Cards like the (a) ATI 5870 Eyefinity support (b) six monitors, which can be combined in any way.

3D Explosions

Most video games produced since 2007 are now ready to be seen in 3D, but the market of 3D monitors has been slow in coming. Currently, several computer monitors and televisions that support 3D are being released. Most video cards that support at least two monitors are capable of running 3D imagery. Sony PlayStation has updated its firmware to support 3D games and movies. So by adding a 3D monitor, and the snazzy glasses that come along, you can move from two dimensions forward into three!

single card that can support up to six monitors. "Surround sight" allows you to merge all six monitors to work as one screen or to combine them into any subset—for example, displaying a movie on two combined screens, Excel on one monitor, Word on another, and a browser spread across the final two.

Review the considerations listed in Figure 32 to see if it might be time for you to upgrade. On a desktop computer, replacing a video card is fairly simple: just insert the new video card in the correct expansion slot on the motherboard.

Evaluating the Audio Subsystem

Computers output sound by means of speakers (or headphones) and a sound card. For many users, a computer's preinstalled speakers and sound card are adequate for the sounds produced by the computer itself—the beeps and so on that the computer makes. However, if you're listening to music, viewing DVDs, hooking into a household stereo system, or playing games with sophisticated sound tracks, you may want to upgrade your speakers or your sound card.

Sound Cards

What does the sound card do? Like a video card, a **sound card**, is an expansion card that attaches to the motherboard inside your system unit. Just as the video card enables your computer to produce images on the monitor, a sound card enables the computer to produce sounds. Most systems have a separate sound card, although low-end computers often have integrated the job of managing sound onto the motherboard itself.

Can I hook up a surround-sound system to my computer? Many computers ship with a basic sound card, which is often a **3D sound card**. The 3D sound technology advances sound reproduction beyond traditional stereo sound (where the human ear perceives sounds as coming from the left or the right of the performance area) and is better at convincing the human ear that sound is omnidirectional, meaning that you can't tell from which direction the sound is coming. This tends to produce a fuller, richer sound than stereo sound. However, 3D sound is not surround sound.

What is surround sound then? **Surround sound** is a type of audio processing that makes the listener experience sound as if it were coming from all directions. The current surround sound standard is from Dolby. There are many formats available, including Dolby Digital EX and Dolby Digital Plus for high-definition audio. Dolby TrueHD is the

Figure 32 | DO YOU NEED TO UPGRADE YOUR VIDEO CARD?

	Current System	Ideal System
Is my video card able to refresh the screen fast enough for the videos and games I play?		
What is the total amount of video memory on my video card?		
How many monitors can this card support?		
Can I import video through my video card?		
Can I send a cable television signal to my video card?		
Does my video card support the highest quality port for my monitor—DVI? HDMI?		

Decades ago, when the electronic photocopier made its debut, book publishers and others who distributed the printed word feared they would be put out of business. They were worried that people would no longer buy books and other printed matter if they could simply copy someone else's original. Years later, when audiocassette and VCR players and recorders arrived on the market, those who felt they would be negatively affected by these new technologies expressed similar concerns. Now, with the arrival of CD-RW, DVD-RW, and BD-RE technology, the music and entertainment industries are worried because users can copy CDs, DVDs, and Blu-ray discs in a matter of minutes.

Although photocopiers and VCRs certainly didn't put an end to the industries they affected, some people still say the music and entertainment industries will take a significant hit with CD-RW, DVD-RW, and BD-RE technology. Industry insiders are claiming that these technologies are unethical, and they're pressing for increased federal legislation against such copying. It's not just the CD-RW, DVD-RW, BD-RE technology that's causing problems, either, because "copies" are not necessarily of the physical sort. Thanks to the Internet, file transfers of copyrighted works—particularly music and films—is now commonplace. According to Music United (**musicunited.org**), more than 243 million files are downloaded illegally every month, and about one-quarter of all Internet users worldwide have downloaded a movie from the Internet.

In a separate survey, the Recording Industry Association of America (RIAA), a trade organization that represents the interests of recording giants such as Sony, Capitol Records, and other major producers of musical entertainment, reported that 23 percent of music fans revealed they were buying less music because they could download it or copy a CD-ROM from a friend.

As you would expect, the music and entertainment industries want to be fairly compensated for their creative output. They blame the technology industry for the creation of means by which artists, studios, and the entertainment industry in general are being "robbed." Although technology that readily allows consumers to transfer and copy music and videos exists, the artists who produce these works do not want to be taken advantage of. However, others claim that the technology industry should not bear the complete burden of protecting entertainment copyrights. The RIAA sums up the future of this debate nicely: "Goals for the new millennium are to work with [the recording] industry and others to enable technologies that open up new opportunities but at the same time to protect the rights of artists and copyright owners."

---

newest standard. It features high-definition and lossless technology, in which no data is lost in the compression process. To create surround sound, Dolby takes digital sound from a medium (such as a DVD-ROM) and reproduces it in eight channels. Seven channels cover the listening field with placement to the left front, right front, and center of the audio stage, as well as the left rear and right rear, and then two extra side speakers are added, as shown in Figure 33. The eighth channel holds extremely low-frequency sound data and is sent to a subwoofer, which can be placed anywhere in the room. To set up surround sound on your computer, you need two things: a set of surround-sound speakers and, for the greatest surround-sound experience, a sound card that is Dolby Digital–compatible.

I don't need surround sound on my computer. Why else might I need to buy an upgraded sound card? Most basic sound cards contain the following input and output jacks (or ports): microphone in, speaker out, and line in. This allows you to hook up a set of stereo speakers and a microphone. But what if you want to hook up a right and left speaker individually, or attach other audio devices to your computer? To do so, you need more ports, which are provided on upgraded sound cards like the one shown in Figure 34.

With an upgraded sound card, you can connect portable minidisc players, portable media players, portable jukeboxes, headphones, and CD players to your computer. Musicians also create music on their computers by connecting special devices (such as keyboards) directly to sound card ports. To determine whether your audio subsystem is meeting your needs, review the table in Figure 35.

Evaluating System Reliability

Many computer users decide to buy a new system not necessarily because they need a faster CPU, more RAM, or a bigger hard drive, but because they are experiencing problems such as slow performance, freezes, and crashes. Over time, even normal use can cause your computer to build up excess files and to become internally disorganized. This excess, clutter, and disorganization can lead to deteriorating performance or, far worse, system failure. If you think your system is

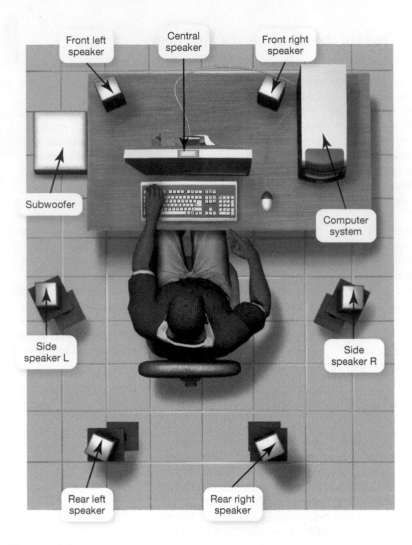

Front left speaker

Central speaker

Front right speaker

Subwoofer

Computer system

Side speaker L

Side speaker R

Rear left speaker

Rear right speaker

Figure 33

Dolby Digital 7.1 surround sound gives you better-quality audio output.

important to you. Right-click on any unnecessary program and select Delete to remove it from the Startup folder. Make sure you delete *only* programs you are absolutely sure are unnecessary. Another way programs sneak their way in is to load themselves into your system tray. Keep an eye on how many icons are in the system tray and uninstall any that you do not use frequently.

2. **Clear out unnecessary files.** Temporary Internet files can accumulate quickly on your hard drive, taking up unnecessary space. Running the Disk Cleanup utility is a quick and easy way to ensure your temporary Internet files don't take up precious hard drive space. Likewise, you should delete any unnecessary files from your hard drive regularly, because they can make your hard drive run more slowly.

3. **Run spyware and adware removal programs.** These often detect and remove different pests and should be used in addition to your regular antivirus package.

4. **Run the Disk Defragmenter utility on your hard drive.** When your hard drive becomes fragmented, its storage capacity is negatively affected. When you defragment (defrag) your hard drive, files are reorganized, making the hard drive work more efficiently.

The utilities that need to be run more than once, like Disk Cleanup, Disk Defragmenter, and the antivirus and spyware programs, can be configured to run automatically at any time interval you want. You can set up a sequence of programs to run one after the other every evening while you sleep, and wake up each day to a reliable, secure system.

My system crashes often during the day. What can I do? Computer systems are complex. It's not unusual to have your system stop responding occasionally. If rebooting the computer doesn't help, you'll need to begin troubleshooting:

1. Check that you have enough RAM, which you learned how to do in the section "Evaluating RAM: The Memory Subsystem" earlier in this

unreliable, see if the problem is one you can fix before you buy a new machine. Proper upkeep and maintenance also may postpone an expensive system upgrade or replacement.

What can I do to ensure my system performs reliably? Here are several procedures you can follow to ensure your system performs reliably:

1. **Clean out your Startup folder.** Some programs install themselves into your Startup folder and run automatically each time the computer starts up, whether you are using them or not. This unnecessary load uses up RAM, leaving less for other programs. To minimize this problem, check your Startup folder by clicking Start > All Programs. Then click on the Startup folder and make sure all the programs listed are

chapter. Systems with insufficient amounts of RAM often crash.

2. Make sure you have properly installed any new software or hardware. If you're using a Windows system, use the System Restore utility to "roll back" the system to a time when it worked more reliably. (To find System Restore, just type "restore" into the Start menu search box.) For Mac systems, Mac OS X Time Machine, shown in Figure 36, provides automatic backup and enables you to look through and restore (if necessary) files, folders, libraries, or the entire system.

3. If you see an error code in Windows, visit the Microsoft Knowledge Base (**support.microsoft.com**), an online resource for resolving problems with Microsoft products. This may help you determine what the error code indicates and how you may be able to solve the problem. If you don't find a satisfactory answer in the Knowledge Base, try copying the entire error message into Google and searching the larger community for solutions.

Can my software affect system reliability?   Having the latest version of software products makes your system much more reliable. You should upgrade or update your operating system, browser software, and application software as often as new patches (or updates) are reported for resolving errors. Sometimes these errors are performance-related; sometimes they are potential system security breaches.

If you are having a problem that can be replicated, use the Problem Steps Recorder to capture the exact steps that lead to it. In Windows 7, go to the Start menu and search for "psr." Run the Problem Steps Recorder and go through the exact actions that create the problem you are having. At any particular step, you can click the Annotate button and add a comment about any part of the screen. PSR then produces a documented report, complete with images of your screen and descriptions of each mouse movement you made. You can then e-mail this report, which is compressed in the WinZip format, to customer support to help technicians resolve the problem.

How do I know whether updates are available for my software?   You can configure Windows so that it automatically checks for, downloads, and installs any available updates for itself, Internet Explorer, and other Microsoft applications such as Microsoft Office. Many other applications now also include the ability to check

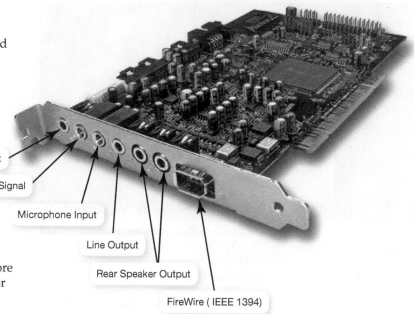

Analog/Digital Output
Line Input Signal
Microphone Input
Line Output
Rear Speaker Output
FireWire (IEEE 1394)

Figure 34

In addition to improving sound quality, upgraded sound cards can provide additional ports for your audio equipment.

Figure 35 | DO YOU NEED TO UPGRADE YOUR AUDIO SUBSYSTEM?

	Current System	Ideal System
Is the speaker quality high enough for the way I am using my computer?		
Is my sound card capable of 3D sound?		
Does my sound card support Dolby Digital surround sound?		
Do I have 5.1-channel surround sound or 7.1-channel surround sound?		
Do I have an HDMI port on the audio card?		

Figure 36

Mac's Time Machine restores files, folders, libraries and, if necessary, the entire system.

system to determine what upgrades might be required before you convert to Windows 7. Be sure to examine the *recommended* (not required) specifications of the new operating system.

2. **Reinstall the operating system.** As a last resort, you might need to reinstall the operating system. To do so, you'll want to back up all of your data files before the installation and be prepared to reinstall all your software after the installation. Make sure you have all of the original discs for the software installed on your system, along with the product keys, serial numbers, and any other activation codes so that you can reinstall them.

for updates. Check under the Help menu of the product, and often you will find a Check for Updates command.

What if none of this helps? Is buying a new system my only option? If your system is still unreliable after these changes, then you have two options:

1. **Upgrade your operating system to the latest version.** There are substantial increases in reliability with each major release of a new operating system. However, upgrading the operating system may require hardware upgrades such as additional RAM, an updated graphics processor, and an even larger hard drive. The Microsoft Windows 7 Upgrade Advisor (a free download from (**microsoft.com**) will scan your

Making the Final Decision

Now that you have evaluated your computer system, you need to shift to questions of *value*. How closely does your system come to meeting your needs? How much would it cost to upgrade the system you have to match what you'd ideally like your computer to do, not only today but also a few years from now? How much would it cost to purchase a new system that meets these specifications?

To decide whether upgrading or buying a new system has better value for you, you need to price both scenarios. Figure 37

Figure 37 | UPGRADE/NEW PURCHASE COMPARISON WORKSHEET

Needs	Hardware Upgrade Cost	Included on New System?	Additional Expense If Not Included on New System
CPU and Memory Subsystems			
CPU upgrade			
RAM upgrade			
Storage Subsystem			
Hard drive upgrade			
SSD drive			
DVD+/-RW burner			
Blu-ray burner			
Video and Audio Subsystems			
Video card upgrade			
Sound card upgrade			

What happened to your last computer? If you threw it away hoping it would be safely recycled with your empty water bottles, think again. Mercury in LCD screens, cadmium in batteries and circuit boards, and flame retardant in plastic housings all are toxic. An alarming, emerging trend is that discarded machines are beginning to create an e-waste crisis.

Instead of throwing your computer away, you may be able to donate it to a nonprofit organization. Many manufacturers, such as Dell, offer recycling programs and have formed alliances with nonprofit organizations to help distribute your old technology to those who need it. Sites like Computers With Causes (**computerswithcauses.org**) organize donations of both working and nonworking computers, printers, and mice. You can also take your computer to an authorized computer recycling center in your area (see Figure 38). The Telecommunications Industry Association provides an e-cycling information site you can use to find a local e-cycling center (**eiae.org**).

However, before donating or recycling a computer, make sure you carefully remove all data from your hard drive, or you may end up having your good deed turn bad by becoming the victim of identity theft. Credit card numbers, bank information, Social Security numbers, tax records, passwords, and personal identification numbers (PINs) are just some of the types of sensitive information that we casually record to our computers' hard drives. Just deleting files that contain proprietary personal information is not protection enough. Likewise, reformatting or erasing your hard drive does not totally remove data, as was proved by two MIT graduate students. In 2003, they bought more than 150 used hard drives from various sources. Although some of the hard drives had been reformatted or damaged so the data was supposedly irrecoverable, the two students were able to retrieve medical records, financial information, pornography, personal e-mails, and more than 5,000 credit card numbers!

The U.S. Department of Defense suggests a seven-layer overwrite for a "secure erase." In other words, they suggest that you fill your hard drive *seven times over* with a random series of 1s and 0s. Fortunately, several programs exist for PCs running Windows, such as Active@ Kill Disk, Eraser, and CyberScrub. Wipe is available for Linux, and ShredIt X can be used for OS X.

These programs provide secure hard drive erasures, either of specific files on your hard drive or of the entire hard drive.

Keep in mind that even these data erasure programs can't provide the ultimate level in security. Computer forensic specialists or supercybercriminals can still manage to retrieve some data from your hard drive if they have the right tools. The ultimate level of protection comes from destroying the hard drive altogether. Suggested methods include drilling holes in the hard drive, burning or melting it, or just taking an old-fashioned sledgehammer to it! For large companies that need to upgrade large quantities of computers and have the options of destroying or recycling their old computers, the problem becomes much worse. In these cases, recycling isn't a good option, and throwing the computers away can create an environmental hazard. Companies such as GigaBiter (**gigabiter.com**) eliminate security and environmental risks associated with electronic destruction by first delaminating the hard drive and then breaking down the computer e-waste into recyclable products. The result of the final step is a sandlike substance that is 100 percent recyclable.

Figure 38

An electronics scrap recycler "demanufactures" printers, computers, and other electronics and then resells the usable parts.

provides an upgrade worksheet you can use to evaluate both the upgrade path and the new purchase path. Be sure to consider what benefit you might obtain by having two systems if you were to buy a new computer. Would you have a use for the older system? Would you donate it to a charitable organization? Would you be able to give it to a family member? Purchasing a new system is an important investment of your resources, and you want to make a well-reasoned, well-supported decision.

1. How can I determine whether I should upgrade my existing computer or buy a new one?

To determine whether you need to upgrade your system or purchase a new one, you need to define your ideal system and what you want it to do. Then you need to perform a system evaluation to assess the subsystems in your computer, including the CPU, memory, storage, video, and audio. Finally, you need to determine if it's economical to upgrade, or whether buying a new computer would be better.

2. What does the CPU do, and how can I evaluate its performance?

Your computer's CPU processes instructions, performs calculations, manages the flow of information through the computer system, and is responsible for processing the data you input into information. CPU speed is measured in gigahertz (billions of machine cycles per second). You can tell whether your CPU is limiting your system performance by watching how busy it is as you work on your computer. The percentage of time that your CPU is working is referred to as CPU usage, which you can determine by checking the Task Manager. Benchmarking software offers direct performance comparisons of different CPUs.

3. How does memory work in my computer, and how can I evaluate how much memory I need?

RAM is your computer's temporary memory. It remembers everything that the computer needs to process data into information. However, it is an example of volatile storage. When the power is off, the data stored in RAM is cleared out. The amount of RAM sitting on memory modules in your computer is your computer's physical memory. The memory your OS uses is kernel memory. At a minimum, you need enough RAM to run the OS plus the software applications you're using, plus a bit more to hold the data you will input.

4. What are the computer's main storage devices, and how can I evaluate whether they match my needs?

Storage devices for a typical computer system may include a hard drive, an SSD drive, a flash drive, and CD and DVD drives. Blu-ray drives are gaining in popularity for viewing and burning high-density media. When you turn off your computer, the data stored in these devices remains. These devices are referred to as *nonvolatile* storage devices. Hard drives have the largest storage capacity of any storage device and are the most economical. Newer SSD drives have the fastest access time and data transfer rate of all nonvolatile storage options. CDs and DVDs have capacities from 700 MB to 17 GB, while Blu-ray discs can hold up to 50 GB. Portable flash drives allow easy transfer of 64 GB or more of data from machine to machine. To determine the storage capacity your system needs, calculate the amount of storage your software needs to reside on your computer. To add more storage or to provide more functionality for your system, you can install additional drives, either internally or externally.

5. What components affect the output of video on my computer, and how can I evaluate whether they match my needs?

How video is displayed depends on two components: your video card and your monitor. A video card translates binary data into the images you see. These cards include their own RAM (video memory) as well as ports that allow you to connect to video equipment. The amount of video memory you need depends on what you want to display on the monitor. A more powerful card will allow you to play graphics-intense games and multimedia.

6. What components affect the quality of sound on my computer, and how can I evaluate whether they match my needs?

Your computer's sound depends on your speakers and sound card. A sound card enables the computer to produce sounds. Users upgrade their sound cards to provide for 3D sound, surround sound, and additional ports for audio equipment.

7. How can I improve the reliability of my system?

Many computer users decide to buy a new system because they are experiencing problems with their computer. However, before you buy a new system because you think yours may be unreliable, make sure the problem is not one you can fix. Run a full scan with antispyware software. Make sure you have installed any new software or hardware properly, check that you have enough RAM, run system utilities such as Disk Defragmenter and Disk Cleanup, clean out your Startup folder, remove unnecessary files from your system, and keep your software updated with patches. If you continue to have troubles with your system, reinstall or upgrade your OS, and, of course, seek technical assistance.

key terms

3D sound card
access time
BD-ROM disc
benchmarks
bit depth
Blu-ray disc
cache memory
clock speed
core
CPU usage
data transfer rate
DVD-RAM
DVD-ROM
DVD-R/RW
DVD+R/RW
external SATA (eSATA)
ExpressCard
front side bus (FSB)
graphics processing unit (GPU)
hard drive
head crash
hyperthreading

kernel memory
latency
memory module (memory card)
Moore's Law
nonvolatile storage
optical media
physical memory
platter
random access memory (RAM)
read/write head
sector
seek time
Serial Advanced Technology
  Attachment (SATA)
solid state drive (SSD)
sound card
surround sound
system evaluation
track
video card (video adapter)
video memory
volatile storage

Word Bank

- access time
- Blu-ray disc
- cache memory
- CPU usage
- data transfer rate
- eSATA

- express cards
- front side bus
- GPU
- hard drive
- memory module
- Moore's law

- RAM
- sound card
- SSD
- surround sound
- system evaluation

Instructions: Fill in the blanks using the words from the Word Bank above.

Joe already has a PC but just heard about a great deal on a new one. He decides to perform a(n) (1) _____ on his computer to see whether he should keep it or buy the new one. First, he runs the Task Manager in Windows. By doing so, he can check the history of (2) _____ as he works through his day. Because he is often over 90 percent, he begins to suspect his system is suffering from too little (3) _____. He has room for an additional two (4) _____ on his motherboard. Adding memory is something he learned how to do this semester, but would that be enough to make this machine do all he needs?

He visits the Intel Web site to check two other important factors on his model of CPU: the amount of (5) _____ memory and the speed of the (6) _____. It looks like the newer i7 processor would be much faster overall. It seems each generation of processors is so much faster than the last. That rule, (7) _____, is still holding true!

He continues to evaluate his system by checking out which components he has and which ones he'll need. He notes the storage capacity of the (8) _____. Recently, he has been wishing his system had a(n) (9) _____ port because adding an external hard drive would give him enough space to start to record HD television shows. As it is, he is running out of space to store files. But the (10) _____, or the amount of time it takes to retrieve data from the disk drive, on any mechanical drive is slow compared to the (11) _____ in the new computer he's eyeing, which has no moving parts at all. Joe also notes that he is unable to do a complete backup of his music library onto optical media now that he has 40 GB of music data. His current system can't burn a (12) _____, but the new system could. The new video card would also include several (13) _____ ports so that six digital monitors can be connected simultaneously. It would be great if he could take advantage of the 5.1 (14) _____ that is on the soundtrack of most of the movies he watches on DVD.

He also has a lot of friends who play video games on their computer systems. However, his current system doesn't meet the minimum requirements for a video card. Newer cards have blindingly fast (15) _____, and some cards even have multiple processors. Overall, with prices dropping, it seems like time to go buy that new system!

Rebecca has already built five or six PCs and tells you she can make a killer desktop system for you for under $1,300. But you do love the idea of having a light, compact notebook computer that could travel with you around campus and back and forth to work.

Instructions: Using the preceding scenario, write an e-mail to Rebecca describing to her what you need in your new system. Examine the specifications for both notebook and desktop systems in this price range and decide which one is best suited to you. Use key terms from the chapter and be sure your sentences are grammatically correct and technically meaningful.

Understanding and Assessing Hardware: Evaluating Your System

Instructions: Answer the multiple-choice and true–false questions below for more practice with key terms and concepts from this chapter.

Multiple Choice

1. Which statement about notebook computers is FALSE?
   a. Notebooks typically have a longer lifespan.
   b. Notebooks are typically less reliable.
   c. Notebooks can be docked to larger monitors.
   d. Notebook are more difficult to expand or upgrade.

2. ROM is classified as what type of storage?
   a. Volatile   c. Flash
   b. Nonvolatile   d. Cache

3. To document a problem you are having, you can use
   a. Disk Cleanup.
   b. Problem Step Recorder.
   c. PC DeCrapifier.
   d. Resource Monitor.

4. If you want your system to run reliably, you should
   a. delete all programs from the Startup folder.
   b. save all of your temporary Internet files.
   c. install programs in the system tray.
   d. defragment the hard drive.

5. Which bests describes RAID 0 technology?
   a. Saved data is spread across two hard drives.
   b. Data is written to one drive and mirrored to a second drive.
   c. RAID 0 allows you to store twice the data.
   d. RAID 0 provides an instant backup of your work.

6. What allows two different programs to be processed at one time?
   a. Hyperthreading
   b. SSD
   c. Benchmarking
   d. GPU

7. Which is *not* a type of memory stored in your system?
   a. RAM
   b. Cache
   c. CPU register
   d. ALU

8. The optimal amount of memory for a video card depends on
   a. the quality of video you will be watching.
   b. the resolution of the monitor.
   c. the number of monitors you have.
   d. All of the above.

9. SuperFetch is a memory-management technique that
   a. determines the type of RAM your system requires.
   b. makes the boot-up time for the system very quick.
   c. preloads the applications you use most into system memory.
   d. defragments the hard drive to increase performance.

10. What is the name for the time it takes a storage device to locate its stored data and make it available for processing?
    a. Clock speed
    b. Access time
    c. Data transfer rate
    d. Seek time

True–False

____ 1. A single CPU can have multiple cores but cannot also use hyperthreading.

____ 2. The memory that your operating system uses is referred to as kernel memory.

____ 3. Motherboards are designed with a specific number of memory card slots.

____ 4. Cache memory is a form of read-only memory that can be accessed more quickly by the CPU.

____ 5. Solid state drives are faster than hard drives and eSATA drives.

Understanding and Assessing Hardware: Evaluating Your System

1. Personalize Your System

Likely you spend many hours each day working on your computer using it for school, work, communication, research, and entertainment. Your computer should be a device that fits you, fits your needs, and expresses who you are.
   a. Begin with the computer's form. Would you select a notebook or a desktop? What features determine that decision?
   b. Next consider performance. Which type of CPU do you need? How much RAM should be installed? What kind of hard drive storage would you select? Give specific price-to-value arguments for each decision.
   c. Now consider expandability. If you need this system to last for four years, what kind of ports and expansion capability are necessary?
   d. Finally, consider style. What components or design decisions can you make so that this system uniquely suits you and represents you?

2. Desktop Replacement

The line between the capabilities of a desktop system and a powerful notebook have become more and more blurred with the arrival of "desktop replacement" systems. These systems often have 17-inch, 18-inch, or larger monitors, weigh 10 pounds or more, and have a battery life of less than two hours. Research the most current entries in the "desktop replacement" category and evaluate them. What kind of user would find this an ideal solution? Do you anticipate this category of computer becoming more popular?

3. Go Small or Stay Home

Manufacturers are releasing a number of systems that are trying to capitalize on size—or the lack of size! Explore some of the small form factor (SFF) computers appearing on the market.
   a. Research the Falcon NorthWest FragBox (falcon-nw.com).
   b. Examine the Apple MacMini (apple.com).
   c. Compare those systems with the Dell Zino HD (dell.com).

Why are these SFF computers appearing? What role do you see these systems fulfilling? What kind of performance and hardware would you recommend for such a system?

4. Do-It-Yourself Computer Design

Visit NewEgg (**newegg.com**) and do a search on "do it yourself". You will find that NewEgg has created a number of bundles, which are a set of components that cover the categories outlined in this chapter: the computer case, processor, RAM, storage, video, and audio.
   a. Which system looks like the best match for your needs for school next semester? Why?
   b. What is the price difference between building the system and purchasing a similar unit from a major manufacturer?
   c. What skills would you need before you could assemble the computer yourself?
   d. What additional components (hardware and software) would you need to complete the system?
   e. What kind of support exists to train you in these skills or to help with questions you might have along the way?

5. How Does Your System Measure Up?

A number of tools are available to measure your system's performance. Explore the following tools and use one to gather data on your current system's performance.
   a. Windows 7 Gadgets: Visit the Windows 7 Personalization Gallery (**windows. microsoft.com**) and find gadgets to help you monitor system performance.
   b. Windows 7 Resource Monitor: Use the Resource Monitor to collect data on CPU utilization and memory usage over a typical school day.
   c. Benchmarking suites: Examine a sample of consumer benchmarking programs like the PassMark's PerformanceTest, Primate Lab's Geekbench, and Maxon's Cinebench. Which subsystems do each of these products evaluate? How do they present their results? Which seems easiest to use?

Understanding and Assessing Hardware: Evaluating Your System

1. In the "Real World"

As you move from an educational environment to a business environment, how you use your computer will inevitably change. Write a description of your ideal computer system for school and for once you are in the workforce. Defend the position you take with information covered in this chapter. To help you in your decision, fill out the worksheet, similar to Figure 2, that is available on the book's companion Website (**pearsonhighered.com/techinaction**).

2. Judging System Performance

As you learned in this chapter, the Resource Monitor provides a detailed breakdown of how the computer is using memory at any given time.

a. Open the Resource Monitor, move to the CPU tab, and open the Processes frame. What is your total CPU Usage? How many "virtual" CPUs does your machine have? Clicking on any of the column titles sorts that column, so clicking the Average CPU column shows you the applications currently using most of the CPU resources. What are the top two most intensive applications?

b. Move to the Memory tab. How much memory is in use? How much is available? Of the memory available, how much has been preloaded with data and files that Windows "thinks" you will need soon?

c. Move to the Disk tab. Click on the Processes With Disk Activity panel. Which programs are making the greatest total demand to read and write to the disk?

3. My Mother(board)

This chapter discussed the qualities of a CPU that are important to consider for system performance. Now examine the features of a motherboard that are critical to the performance and expandability of a system. Visit NewEgg (**newegg.com**) and search for "Intel Motherboards"; then sort by "Best Rated".

a. Which model has the best reviews?

b. How many ports and what type of ports does it have?

c. What kind of CPU does it support?

d. What kind of memory does it use, and what is the maximum memory it supports?

e. How many hard drives can it run? Does it support both RAID 0 and RAID 1?

f. Does it have integrated video? Audio?

4. Room to Move

You are responsible for specifying the storage solution for an accounting customer's computer system. Your customer needs to always have redundancy—that is, multiple copies of the work they are doing—because of the secure nature of the records they keep and the length of time they are required to keep records. Prepare a report that describes the type of hard drive and optical storage you would recommend. Be sure to include performance specifications and price. Devise a list of additional questions you would need to ask your customer to be sure they have a system that meets their expectations.

5. A Picture Is Worth a Thousand Words

You work in a financial analysis firm. It is necessary to watch small fluctuations in many different international monetary funds and markets each day. This data is then fed into your own prediction software, tied to Excel calculations, and then plotted with three different statistical analysis packages. What video solution would be ideal for this environment? Would it require a video card with a single or dual GPU? Multiple video cards? Multiple monitors?

6. Let Me Tell You My Problem

You may be responsible for helping others solve various computer problems. Test out the Problem Steps Recorder in Windows 7 to see how the program can help you help them. Click the Start button and search for "psr". Run the program and click Record. Then just click between different applications, visit the Control Panel, and add an annotation. Save the file to your desktop and close the Problem Steps Recorder. View the annotated report. How could you use the Problem Steps Recorder to describe a problem or to gather information?

Understanding and Assessing Hardware: Evaluating Your System

Instructions: Albert Einstein used *Gedankenexperiments*, or critical thinking questions, to develop his theory of relativity. Some ideas are best understood by experimenting with them in our own minds. The following critical thinking questions are designed to demand your full attention but require only a comfortable chair—no technology.

1. And Google Says...

In a presentation in Dublin, Ireland in March 2010, Google sales chief Jim Haley stated that desktops would be irrelevant in three years (**SiliconRepublic.com**). Smartphones, notebooks, and the amount of information available online will converge to create a different kind of future than what we've known, according to Haley. Do you agree? Why or why not? What impact would that have on the types of hardware and software that are the most in demand?

2. Emerging Technologies

Touchscreens are now available in a range of sizes, from smartphones to iPads to larger products like the Microsoft Surface. Windows 7 has integrated support for touchscreens. "Surround Sight" and 3D monitors are available in increasing numbers. What new technologies will last and become part of our collective experience? How will these technologies and devices change entertainment and how people interact with information? What future technologies that would be on your wish list?

3. The Early Adopter

We are all aware of the technology price curve: when first introduced, products have the highest prices and the most instability. As these products settle into the market, they become more reliable and the price falls, sometimes very quickly. People who make those first release purchases are called *early adopters*. What are the advantages to being an early adopter? What are the disadvantages? How do you decide at what point you should step into the technology price curve for any given product?

4. A Green Machine

Review the impacts of your computer during its entire lifecycle. How do the production, transportation, and use of the computer impact the increase of greenhouse gas emissions? How does the selection of materials and packaging impact the environment? What restricted substances (like lead, mercury, cadmium, and PVC) are found in your machine? Could substitute materials be used? How would the ultimate "Green Machine" be designed?

5. System Longevity

If you purchase a computer system for business purposes, the Internal Revenue Service (IRS) allows you to depreciate its cost over five years. The IRS considers this a reasonable estimate of the useful lifetime of a computer system. What do you think most home users expect in terms of how long their computer systems should last? How does the purchase of a computer system compare with other major household appliances in terms of cost, value, benefit, life span, and upgrade potential?

team time

Many Different Computers for Many Different Needs

Problem

Even within one discipline, there are needs for a variety of types of computing solutions. Consider the Communications department in a large university. Because it is such an interdisciplinary area, there are some groups involved in video production, some groups producing digital music, and some groups responsible for creating scripts and screenplays. The department as a whole needs to decide on a complete computing strategy.

Process

Split your class into teams.

1. Select one segment of the Communications department that your team will represent: video production, digital music, or scripting. The video production team requires their labs to be able to support the recording, editing, and final production and distribution of digital video. The digital music group wants to establish a collegiate recording studio (in the model of the Drexel University recording label, Mad Dragon Records). The scripting group needs to support a collaborative community of writers and voice-over actors.
2. Analyze the computing needs of that division, with particular focus on how they need to outfit their computer labs.
3. Price the systems you would recommend and explain how they will be used. What decisions have you made to guarantee they will still be useful in three years?
4. Write a report that summarizes your findings. Document the resources you used and generate as much enthusiasm as you can for your recommendations.

Conclusion

The range of available computing solutions has never been so broad. It can be a cause of confusion for those not educated in technology. But with a firm understanding of the basic subsystems of computers, it is precisely the pace of change that is exciting. Being able to evaluate a computer system and match it to the current needs of its users is an important skill.

Understanding and Assessing Hardware: Evaluating Your System

In this exercise, you will research and then role-play a complicated ethical situation. The role you play might or might not match your own personal beliefs; in either case, your research and use of logic will enable you to represent the view assigned. An arbitrator will watch and comment on both sides of the arguments, and together the team will agree on an ethical solution.

Topic: Light Peak

We have seen many dramatic increases in connectivity speed. The USB standard is now in its third revision, with each being many fold faster than its predecessor. Currently, Intel is developing a technology named Light Peak that could replace all of the cables you currently see dangling from computers with one fiber-optic cable—one very fast fiber-optic cable. This technology will allow for smaller notebook computer designs, because they won't need to have a huge set of ports along the side. Intel feels Light Peak could become the universal port, replacing USB, HDMI, FireWire, DVI, and others. And using Light Peak, an entire high-definition movie could be transferred in 30 seconds.

Research Areas to Consider

- Durability of fiber-optic cables for consumers

- Protection of intellectual content as transfer speeds increase

- Building consensus in the market for new technologies

- 2009 Nobel Prize for Physics

Process

Divide the class into teams.

1. Research the areas cited above from the perspective of either an Intel engineer working on Light Peak, a notebook designer, a producer of high-definition videos, or an arbitrator.

2. Team members should write a summary that provides factual documentation for the positions and views their character takes around the issue of increasingly high speed data transfer and intellectual property rights. Then, team members should create an outline to use during the role-playing event.

3. Team members should arrange a mutually convenient time to meet for the exchange, either using the chat room feature of MyITLab, the discussion board feature of Blackboard, or meeting in person.

4. Team members should present their case to the class, or submit a PowerPoint presentation for review by the rest of the class, along with the summary and resolution they developed.

Conclusion

As technology becomes ever more prevalent and integrated into our lives, more and more ethical dilemmas will present themselves. Being able to understand and evaluate both sides of the argument, while responding in a personally or socially ethical manner, will be an important skill.

Understanding and Assessing Hardware: Evaluating Your System

3D sound card An expansion card that enables a computer to produce sounds that are omnidirectional or three dimensional.

access time The time it takes a storage device to locate its stored data.

BD-ROM disc BD-ROM is defined as BluRay Disc Read Only Memory. BD-ROM is an optical disc storage media format for high-definition video and data storage.

benchmark A measurement used in comparing software and hardware performance. Benchmarks are created using software applications that are specifically designed to push the limits of computer performance.

bit depth The number of bits a video card uses to store data about each pixel on the monitor.

Blu-ray disc A method of optical storage for digital data, developed for storing high-definition media. It has the largest storage capacity of all optical storage options.

cache memory Small blocks of memory, located directly on and next to the central processing unit (CPU) chip, that act as holding places for recently or frequently used instructions or data that the CPU accesses the most. When these instructions or data are stored in cache memory, the CPU can more quickly retrieve them than if it had to access the instructions or data from random access memory (RAM).

clock speed The steady and constant pace at which a computer goes through machine cycles, measured in hertz (Hz).

core A complete processing section from a CPU, embedded into one physical chip.

CPU usage The percentage of time a central processing unit (CPU) is working.

data transfer rate (bandwidth) The maximum speed at which data can be transmitted between two nodes on a network; usually measured in megabits per second (Mbps).

DVD-RAM One of three competing technologies for rewritable DVDs.

DVD-ROM DVD format in which data can only be read and not written.

DVD-R/RW One of two recognized DVD formats that enable you to read, record (R), and rewrite (RW) data on the disc.

DVD+R/RW One of two recognized DVD formats that enables you to both read, record (R), and rewrite (RW) data on the disc.

external SATA A fast data transfer point where a user can easily add peripheral devices.

ExpressCard An electronic card that when plugged into notebook computers provides functionality such as wireless network connections, USB ports, or FireWire ports.

front side bus (FSB) Located on the motherboard, this bus runs between the central processing unit (CPU) and the main system memory.

graphics processing unit (GPU) A specialized logic chip that is dedicated to quickly displaying and calculating visual data such as shadows, textures, and luminosity.

hard drive A device that holds all permanently stored programs and data; can be located inside the system unit or attached to the system unit via a USB port.

head crash Impact of read/write head against magnetic platter of the hard drive; often results in data loss.

hyperthreading A technology that permits quicker processing of information by enabling a new set of instructions to start executing before the previous set has finished.

kernel memory The memory that the computer's operating system uses.

latency The process that occurs after the read/write head of the hard drive locates the correct track, and then waits for the correct sector to spin to the read/write head.

memory module (memory card) A small circuit board that holds a series of random access memory (RAM) chips.

Moore's Law A prediction, named after Gordon Moore, the cofounder of Intel; states that the number of transistors on a CPU chip will double every two years.

nonvolatile storage Permanent storage, as in read-only memory (ROM).

optical media Portable storage devices, such as CDs, DVDs, and Blu-ray discs, that use a laser to read and write data.

physical memory The amount of random access memory (RAM) that is installed in a computer.

platter A thin, round, metallic storage plate stacked onto the hard drive spindle.

random access memory (RAM) The computer's temporary storage space or short-term memory. It is located in a set of chips on the system unit's motherboard, and its capacity is measured in megabytes or gigabytes.

read/write head The mechanism that retrieves (reads) and records (writes) the magnetic data to and from a data disk. They move from the outer edge of the spinning platters to the center, up to 50 times per second.

sector A section of a hard drive platter, wedge-shaped from the center of the platter to the edge.

seek time The time it takes for the hard drive's read/write heads to move over the surface of the disk, between tracks, to the correct track.

Serial Advanced Technology Attachment (Serial ATA) A type of hard drive that uses much thinner cables, and can transfer data more quickly, than IDE drives.

solid state drive (SSD) A drive that uses the same kind of memory that flash drives use, but can reach data in only a tenth of the time a flash drive requires.

Understanding and Assessing Hardware: Evaluating Your System

glossary

sound card An expansion card that attaches to the mother-board inside the system unit and that enables the computer to produce sounds by providing a connection for the speakers and microphone.

surround sound A type of audio processing that makes the listener experience sound as if it were coming from all directions.

system evaluation The process of looking at a computer's subsystems, what they do, and how they perform to determine whether the computer system has the right hardware components to do what the user ultimately wants it to do.

track A concentric circle that serves as a storage area on a hard drive platter.

video card (video adapter) An expansion card that is installed inside a system unit to translate binary data (the 1s and 0s the computer uses) into the images viewed on the monitor.

video memory RAM that is included as part of a video card.

volatile storage Temporary storage, such as in random access memory (RAM). When the power is off, the data in volatile storage is cleared out.

credits

networking:
connecting computing devices

From Chapter 7 of *Technology in Action Complete,* Eighth Edition, Alan Evans, Kendall Martin, Mary Anne Poatsy.

networking:
connecting computing devices

how cool is *this?*

As you have probably already experienced, wireless connectivity is not always free. Many businesses, such as Starbucks, **charge** customers for each device they want to connect, which can become expensive for groups of friends trying to surf the Internet while waiting to **catch a flight** at the airport. Connectify is free software that takes an existing Internet connection and turns it into a wireless hotspot. So if you are connected to the Internet on your notebook, the **Connectify** software turns your notebook computer into a wireless hotspot so that you and your friends can connect other WiFi-enabled devices such as a cell phone or **gaming** system through the same Internet connection. The hotspot you create features easy connectivity and encryption of data for solid **security**.

Networking Fundamentals

Now that we are into the second decade of the 21st century, most homes have more than one computing device that is capable of connecting to the Internet. A typical family, like the Diaz family (see Figure 1), might be engaged in the following: Carlos (the father) is watching a movie, which he downloaded yesterday on the large-screen HDTV in the living room while checking his Gmail

Figure 1

By setting up a home network, everyone in the family can connect their computers and others devices whenever and wherever they desire.

Networking: Connecting Computing Devices

on his smartphone. Camila (the mother) is in the kitchen fixing lunch while checking the weather forecast and watching YouTube videos. Antonio, their fifteen-year-old son, is in his bedroom playing an online game with his friends (via his PlayStation) and is uploading a video he made for a class project to a Web site at school. Adriana, Antonio's older sister, is in the den using her notebook computer to finish a report for school. She's also watching a Blu-ray disc of *Avatar*, which is one of her all-time favorite movies. Grandma Cecilia is in the family room viewing pictures from the family's last vacation and is uploading to Facebook the pictures that she took of her grandchildren during their trip to Disneyland last week. And Angel, the youngest daughter, is playing with Sparky in the backyard and uploading video that she took of him with her phone so that everyone can see it in the family room while they eat lunch. And because both Carlos and Camila work outside the home, they use webcams to monitor activities in the house, like ensuring their kids arrive home safely from school, while they are at work. What makes all this technology transfer and sharing possible? A home network!

What is a computer network?
A computer **network** is simply two or more computers that are connected via software and hardware so that they can communicate with each other. You access networks all the time whether you realize it or not. When you use an ATM, get gasoline, or use the Internet (the world's largest network), you are interacting with a network. Each device connected to a network is referred to as a **node**. A node can be a computer, a peripheral (such as an all-in-one printer), a game console (such as a

PlayStation or a Wii), a digital video recorder (such as a TiVo), or a communications device (such as a modem). The main function for most networks is to facilitate information sharing, but networks provide other benefits.

What are the benefits of networks?
There are several benefits to having computers networked. Most home users want a network to facilitate resource sharing. For example, a network allows you to share the high-speed Internet connection coming into your home. Networks also allow you to share peripheral devices, such as printers. Figure 2a shows two computers that are not networked. Computer 1 is connected to the printer, but Computer 2 is not. To print files from Computer 2, users have to transfer them using a flash drive or another storage medium to Computer 1, or they have to disconnect the printer from Computer 1 and connect it to Computer 2. By networking Computer 1, Computer 2,

Figure 2

(a) Computers 1 and 2 are not networked, and Computer 2 cannot access the printer. (b) Networking allows sharing of the printer.

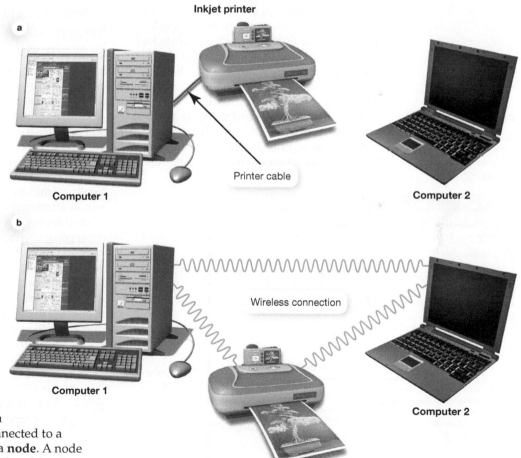

and the printer, as shown in Figure 2b, both computers can print from the printer without transferring files or attaching the printer to a particular computer. Using a wired or wireless network to share a printer saves the cost of buying one printer for each computer.

Besides peripheral and Internet connections, does networking facilitate any other types of resource sharing? You can also easily share files between networked computers without having to use portable storage devices such as flash drives to transfer the files. In addition, you can set sharing options in Windows or OS X that allow the user of each computer on the network to access files (such as music or videos) stored on any other computer on the network, as shown in Figure 3.

This Windows network has five computers attached to it. ALAN-DESKTOP, ALAN-NOTEBOOK, and PAT-NOTEBOOK are running the Windows operating system. The two MACBOOKs are running OS X. The Public folders enable file sharing because the user of any computer on the network can access the Public folder's contents. And note the final advantage of networking: computers running different operating systems (such as Windows and OS X) can communicate on the same network.

Are there disadvantages to setting up a network? Networks involve the purchase of additional equipment to set them up, so cost is one disadvantage. Also,

networks need to be administered, at least to some degree. **Network administration** involves tasks such as: 1) installing new computers and devices, 2) monitoring the network to ensure it is performing efficiently, 3) updating and installing new software on the network, and 4) configuring, or setting up, proper security for a network. Fortunately, most home networks do not require a great deal of administration after their initial configuration, and the benefits of using a network usually outweigh the disadvantages.

Network Architectures

The term **network architecture** refers to the design of a network. Network architectures are classified according to the way in which they are controlled and the distance between their nodes.

Describing Networks Based on Network Administration

What different types of control do I have over my network? A network can be administered, or managed, in either of two main ways: locally or centrally. Local administration means that the configuration and maintenance of the network must be performed on each individual computer attached to the network. A peer-to-peer network is the most common example of a locally administered network. Central administration means that tasks can be performed from one computer and affect the other computers on the network. The most common type of centrally administered network is a client/server network.

What is a peer-to-peer network? In a **peer-to-peer (P2P) network**, each node connected to the network can communicate directly with every other node on the network. Thus, all nodes on this type of network are peers (equals). When printing, for example, a computer on a P2P network doesn't have to go through the computer that's connected to the printer. Instead, it can communicate directly with the printer. Figure 2b, shown earlier, shows a very small peer-to-peer network.

Figure 3

Windows Explorer showing five networked computers set up for sharing.

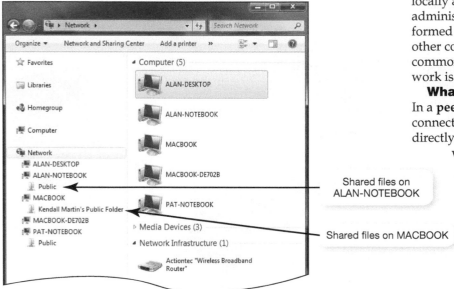

Shared files on
ALAN-NOTEBOOK

Shared files on MACBOOK

Step 1:
Client computer requests a service.

Step 2:
Server computer provides service.

Computer A (client)

Computer B (server)

Figure 4

In a client/server network, a computer acts either as a client making requests for resources or as a server providing resources.

Because they are simple to set up, P2P networks are the most common type of home network. Very small schools and offices may also use P2P networks. However, most networks that have 10 or more nodes are client/server networks.

What are client/server networks?
A **client/server network** contains two different types of computers: clients and servers. A **client** is a computer on which users accomplish specific tasks (such as construct spreadsheets) and make specific requests (such as printing a file). The **server** is the computer that provides information or resources to the client computers on the network. The server on a client/server network also provides central administration for network functions such as printing. Figure 4 illustrates a client/server network in action.

The Internet is an example of a client/server

Figure 5

At only 8 inches high, the Acer Aspire easyStore server can perform a variety of tasks to simplify media management on a home network.

network. When your computer is connected to the Internet, it is functioning as a client computer. When it accesses the Internet through an Internet service provider (ISP), your computer connects to a server computer maintained by the ISP. The server "serves up" resources to your computer so that you can interact with the Internet.

Are client/server networks ever used as home networks?
Although client/server networks can be configured for home use, P2P networks are more often used in the home because they cost less than client/server networks and are easier to configure and maintain. However, specialized types of servers (such as servers for sharing files) are now appearing on P2P networks in the home.

Nowadays, the individuals in most homes are accumulating vast amounts of media files from digital cameras, camcorders, video downloads, and music downloads. Because users often want to share this media, specialized home network servers such as the Acer Aspire easyStore servers featuring Windows Home Server are now available for home networks. A **home network server** is designed to store media, share media across the network, and back up files on computers connected to the network (see Figure 5). All computers connected to the network can access the server.

Even though a server may now be attached to a home network, that does not change the architecture of a home network from a P2P network to a client/server network. Except for the specialized functions of the home network server, all network administration tasks (such as installation of software and changing of configuration settings) must still be performed locally, and all the nodes on the network are still peers to each other.

Describing Networks Based on Distance

How does the distance between nodes define a network? The distance between nodes on a network is another way to describe a network. A **local area network (LAN)** is a network in which the nodes are located within a small geographic area. Examples include a network in a computer lab at school or at a fast-food restaurant. A **home area network (HAN)** is a network located in a home. HANs are used to connect all of a home's digital devices, such as computers, peripherals, phones, gaming devices, digital video recorders (DVRs), and televisions.

Is it possible to connect LANs? A **wide area network (WAN)** is made up of LANs connected over long distances. Say a school has two campuses (east and west) located in different towns. Connecting the

LAN at the east campus to the LAN at the west campus by telecommunications lines would allow the users on the two LANs to communicate. The two LANs would be described as a single WAN.

Are wireless networks that cover large areas like cities considered WANs? Technically, wireless networks like the one deployed in Minneapolis, which provides Internet access to city residents and visitors, are WANs. However, when a network is designed to provide access to a specific geographic area, such as an entire city, the network is usually called a **metropolitan area network (MAN)**. Many cities in the United States are now deploying MANs to provide Internet access to residents and provide convenience for tourists.

Network Components

To function, all networks must include (1) a means of connecting the nodes on the network (cables or wireless technology), (2) special devices that allow the nodes to communicate with each other and to send data, and (3) software that allows the network to run. We discuss each of these components in this section (see Figure 6).

Figure 6

Network components.

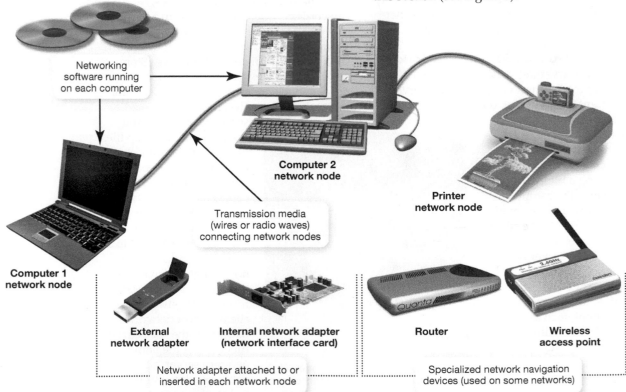

Transmission Media

How are nodes on a network connected?
All network nodes are connected to each other and to the network by transmission media. **Transmission media** establishes a communications channel between the nodes on a network and can either be wireless or wired.

Wireless networks use radio waves to connect nodes. With the proliferation of portable devices being connected to home networks, a network with at least some wireless connectivity is preferred in most homes.

Wired networks use various types of cable (wires) to connect nodes. **Twisted-pair cable** is made up of copper wires that are twisted around each other and surrounded by a plastic jacket. Normal telephone cable is a type of twisted-pair cable, although phone cable won't work for connecting a home network and a slightly different type of twisted-pair cable is used. **Coaxial cable** consists of a single copper wire surrounded by layers of plastic. If you have cable TV, the cable running into your TV or cable box is most likely coaxial cable. **Fiber-optic cable** is made up of plastic or glass fibers that transmit data at extremely fast speeds. Verizon's FiOS service uses fiber-optic cable to run very fast data connections directly up to your home, although fiber-optic cable is not usually run inside the home. On a FiOS network, twisted-pair or coaxial cable is still used inside the home to transport the network signals.

Does it matter what type of media you use to transfer data?
The media you choose depends on the requirements of a network's users. Using wireless media is critical when portable computing devices (such as smartphones) need to be connected to a network. However, higher speed connections (than can be achieved by wireless connectivity) are required for certain types of network activities, such as downloading large files such as movies. Different types of transmission media transmit data at different speeds.

Data transfer rate (also called **bandwidth**) is the maximum speed at which data can be transmitted between two nodes on a network. **Throughput** is the actual speed of data transfer that is achieved. Throughput is always less than or equal to the data transfer rate. Data transfer rate and throughput are usually measured in megabits per second (Mbps). (A megabit is 1 million bits.) Twisted-pair cable, coaxial cable, and wireless media usually provide enough bandwidth for most home networks.

Network Adapters

How do the different nodes on the network communicate?
Network adapters are devices connected to or installed in network nodes that enable the nodes to communicate with each other and to access the network. All desktop and notebook computers (and many peripherals) sold today contain network adapters installed *inside* the device. This type of adapter is referred to as a **network interface card (NIC)**. Different NICs are designed to use different types of transmission media. Most NICs included in computing devices today are built to use wireless media but many can use wired media as well. Your notebook computer most likely has a wireless NIC in it that allows you to connect to wireless networks (home, school, or the coffee shop). But most notebooks also have a port on the side that accommodates cable for a wired connection to a network.

> **"All computers sold today contain network adapters."**

Why would I ever consider using a wired connection with my notebook computer?
Wired connections can sometimes provide greater throughput than current high-speed wireless networks. Here are some common reasons why wireless signals may have decreased throughput:

- Wireless signals are more susceptible to interference from magnetic and electrical sources.
- Other wireless networks (such as your neighbor's network) can interfere with the signals on your network.
- Certain building materials (such as concrete and cinderblock) and metal (a refrigerator) can decrease throughput.
- Throughput varies depending on the distance from your networking equipment.

Wireless networks usually use specially coded signals to protect their data whereas

Sharing Your Internet Connection with Your Neighbors: Legal? Ethical? Safe?

With the advances in wireless equipment, signals can travel well beyond the walls of your home. This makes it possible in an apartment or single family home (where homes are close together) for a group of neighbors to share a wireless signal and potentially save money by splitting the cost of one Internet connection among them. However, before jumping into this venture, you need to weigh a few issues carefully.

You probably aren't legally prohibited from sharing an Internet connection, but you should check on the state and local laws. Most laws are designed to prohibit piggybacking, which is using a network without the account holder's consent. However, if you are giving neighbors permission to share your connection, you probably don't violate any piggybacking laws.

Of course, your ISP might not permit you to share your Internet access with anyone. You probably have a personal account that is designed for one household. The terms of your agreement with the Internet provider might prohibit you from sharing your connection with people outside your household. If you aren't allowed to share the type of account you have now, your ISP probably offers a type of account (such as a small business account) that will allow you to share a connection, but it will most likely be more expensive. The ISPs know that the more people that share an account, the more likely that account is to use bandwidth; so they price their accounts accordingly. You might be able to share a personal account without being detected by your ISP, but that certainly would be unethical because you should be paying for a higher level of access. Therefore, make sure to check with your ISP to determine that you have the right type of account.

The next thing you need to consider is whether the shared access should be open to all neighbors, or just to the neighbors that are contributing to the cost of the Internet connection. You could leave the connection open (like the connections at Panera Bread) and let anyone who finds it log on and surf. You might consider this a very ethical action, because you are providing free Internet access for anyone who needs it. You could register your free hot spot with a service like JiWire, and then people would know where it is. However, your neighbors who are helping pay the cost might have a different viewpoint and not want to fund free surfing for everyone. Make sure you work this out before proceeding.

If you are going to host a free and open hot spot, you still need to make sure that you set it up safely. You want to maintain a secure network for you and your neighbors while still allowing the occasional visiting surfer to use the connection. There are WiFi sharing services (see Figure 7) such as Fon (**fon.com**), Whisher (**whisher.com**, now owned by **wifi.com**), and WeFi (**wefi.com**) that can provide you with special hardware (a router) or software that allows you to configure your hot spot so your network remains secure.

While offering free access to anyone will earn you lots of good karma, additional risks exist because you don't know what mischief or criminal activities someone might engage in while connected to the Internet through your account. Think very carefully before you proceed down the sharing path, and make sure you set your hot spot up to protect your internal network.

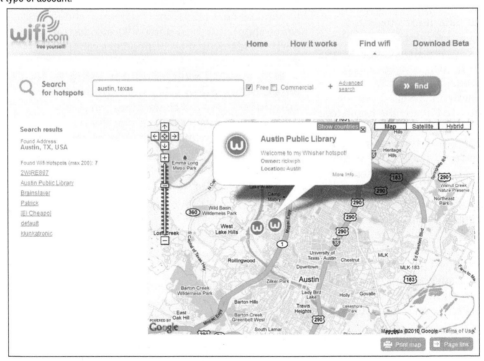

Figure 7

At Wifi.com you can search and find free hot spots hosted by other Whisher users.

wired connections don't protect their signals. This process of coding signals can slightly decrease throughput, although once coded, data travels at usual speeds.

Therefore, in situations where you want to achieve the highest possible throughput (transferring a large video), you may want to connect your notebook (or other portable device) to your home network using a wire (at least temporarily). We'll discuss this type of connection in more depth when we talk about home Ethernet networks later in this chapter.

Network Navigation Devices

How is data sent through a network? Network navigation devices facilitate and control the flow of data through a network. Data is sent over transmission media in bundles. Each bundle is called a **packet**. For computers to communicate, these packets of data must be able to flow between network nodes. Network navigation devices, which are themselves nodes on a network, enable the transmission of data between other nodes on the network that contain NICs.

What network navigation devices will I use on my home network? The two most common navigation devices are routers and switches. A **router** transfers packets of data between two or more networks. For example, if a home network is connected to the Internet, a router is required to send data between the two networks (the home network and the Internet). A **switch** is a "traffic cop" on a network. Switches receive data packets and send them to their intended nodes on the same network (not between different networks). All routers sold for home use have switches integrated into them. We discuss routers for home networks in more detail later in the chapter.

SOUND BYTE

Installing a Home Computer Network

Installing a network is relatively easy if you've seen someone else do it. In this Sound Byte, you'll learn how to install the hardware and configure Windows for a wired or wireless home network.

Networking Software

What software do home networks require? Home networks need operating system (OS) software that supports P2P networking. The Windows, OS X, and Linux operating systems all support P2P networking. You can connect computers running any of these OSs to the same home network (we also cover configuring software for home networks later in the chapter).

Is the same software used in client/server networks? Client/server networks are controlled by centralized servers that have specialized **network operating system (NOS)** software installed on them. This software handles requests for information, Internet access, and the use of peripherals for the rest of the network nodes. As opposed to P2P networks, the nodes on a client server network do not communicate directly with each other but communicate through a server. Communicating through a server is more efficient in a network with a large number of nodes, but requires more complex NOS software than is necessary for P2P networks. Examples of NOS software include Windows Server 2008 R2 and SUSE Linux Enterprise Server.

> **"Home networks need operating system software that supports P2P networking."**

Home Ethernet Networks

Now that you understand the basic components of a home network, you are probably wondering where to start on installing your home network. In the following sections, we'll discuss the most common types of networks found in the home and how to get the fastest data transfer rates from your home network. We'll also explore the various types of cabling used in wired networks.

Ethernet Home Networks

What type of peer-to-peer network should I install in my home? The vast majority of home networks are Ethernet networks. An **Ethernet network** is so named because it uses the Ethernet protocol as the means (or standard) by which the nodes on the network communicate. The Ethernet protocol was developed by the Institute of

Wake Up Your Computer Remotely

Having your computer on a home network with a shared Internet connection makes it possible to access your computer and its files even when you aren't at home. But if your computer is asleep, you need some way to "wake it up." Otherwise, you can't access it through the Internet. Fortunately for Mac users, there is an application called iNet WOL (Wake on LAN) designed to do this (see Figure 8). iNet WOL is compatible with the iPhone, iPod Touch, and iPad. The application allows you to use your portable device to wake up your computer via the Internet. Once your computer is awake, you can then use your remote access software to access it. Think of iNet WOL as an alarm clock for your computer.

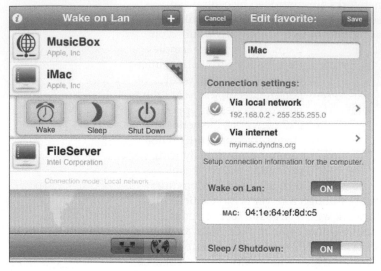

Figure 8

The application iNet WOL (Wake on LAN) lets you use your iPhone to wake up your computer from a remote location.

Electrical and Electronics Engineers (IEEE). This nonprofit group develops many standard specifications for electronic data transmission that are adopted throughout the world. Each standard the IEEE develops is numbered, with 802.11 (wireless) and 802.3 (wired) being the standards for Ethernet networks. The Ethernet protocol makes Ethernet networks extremely efficient at moving data. Ethernet networks use both wireless and wired transmission media.

What is the current wireless standard for Ethernet networks? The current standard that governs wireless networking for Ethernet networks is the **802.11n standard**, which was ratified in 2009. Establishing standards for networking is important so that devices from different manufacturers will work well together. The

802.11 standard is also known as **WiFi**. Four standards are currently defined under the 802.11 WiFI standard: 802.11a, 802.11b, 802.11g, and 802.11n. Since 802.11n features the fastest data transfer rates, it is now the most desirable choice for home networks. Devices using older standards (such as 802.11g) will still work with 802.11n networks, but they will operate with slower data transfer rates. This accommodation of current devices being able to use previously issued standards in addition to the current standards is known as **backward compatibility**.

How do 802.11n wireless devices work? Wireless routers and network adapters contain transceivers. A **transceiver** is a device that translates the electronic data that needs to be sent along the network into radio waves and then broadcasts these radio waves to other network nodes. Transceivers serve a dual function because they also receive the signals from other network nodes. Devices that use the 802.11n standard achieve higher throughput by using a technology known as Multiple Input Multiple Output (MIMO).

Devices using wireless standards developed prior to the 802.11n standard only utilized one antenna for transmitting and receiving data. Devices that use **Multiple Input Multiple Output (MIMO)** technology are designed to use multiple antennas for transmitting and receiving data. The multiple antennas break the data into multiple data streams and allow for faster transmission of the data. 802.11n devices can achieve throughput of up to 300 Mbps under ideal conditions. But as mentioned previously, many factors can reduce the throughput of a wireless connection.

Throughput Speeds

How can I tell how fast the wireless connection to my network is on my computer? You can install various utilities, such as Net Meter (available at download.com), on your computer that will measure your throughput. Net Meter (see Figure 9) shows you the throughput you are achieving on your computer's wireless connection to your network over a period of time. Hopefully, you'll achieve throughput in the range of 50 to 200 Mbps on your wireless network, which should be sufficient

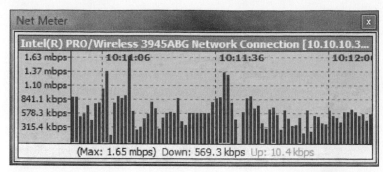

Figure 9

Net Meter shows this computer is achieving a rather slow maximum connection of 1.65 mbps on a shared wireless network at a hotel.

for most applications (even watching video). However, if you don't achieve acceptable throughput, you might want to consider a wired Ethernet connection.

What kind of throughput is achievable with wired network connections? Up to one gigabit per second (1,000 Mbps) of throughput is possible using the **gigabit Ethernet** standard, which is the most commonly used wired Ethernet standard deployed in devices designed for home networks. Wired Ethernet networks use cables to transmit data as opposed to the radio waves used on wireless networks. Because cabling is much less susceptible to interference, a wired connection can achieve higher rates of throughput.

Network Cabling

What type of cable do I need to connect to a wired Ethernet network? The most popular transmission media option for wired Ethernet networks is **unshielded twisted-pair (UTP) cable**. UTP cable is composed of four pairs of wires that are twisted around each other to reduce electrical interference. You can buy UTP cable in varying lengths with RJ-45 connectors (Ethernet connectors) already attached. RJ-45 connectors resemble standard phone connectors (called RJ-11 connectors) but are slightly larger and have contacts for eight wires (four pairs) instead of four wires (see Figure 10). You must use UTP cable with RJ-45 connectors on an Ethernet network because a phone cable will not work.

Do all wired Ethernet networks use the same kind of UTP cable? Figure 11 lists the three main types of UTP

cable you would consider using in home-wired Ethernet networks—Cat 5E, Cat 6, and Cat 6a—and their data transfer rates. Although Cat 5E cable is the cheapest and is sufficient for many home networking tasks it was designed for 100 Mpbs wired Ethernet networks that were popular before gigabit Ethernet networks became the popular standard for home networking. Therefore, you should probably not install Cat 5E cable although it is still available in stores. Since **Cat 6 cable** is designed to achieve data transfer rates that support a gigabit Ethernet network, it is probably the best choice for home networking cable. Cat 6a cable is designed for Ultra-Fast Ethernet (10 gigabit Ethernet) networks that run at

BITS AND BYTES

Blazingly Fast Wireless Connections on the Horizon

Although most people want wireless connectivity throughout their home, wired connections still provide the best throughput. But a joint effort between the Wireless Gigabit Alliance and the WiFi Alliance aims to change this. The next generation of wireless standards is called Wi-Gig and will be designed to provide up to 7 Gbps of throughput. This speed will blow away current WiFi standards (with a current theoretical maximum transfer rate of 600 Mbps) and wired gigabit connectivity. Whereas WiFi currently operates in the 5 GHz and 2.4 GHz bands, Wi-Gig will operate in the 60 GHz band, which is currently unlicensed by the FCC. This should prevent many of the interference issues that WiFi users currently experience. But don't start looking in the stores for this equipment just yet; this standard will take several years to develop.

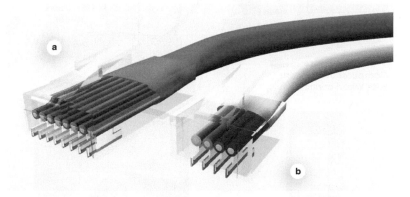

Figure 10

(a) An RJ-45 (Ethernet) connector, which is used on UTP cables; and (b) a typical RJ-11 connector, which is used on standard phone cords.

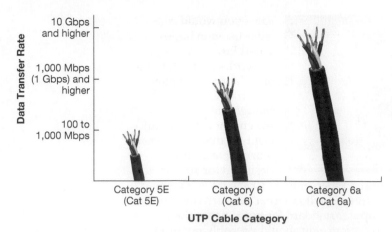

Figure 11

Data Transfer Rates for
Popular Home Network
Cable Types

Figure 12

Wired and wireless
connections in the same
home network.

speeds as fast as 10 Gbps. Installing a 10 gigabit Ethernet network in the home is probably unnecessary because today's home applications don't require this rate of data transfer

What precautions should I taken when running UTP cable? UTP cable is no more difficult to install than normal phone cable but there are a few things to avoid. Do not put sharp bends into the cable when running it around corners because this can damage the copper wires inside and lead to breakage. Also, run the cable around the perimeter of the room (instead of under

a rug, for example) to prevent damage to wires from foot traffic.

How long can an Ethernet cable run be? Regardless of the type of Ethernet cable you use, runs for UTP cable can't exceed 100 meters (328 feet) or the signal starts to degrade. Even for short cable runs, you should use continuous lengths of cable. Although two cables can be spliced together with a connecting jack, this creates a point of failure for the cable, because connectors can loosen in the connecting jack and moisture or dust can accumulate on the contacts.

Fortunately, you don't have to choose between a wired or a wireless network. Ethernet networks can handle your wired and wireless needs on the same network. This gives you the best of both worlds (portability and high throughput).

Wired and Wireless on One Network

Can I have wired and wireless nodes on one Ethernet network? Yes, one Ethernet network can support nodes with both wireless and wired connections. Most people will want to connect portable devices (such as notebooks and smartphones) that are constantly being moved around the home wirelessly to their network. However, many of the devices that are connected to a network (such as televisions, DVRs, and Blu-ray players) usually stay in one location. Although these devices probably feature wireless connectivity also, it may be desirable to hook them up to wired connections to take advantage of faster throughput achieved by wired connectivity. Routers sold for home networks facilitate wired and wireless connections. Figure 12 shows an example of a network with a wireless/wired router attached.

Are there other types of P2P networks that can be installed in the home? Non-Ethernet networks in the home are extremely rare. Because Ethernet networks 1) are based on a well-established standard, 2) feature easy

Wireless DSL/Cable router

Computer in bedroom with wired connection

Notebook on back porch with wireless connection

Smartphone in kitchen with wireless connection

HDTV with wireless connection

set-up, 3) provide good throughput for home networking needs, and (4) are cost effective, manufacturers of home networking equipment have overwhelmingly embraced Ethernet networks.

Does the type of operating system I'm using affect my choice of a home networking standard? Windows, OS X, and Linux built in P2P networking software will all support connection to an Ethernet network. Therefore, an Ethernet network is appropriate for all computers using these three operating systems.

Home Ethernet Equipment

By now you should have enough information to decide what nodes on your network need be connected wirelessly and which devices would benefit from wired connections. In this section, we'll explore the various types of equipment (such as a router) that you need to obtain to configure your home network. And we'll explore what devices your nodes need to contain to enable them to connect to your network.

Routers and Switches: Moving Data Around Your Network

What equipment do I need for a home Ethernet network? Ethernet networks need network navigation devices to make them work and therefore the first piece of equipment to consider is a router. Recall that routers are designed to transfer packets of data between two (or more) networks—in this case, your home network and the Internet. A router is essential on a home network to allow sharing of an Internet

connection. For an Ethernet network to function properly, data must also be transmitted efficiently around the network. A switch is the device that is used on Ethernet networks to route the data between nodes on the same network.

Because both a router and a switch are needed on home Ethernet networks, the manufacturers of home networking equipment make devices that are a combination of routers and switches. In most instances, these devices are called *routers* or *broadband routers*. But despite the name, these devices do include integrated switches. Although manufacturers do make routers with only wired capabilities, for the vast majority of home networks, people buy routers with wireless capabilities.

What do switches do on an Ethernet network? Data is transmitted through the transmission medium of an Ethernet network in packets. Imagine the data packets on an Ethernet network as cars on a road. If there were no traffic signals or rules of the road (such as driving on the right-hand side), we'd see a lot more collisions between vehicles, and people wouldn't get where they were going as readily (or at all). Data packets can also suffer collisions. If data packets collide, the data in them is damaged or lost. In either case, the network doesn't function efficiently. The routers you buy for home networks have a switch integrated into them, so you won't need to buy a standalone switch for your home network.

As shown in Figure 13, a switch in an Ethernet network acts like a traffic signal (or a traffic cop) by enforcing the rules of the

Figure 13

A simplified explanation is that switches (working in conjunction with NICs) act like traffic signals or traffic cops. They enforce the rules of the data road on an Ethernet network and help prevent data packets from crashing into each other.

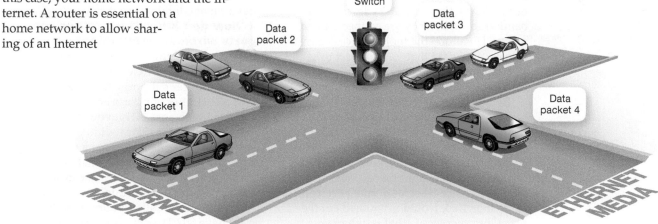

Networking: Connecting Computing Devices

111

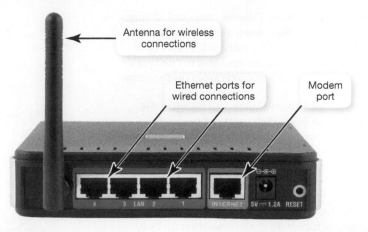

Figure 14

Rear view of typical wireless/wired router.

Antenna for wireless connections

Ethernet ports for wired connections

Modem port

data road on the transmission media. The switch keeps track of the data packets and, in conjunction with network interface cards, helps the data packets find their destinations without running into each other. The switch also keeps track of all the nodes on the network and sends the data packets directly to the node for which they are headed. This keeps the network running efficiently.

In the next section, we'll explore connecting your computing devices to your router.

Connecting Devices to Routers

How many computers and other devices can be connected to a router in a home network? Most home wireless routers can support up to 253 wireless connections at the same time. This number is a theoretical maximum, however—most home networks probably have fewer than ten wireless devices connected to the network. But regardless of how few or how many devices your home network has, those wireless devices share bandwidth when they are connected to a router. Therefore, the more devices actively transmitting data that you connect to a single router, the smaller the portion of the router's bandwidth each device receives.

To look at this another way, consider you have a pizza which represents your router's bandwidth. You can cut the pizza into six or eight pieces (that is, you can connect either six or eight devices to the network). If you cut the pizza into eight pieces, each person who gets a slice receives a smaller portion of pizza than they would if you had cut the pizza into six pieces. (that is, when you connect eight devices to the network, each

device has less bandwidth than it would have if only six devices were connected to the network).

Does my wireless router support wired connections? Most home wireless routers have three or four Ethernet ports on the back of the router to support wired connections via twisted-pair cable (see Figure 14). If you have a lot of devices (such as a game console, HDTV, and a notebook) in your home that may be used simultaneously, you might want to consider connecting some of them via a wired connection to increase allocated bandwidth to each wireless device. This will help increase the throughput to each wireless device.

If you find that you need additional ports for plugging in wireless connections to your network, you can buy a standalone switch and plug that into one of the ports on your router. This will give you additional ports for making wired connections to your network. Do not mistakenly buy another router (with an embedded switch) and try adding that to your network because the two routers will cause conflicts as they fight for control over network navigation.

Where do I obtain a router for my home network? You can purchase a router at any store (such as Best Buy) or online stores (**tigerdirect.com**, **newegg.com**) that carry home networking equipment. Also, since networks are so common in homes now, many ISPs offer home subscribers a device that combines a broadband modem and a wireless router. ISPs typically charge either a one-time or a monthly fee for this combination device. If you already have broadband access in your home, you at least have a modem. Check with your ISP if you are not sure whether you also already have a device that contains a router.

How do I know if my router supports wireless networking? If you do have a router provided by your ISP, make sure to ask what wireless networking standard the router supports. If it does not support 802.11n but supports and older standard such as 802.11g, you should consider having your ISP provide you with a new router. You want to have a router that supports the fastest wireless networking standard (802.11n) so that you can achieve the highest possible throughput on your wireless nodes. If all of your wireless devices have 802.11n network adapters, but your router supports 802.11g, you will not achieve the best throughput available to you because 802.11g devices feature much slower transfer rates than 802.11n devices (about four to six times slower).

Where do I place the router on my network? Your router should be connected directly to your broadband modem (see Figure 15). The connection is usually an Ethernet cable (Cat 6 cable) running from an Ethernet port on your modem to the modem port on your router.

Are wireless routers for Windows and OS X networks different? All routers that support the 802.11n standard should work with computers running Windows or OS X. However, Apple has designed routers that are optimized for working with Apple computers. So if you are connecting Apple computers to your network, you may wish to consider using an Apple AirPort router. (Windows machines can also connect to the AirPort routers.) The Apple AirPort Extreme (Figure 16) is a good choice for a home network. It supports up to 50 simultaneous wireless connections and has three gigabit Ethernet ports for wired connections.

How do I set up my router so that I can use it to connect to the Internet? First, contact your ISP and find out about any special settings that you may need to configure your router to work with your ISP. Next, access your router from Internet Explorer (or another Web browser) by entering the router's IP address or default URL. You can usually find this information in the documentation that came with the router. You'll also need a username and password to log on to the router. You'll probably find these, too, in the documentation that came with the router.

Many routers feature their own wizard (different from the Windows Networking wizards) that takes you through special configuration screens. A sample screen from a router is shown in Figure 17. The documentation that came with your router will provide a URL to use to log on to the router. If you're unsure of any information that

needs to be entered to configure the router (such as whether IP addresses are assigned dynamically—meaning you are assigned a new IP address by your ISP each time you connect to the Internet), contact your ISP and ask for guidance.

After ensuring that your router is set up properly, you are ready to begin connecting your computing devices to your network. You now need to ensure that all your nodes have the proper equipment to enable them to connect to your network.

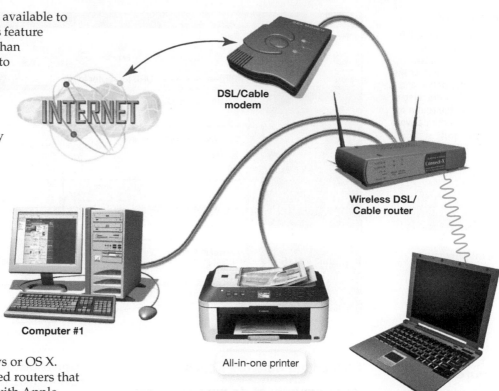

DSL/Cable modem

Wireless DSL/ Cable router

Computer #1

All-in-one printer

Computer #2

Figure 15

A small network with a wireless router attached.

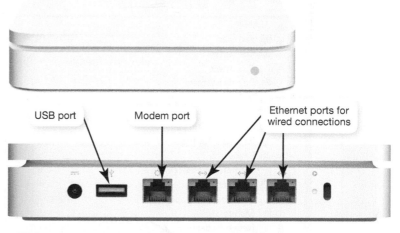

USB port   Modem port   Ethernet ports for wired connections

Figure 16

The AirPort Extreme router is often used for home networks with Apple computers.

Figure 17

Although setups differ from router to router, you will need basic information such as the logon information and the type of IP addressing to configure the router to work with your network and your ISP.

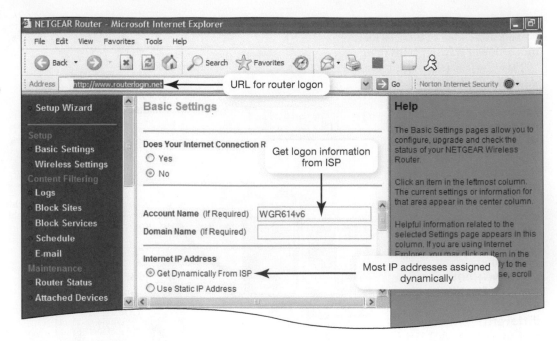

Figure 18

This Windows device manager shows a wireless and a wired network adapter installed in a notebook.

>To access Device Manager: Click the **Start Button**, select **Control Panel**, click on the **Hardware and Sound Group**, then click on **Device Manager**.

Connecting Network Nodes

What equipment do my computers need to communicate with wireless media on an 802.11n wireless network? Your computers need to have wireless network interface cards (NICs) installed in them. Notebooks and netbooks sold over the last several years most likely contain 802.11n NICs. For older computers, as long as they have wireless Ethernet adapters that are compatible with a previous standard (802.11g or 802.11b) they will be able to connect to your 802.11n router. However, the throughput will be at the lower 802.11g and b data transfer rates.

How can I tell what network adapters are installed in my computer? To see which network adapter(s) are installed in your Windows computer and to check whether the adapter is working, you should use the Device Manager utility program (see Figure 18). The installed adapters will be shown and then you search for information on the Internet to determine the adapter's capability if you aren't sure which wireless standard it supports.

Connecting Other Devices to Networks

Because sharing peripherals is a major benefit of installing a network, many peripheral devices, such as scanners and printers, now come with built-in Ethernet adapters. Also, many home entertainment devices (such as televisions, Blu-ray players, and gaming systems), portable devices (such as smartphones, and iPod Touches and iPads), and power monitoring devices to reduce energy consumption in the home are also designed to attach to home networks. Such devices are usually described as being "network-ready."

Networking: Connecting Computing Devices

114

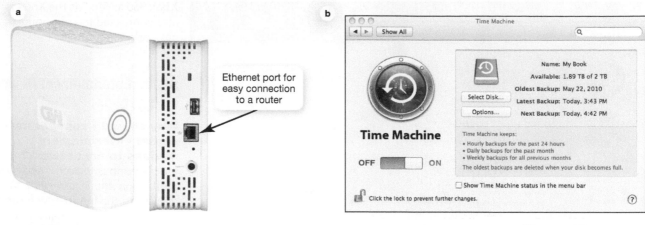

a

b

Ethernet port for
easy connection
to a router

Time Machine

Show All

Name: My Book
Available: 1.89 TB of 2 TB
Oldest Backup: May 22, 2010
Latest Backup: Today, 3:43 PM
Next Backup: Today, 4:42 PM

Select Disk...
Options...

Time Machine

OFF [====] ON

Time Machine keeps:
• Hourly backups for the past 24 hours
• Daily backups for the past month
• Weekly backups for all previous months
The oldest backups are deleted when your disk becomes full.

☐ Show Time Machine status in the menu bar

🔒 Click the lock to prevent further changes.

Figure 19

(a) The My Book drives
from Western Digital
feature NAS devices that
can store 2 TB of data in a
device the size of a small
book. (b) Time Machine
in conjunction with an
external hard drive
provides easy backups of
Macs on a network.

Network-Ready Devices

What is a network-ready device? A
network-ready device (or Internet ready)
can be connected directly to a router instead
of to a computer on the network. Network-
ready devices usually contain wireless and/
or wired network adapters inside them. A
few devices (such as TiVo or the Xbox 360)
still have external network adapters that
connect to the device via a USB port but
these eventually should be phased out in
favor of internal adapters. The eventual goal
may be to have all electronic devices in your
home be nodes on your network.

**Why should I connect my peripher-
als to my home network?** There is
an advantage to connecting peripherals
wirelessly to your network. If a printer were
connected directly to another computer (via
a cable) on the network instead of being a
node on the network, that computer would
need to be switched on so other computers
could access the printer. With a network-
ready printer, only the printer needs to be
powered on for any computer on the network to print to it.

**What can I attach to my network
to facilitate file sharing and back up
of data?** Network attached storage
(NAS) devices are specialized computing
devices designed to store and manage your
data. People are generating tremendous
quantities of data today with digital cameras
and camcorders, as well as buying music
files, and these files need to be stored and
shared. Although data can always be stored
on individual hard drives in computers on a
network, NAS devices provide for centralized data storage and access.

Popular for years on business networks,
NAS devices are now being widely marketed for home networks. You can think of
them as specialized external hard drives.
NAS devices, like the My Book series from
Western Digital (see Figure 19a), connect
directly to the network through a router or
switch. Specialized software can then be
installed on computers attached to the
network to ensure that all data saved to an
individual computer is also stored on the
NAS as a backup.

For Apple computers, the Time Capsule is
a wireless router combined with a hard
drive for facilitating backups of all computers connected to the network. The Time
Capsule looks very similar to the AirPort
router and it works in conjunction with the
Time Machine backup feature of OS X (see
Figure 19b). If you buy a Time Capsule,
you won't need to buy an AirPort router
(or other router) as the Time Capsule fulfills
this function on your network also. When
the Time Capsule is installed on your
network, Macs connected to the network
will ask the user if they want to use the Time
Capsule as their source for Time Machine
backups. The Time Capsule is another type
of NAS device.

**Besides external hard drives, are
their other NAS devices I could use
on my network?** A more sophisticated
type of NAS device is a home network
server. Home network servers are specialized devices that are designed to provide a
specific set of services to computers on a
home network. Home servers do not convert a home peer-to-peer network into a
client/server network because these servers
only perform only a limited set of functions

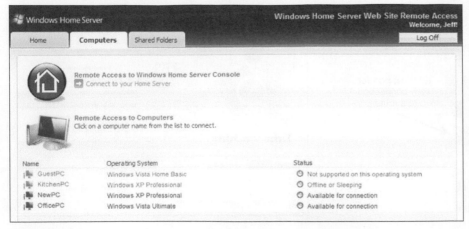

Figure 20

Windows Home Server remote access interface.

Figure 21

Searching for the right remote? New software apps make it easy to just use your phone instead.

instead of all the functions performed on client/server networks.

Home network servers, like the Acer Aspire easyStore server (shown earlier in Figure 5), are often configured with Windows Home Server and connect directly as a node on your network. Home servers have the functionality of NAS devices and often handle the following tasks:

- Automatically back up all computers connected to the network.
- Act as a repository for files to be shared across the network (such as music and video files).
- Function as an access gateway to allow any computer on the network to be accessed from a remote location via the Internet (see Figure 20).

And you can access the media stored on your Windows Home Server through your

Xbox 360 as long as the Xbox is also connected to your home network.

Digital Entertainment Devices on a Network

Why should I connect my digital entertainment devices to my network? The main reason is to access and share digital content. When you attach devices to the Internet, you can purchase (or even obtain for free) more content for you to enjoy such as movies, videos, or music files. You can also use gaming devices to play multiplayer games with players all over the world. The content you access is either downloaded or streamed to your entertainment devices. Viewing Netflix movies delivered over the Internet on your computer is an example of streaming media.

When media is *streamed*, it is sent directly to a device (such as a computer or HDTV) without being saved to a hard drive. This requires a lot of bandwidth so a broadband connection is required to effectively view streaming media. Media can also be *downloaded* (saved) to a hard drive for viewing at a later time. Although the Amazon Video on Demand service now offers streaming movies, they still offer the ability to download content to your computer or your TiVo so you can view it later.

What types of digital entertainment devices can I use to view streaming or downloaded media? Network-ready televisions and home theater systems allow for direct connection to your home network (wireless or wired). These devices are configured to receive streaming media directly from the Internet. Waiting for a DVD to come in the mail from Netflix is so passé when you can have it available immediately on your television through your home network!

However, many people prefer to own media and buy it on permanent formats such as Blu-ray discs. Blu-ray disc players, such as the Sony 3D Blu-ray disc players offer not only high-definition resolution but also the capability to display 3D video. These Blu-ray players feature integrated wireless connectivity for connection to your network as well as the ability to receive streaming media from various Internet providers. You can even view videos from YouTube and listen to Pandora Internet Radio right through your Blu-ray player.

In terms of controlling your devices such as televisions and Blu-ray players, more companies are developing applications that enable your handheld devices (such as PSPs or iPhones) to act as remote controls. The BD Remote app by Sonoran Blue (see Figure 21) for the iPhone allows you to control Sony Blu-ray players.

Digital video recorders (DVRs), like the TiVo Premiere, are often used in the home to record high-definition television programs. Connecting your TiVo to your network makes it possible to receive downloads of movies directly to your TiVo from services such as Amazon Video on Demand. And some home network servers, like the Hewlett Packard MediaSmart servers, now work in conjunction with TiVo devices to provide additional storage for your TiVo devices. The TiVo Desktop software (see Figure 22), which you download from **tivo.com**, allows you to transfer shows recorded on your TiVo to your computer or to portable devices such as an iPod, iPhone, BlackBerry, or PSP.

Can I connect my gaming consoles to my home network? Current gaming systems, like the PlayStation 3, offer much more than just games as they can function as a total entertainment platform when connected to your network (and therefore to the Internet). The PlayStation 3 (PS3) has a built-in Blu-ray drive and can play Blu-ray discs as well as DVDs and music files. You can download movies, games, and videos directly to the PlayStation. It can also be used to share media across your network and import photos or video from cameras and camcorders. And if you have a PSP, you can use an application called Remote Play (see Figure 23) to access features of your PlayStation from your PSP. You can use the PSP to turn your PlayStation on and off,

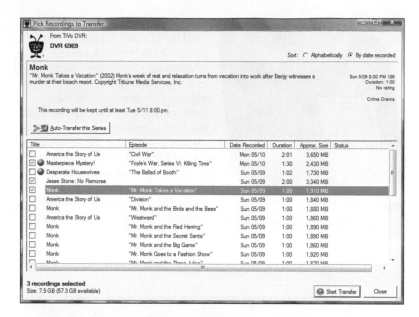

Figure 22

The TiVo Desktop software facilitates transfer of recorded shows to portable devices so you can enjoy your content on the go.

access music and video files, access photos stored on your PlayStation, play games, and browse the Internet. Media is transmitted from your PlayStation and displayed on the PSP screen.

Specialized Home Networking Devices

What if I don't need the full functionality of a PC, but I still want to access Internet content? The launch of the Apple iPad signaled a resurgence of Internet appliances. The main function of an **Internet appliance** is easy access to the Internet, social networking sites, e-mail, video,

Figure 23

The Remote Play feature of the PSP and the PlayStation 3 (PS3) allows users to access PS3 features, like the PlayStation Store, directly from their PSP.

ACTIVE HELP-DESK Understanding Networking

In this Active Helpdesk call, you'll play the role of a helpdesk staffer, fielding calls about home networks—their advantages, their main components, and the most common types—as well as about wireless networks and how they are created.

Networking: Connecting Computing Devices

Figure 24

Quick access to information and entertainment is the key feature of Internet appliances.

news, and entertainment. These devices fall into a category somewhere between smartphones and full-blown computers. They are light on calculation, but high on easy content delivery. Devices such as the Sony Dash Personal Internet viewer (see Figure 24) are popular in kitchens and bedside tables where access to Internet radio stations, short videos, and quick information updates (like Facebook updates and current weather conditions) are needed. Originally, Internet appliances

Featuring a touch screen interface, this frame can access photos stored on your network or on an online photo-sharing site and display them. You can set up an e-mail address for the picture frame so that friends and family can e-mail pictures directly to the frame as soon as they are taken. Wouldn't it be nice to come home to new photos of your friend's trip to Cancun tonight?

How can I use my home network to enhance my home security?
Monitoring cameras, both for indoor and outdoor use, are now available for the home and feature wireless connectivity. The cameras can connect to your network and be monitored by software like the Logitech Digital Video Security System (Figure 26). Security monitoring software allows you to view real-time images from the cameras at your home. The software can be configured to alert you via e-mail or text message when the cameras detect movement. Some systems also allow you to receive alerts when there is a lack of movement. This can be useful for monitoring an aging relative (who may need help if they stop moving) or for monitoring the arrival of children coming home from school at a certain time.

Figure 25

Sending pictures directly to an electronic frame from your phone is possible when the frame is connected to your network.

were marketed toward older computer users since these devices feature easy operation and a shallow learning curve. But the Apple iPad is propelling this category of devices into the hands of much younger users.

How can I use my home network to enhance photo sharing? Digital picture frames that display an array of changing digital photos have become quite popular with the rise in digital photography. Now digital picture frames such as the eStarling TouchConnect (see Figure 25) come with built-in wireless adapters for easy connection to home networks.

Figure 26

Logitech security products can help you remotely monitor your home's security.

As time goes on, many more types of entertainment devices and home gadgets will eventually be connected to your home network.

Securing Wireless Networks

All computers that connect to the Internet (whether or not they are on a network) need to be secured from intruders. This is usually accomplished by using a **firewall**, which is a hardware or software solution that helps shield your network from prying eyes. Wireless networks present special vulnerabilities; therefore, you should take additional specific steps to keep your wireless network safe. It is important to configure your network security before setting up and connecting all the nodes on your network.

Why is a wireless network more vulnerable than a wired network? With a wired network, it is fairly easy to tell if a **hacker** (someone who breaks into computer systems to create mischief or steal valuable information) is using your network. However, wireless 802.11n networks have wide ranges that may extend outside of your house. This makes it possible for a hacker to access your network without your knowledge.

Why should I be worried about someone logging onto my wireless network without my permission? Some use of other people's wireless networks is unintentional. Houses are built close together. Apartments are clustered even closer together. Wireless signals can easily reach a neighbor's residence. Most wireless network adapters are set up to access the strongest wireless network signal detected. If your router is on the east side of your house and you and your notebook are on the west side, then you may get a stronger signal from your neighbor's wireless network than from your own. **Piggybacking** is connecting to a wireless network (other than your own) without the permission of the owner. This practice is illegal in many jurisdictions but often happens inadvertently between neighbors.

Your neighbor probably isn't a hacker, but he might be using a lot of bandwidth—your bandwidth! If he's downloading a massive movie file while you're trying to do research for a term paper, he's probably slowing you

down. In addition, when some less-than-honest neighbors discover they can log onto your wireless network, they may cancel their own Internet service to save money by using yours. Some neighbors might even be computer savvy enough to penetrate your unprotected wireless network and steal personal information, just as any other hackers would.

In addition, because computer criminal activities are traceable, hackers love to work their mischief from public computers (such as those in a library or college) so they can't be identified. If a hacker is sitting in her car outside your house and logging on to your wireless network, any cyberattacks she launches might be traced back to your IP address, and you might find law enforcement officials knocking on your door.

How is my wireless network vulnerable? Packets of information on a wireless network are broadcast through the airwaves. Savvy hackers can intercept and decode information from your transmissions that may allow them to bypass any standard protections, such as a firewall, which you have set up on your network. Therefore, to

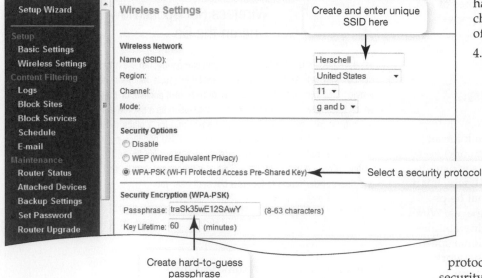

Figure 27

By running your router configuration wizard, you can configure the security protocols available on your router and change the SSID, which helps protect your wireless network.

secure a wireless network, you should take the additional precautions described in the Sound Byte "Securing Wireless Networks" and as summarized below:

1. **Change your network name (SSID).** Each wireless network has its own name to identify it, which is known as the **service set identifier** or **SSID**. Unless you change this name when you set up your router, the router uses a default network name that all routers from that manufacturer use (such as "Wireless" or "Netgear"). Hackers know the default names and access codes for routers. If you haven't changed the SSID, it's advertising the fact that you probably haven't changed any of the other default settings for your router, either.

2. **Disable SSID broadcast.** Most routers are set up to broadcast their SSIDs so that other wireless devices can find them. If your router supports disabling SSID broadcasting, turn it off. This makes it more difficult for a hacker to detect your network and nearly impossible for a neighbor to inadvertently connect to your network.

3. **Change the default password on your router.** Hackers know the default passwords of most routers, and if they can access your router, they can probably break into your network. Change the password on your router to something

hard to guess. (Use at least eight characters that are a combination of letters, symbols, and numbers.)

4. **Turn on security protocols.** Most routers ship with security protocols such as Wired Equivalent Privacy (WEP) or WiFi Protected Access (WPA). Both use encryption (a method of translating your data into code) to protect data in your wireless transmissions. WPA is a much stronger protocol than WEP, so enable WPA if you have it; enable WEP if you don't. When you enable these protocols, you are forced to create a security encryption key (passphrase). When you attempt to connect a node to a security-enabled network for the first time, you'll be required to enter the encryption key. The encryption key or passphrase (see Figure 27) is the code that computers on your network need to decrypt (decode) data transmissions. Without this key, it is extremely difficult, if not impossible, to decrypt the data transmissions from your network. This prevents unauthorized access to your network because hackers won't know the correct key to use. The Windows 7 Connect to a network dialog box shows all wireless networks within range (see Figure 28a). Clicking on one allows you to connect to it, or prompts you for more information such as the SSID name and security key (see Figure 28b).

5. **Implement media access control.** Each network adapter on your network has a unique number (like a serial number) assigned to it by the manufacturer. This is called a **media access control (MAC) address**, and it is a number printed right on the network adapter. Many routers allow you to restrict access to the network to only certain MAC addresses. This helps ensure that only authorized devices can connect to your network.

6. **Limit your signal range.** Many routers allow you to adjust the transmitting power to low, medium, or high. Cutting down the power to low or medium could prevent your signal from

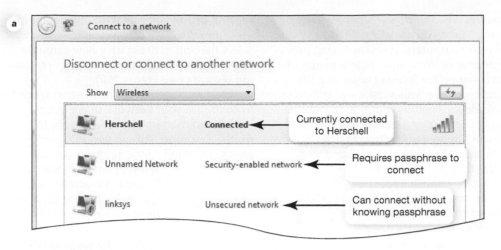

a

Connect to a network

Disconnect or connect to another network

Show Wireless ▼

Herschell	Connected ◄──	Currently connected to Herschell
Unnamed Network	Security-enabled network ◄──	Requires passphrase to connect
linksys	Unsecured network ◄──	Can connect without knowing passphrase

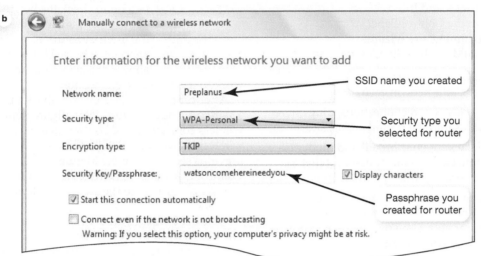

b

Manually connect to a wireless network

Enter information for the wireless network you want to add

Network name: Preplanus ◄──   SSID name you created

Security type: WPA-Personal ▼ ◄──   Security type you selected for router

Encryption type: TKIP ▼

Security Key/Passphrase: watsoncomehereineedyou ◄──   ☑ Display characters

☑ Start this connection automatically   Passphrase you created for router

☐ Connect even if the network is not broadcasting
Warning: If you select this option, your computer's privacy might be at risk.

Figure 28

(a) The Windows 7 Connect to a network dialog box. (b) Manually connecting to a wireless network allows you to establish a connection if you know the network encryption key and the SSID name.

>You can access the **Connect to a network** dialog box by right-clicking the **Network Connection** icon on the taskbar and selecting **Connect to a network** from the shortcut menu. You can access the **Manually connect to a wireless network** dialog box by accessing the **Control Panel**, clicking on **Network and Internet**, selecting **Network and Sharing Center**, choosing the **Set up a new connection or network** option, and then clicking on **Manually connect to a wireless network**.

reaching too far away from your home, making it tougher for interlopers to poach your signal.

7. **Apply firmware upgrades.** Your router has read-only memory that has software written to it. This software is known as **firmware**. As bugs are found in the firmware (which hackers might exploit), manufacturers issue patches, just as the makers of operating system software do. Periodically check the manufacturer's Web site and apply any necessary upgrades to your firmware.

If you follow these steps, you will greatly improve the security of your wireless network. There are many other ways to keep your computer safe from malicious individuals on the Internet and ensure that your digital information is secure.

Configuring Software for Your Home Network

Once you install the hardware for your network, you need to configure your operating system software for networking on your computers. In this section, you'll learn how to do just that using special Windows tools. Although configuration is different with Mac OS X, the setup is quick and easy. Linux is the most complex operating system to configure for a home network, though the difficulties are not insurmountable.

Windows Configuration

Is configuring software difficult?
Windows makes configuring software relatively simple if you are using the same version of Windows on all of your

computers. The Windows examples in this section assume you are using Windows 7 on all of your computers. If you are using previous versions of Windows, there is plenty of information on the Internet regarding the connection of previous versions of Windows to a Windows 7 network. In Windows 7, the process of setting up a network is fairly automated by various software wizards. A wizard is a utility program included with software that you can use to help you accomplish a specific task. You can launch the Windows wizards from the Network and Sharing Center, which can be accessed via the Network and Internet group in the Control Panel. Before running any wizards, you should do the following:

> **The HomeGroup feature in Windows 7 facilitates file and peripheral sharing.**

1. Make sure there are network adapters on each node.

2. For any wired connections, plug all the cables into the router, nodes, and so on.

3. Make sure your broadband modem is connected to your router and that the modem is connected to the Internet.

4. Turn on your equipment in the following order (allowing the modem and the router about one minute each to power up and configure):

   a. your broadband modem,

   b. your router, and

   c. all computers and peripherals (printers, scanners, and so on).

Other devices, such a televisions, Blu-ray players and gaming consoles can be added to the network after configuring the computers.

By completing these steps, you enable the wizards to make decisions about how best to configure your network. After you have completed these steps, open the Network and Sharing Center from the Control Panel (see Figure 29a). You can see the network to which you are currently connected on this screen. On the lower portion of the Network and Sharing Center screen, you can set sharing options for your network. Ensure that network discovery is shown as "on," because this allows your computer to locate other computers and peripherals on the network. You should also verify that the options for file and printer sharing and public folder sharing are shown as "on" to enable

file and printer sharing with other computers. From the Network and Sharing Center, select the option to Set up a new connection or network to access the Windows networking wizards (see Figure 29b).

Select the Connect to the Internet wizard to configure your network to use your broadband modem to connect to the Internet for the first time. This wizard also configures your wired connections on your network (if any). On the information screen (see Figure 29c), enter the access information provided by your ISP. Enter a memorable name for your network and check the box to allow other people to use the Internet connection you are establishing. This will allow all users on the network to use the same connection.

After running this wizard, run the Set Up a Wireless Router wizard to configure your wireless connectivity. If you set up a secured wireless network (as detailed in the previous section), use the Manually Connect to a Wireless Network wizard to connect computers to the secure wireless network.

What if I don't have the same version of Windows on all my computers? Computers with various versions of Windows can coexist on the same network. Always set up the computers running the newest version of Windows first (Windows 7). Then consult the Microsoft web site for guidance on how to proceed for configuring computers with previous versions of Windows on a Windows 7 network.

How do I differentiate the computers on my network? When you set up your Windows computer, you gave it a name. Each computer on a network needs a name that is different from the names of all other computers on the network so that the network can identify it. This unique name ensures that the network knows which computer is requesting services and data and can deliver data to the correct computer.

For ease of file and peripheral sharing, Windows 7 created a feature known as HomeGroup. If you have all Windows 7 computers on your network, you simply all join the same HomeGroup. When you set up your first Windows 7 computer on your network, you can set a password for the HomeGroup.

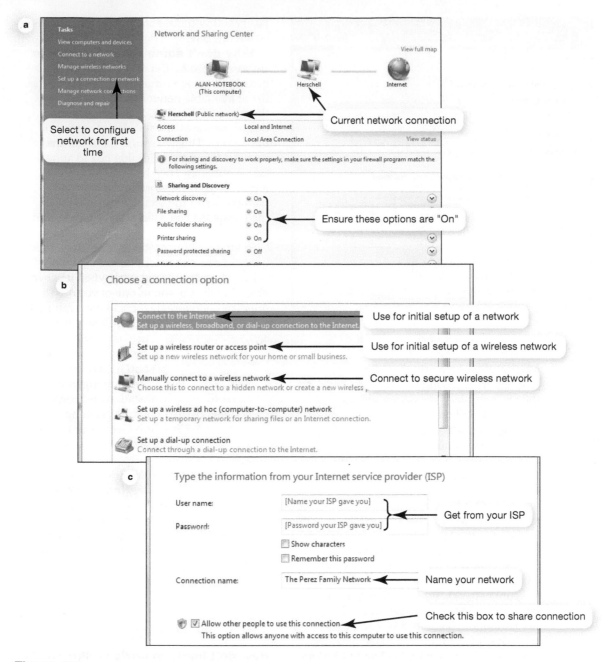

Figure 29

(a) The Windows Network and Sharing Center helps you configure your home network. Selecting the appropriate sharing options allow others to share resources on your computer. (b) Selecting the appropriate option provides access to wizards that will assist you. (c) Fill in the information provided by your ISP. The wizard will then set up your connection and connect your computer to the Internet.

>The Windows Network and Sharing Center is found in the Control Panel.

All other computers that subsequently are added to the network will need the password to join the HomeGroup. When you configure a HomeGroup, you have the option of deciding what files and peripherals on your computer will be shared with other computers on the network (see Figure 30).

How do Macs connect wirelessly to networks? Generally, connecting Macs to a wireless network is a much easier process than connecting with Windows computers. You set up the security for a router on a Mac network just as was illustrated in the previous section on securing

Figure 30

The Change HomeGroup settings screen allows you to configure sharing options for a particular computer.

>The **Change HomeGroup settings** screen can be accessed by clicking the **Computer link** on the **Start** menu, then clicking the **HomeGroup** icon, and then clicking the **View HomeGroup settings** link.

your wireless network. Therefore, logging your Mac onto the network will require knowing the SSID and its passphrase. When you boot up your Mac, the wireless card should be on by default. The network login screen (see Figure 31) should appear with a list of available networks (that is, the ones the NIC in your Mac can detect). The locks next to the network names indicate a secure network, which will require a password. Enter the password for the network in the password box and click the Join button to connect to the network. For unsecure networks, the Join button can

Figure 31

The OS X available wireless networks dialog box.

be clicked without entering anything in the password box.

Why don't some networks appear as available? But networks with SSID broadcast turned off will not appear on the list of available networks. To join one of these secure networks, click the Other button on the available wireless network dialog box. This will cause the Enter the name of the network dialog box to appear (see Figure 32). Then just enter the SSID name for your network in the Network name box and the security passphrase in the password box. Clicking the join button will then connect you to the network. Checking the Remember this network check box will cause the computer to automatically connect to the network when it is available (that is, it becomes one of your preferred networks). You can have multiple preferred networks such as your home, school and local coffee shop networks.

Assuming you installed and configured everything properly, your home network should now be up and running, allowing you to share files, Internet connections, and peripherals. You are now ready to configure other non-computer devices to connect them to your network.

Wireless Node Configuration

How do I hook up devices like a TiVo or gaming console to my network? For a wired connection, you would simply plug a cable into the device and your router. For wireless connections, there is usually a set of steps to follow in the setup menu for the device you are configuring. Assuming you set up a secure wireless network as described in the security section of this chapter, you'll need to know the SSID name of your network and the security passphrase. Although each device's configuration steps will be slightly different, eventually, you will get to a screen where you need to input the SSID name and the

Figure 32

The OS X secure wireless networks dialog box.

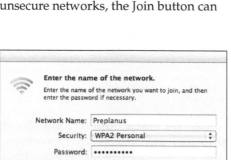

You probably have a lot of data on your home network such as music and video files. And you probably generate more data every day. But this pales in comparison to the data generated by most businesses. The vast quantities of data on business and government networks also require much higher levels of protection than the data on your home network. With billions of dollars spent on e-commerce initiatives every year, companies have a vested interest in keeping their information technology (IT) infrastructures humming along. The rise in terrorism has shifted the focus slightly—from protecting virtual assets and access, to protecting these plus physical assets and access points. The increased need for virtual and physical security measures means there should be a robust job market ahead for computer security experts.

The National Security Agency and the Office of Homeland Security are both encouraging information security professionals to be proficient in information assurance. As defined by the NSA, *information assurance* is "the set of measures intended to protect and defend information and information systems by ensuring their availability, integrity, authentication, confidentiality, and non-repudiation. This includes providing for restoration of information systems by incorporating protection, detection, and reaction capabilities." The five key attributes of secure information systems are as follows:

1. **Availability:** The extent to which a data-processing system is able to receive and process data. A high degree of availability is usually desirable.

2. **Integrity:** A quality that an information system has if the processing of information is logical and accurate and the data is protected against unauthorized modifications or destruction.

3. **Authentication:** Security measures designed to protect an information system against acceptance of a fraudulent transmission of data by establishing the validity of a data transmission or message, or the identity of the sender.

4. **Confidentiality:** The assurance that information is not disclosed to unauthorized persons, processes, or devices.

5. **Nonrepudiation:** A capability of security systems that guarantees that a message or data can be proven to have originated from a specific person and was processed by the recipient. The sender of the data receives a receipt for the data, and the receiver of the data gets proof of the sender's identity. The objective of nonrepudiation

is to prevent either party from later denying having handled the data.

The Global Information Assurance Certification, or GIAC (**giac.org**), is an industry-recognized certification that provides objective evidence (through examinations) that security professionals have mastered key skills in various aspects of information assurance.

What skill sets will be most in demand for security professionals? In addition to information assurance technical skills (with an emphasis on network engineering and data communications), broad-based business experience is also extremely desirable. IT security professionals need to understand the key issues of e-commerce and the core areas of their company's business (such as marketing, sales, and finance). Understanding how a business works is essential to pinpointing and correcting security risks that could be detrimental to a company's bottom line. Because of the large number of attacks by hackers, security and forensic skills and related certifications also are in high demand. Working closely with law enforcement officials is essential to rapidly solving and stopping cybercrime.

Another important attribute of security professionals is the ability to lead and motivate teams. Security experts need to work with diverse members of the business community, including customers, to forge relationships and understanding among diverse groups. Security professionals must conduct skillful negotiations to ensure that large project implementations are not unduly delayed by security initiatives or pushed through with inadequate security precautions. Diplomacy is therefore a sought-after skill.

Look for more colleges and universities to roll out security-based degree and certificate programs as the demand for security professionals increases. These programs will most likely be appropriate for experienced networking professionals who are ready to make the move into the IT security field. If you're just starting to prepare for a career, consider a degree in network engineering, followed by network security training while you're working at your first job. A degree program that is also designed to prepare you for security certification exams is particularly desirable. Networking and security degrees, combined with passing grades on certification exams, should help you make a smooth transition into the exciting world of cybersecurity.

---

passphrase. The Xbox 360 configuration screens are shown in Figure 33.

Once all your devices are connected to your network, you might want to check your Internet connection speed to see what kind of throughput you are achieving. You can check your speed on any device on your network that can access the Internet with a browser.

How can I test my Internet connection speed? Your ISP may have

promised you certain speeds of downloading and uploading data. How can you tell if you are getting what was promised? There are numerous sites on the Internet, such as **Speedtest.net** (see Figure 34) and **broadband.gov**, where you can test the speed of downloading files to your computer and uploading files to other computers. You can then see how your results compare to those of other users in your state and across the United States. Many factors

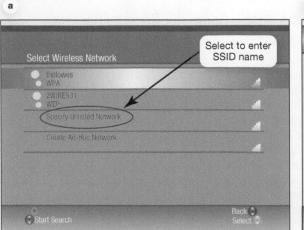
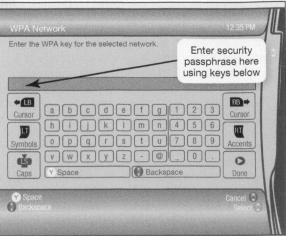

Figure 33

Xbox 360 wireless configuration screens. (a) The Xbox will detect available networks. Select the Specify Unlisted Network option to enter the SSID name of your network. (b) Enter the security passphrase on the appropriate security screen.

can influence your Internet speeds, so be sure to run the test at several different times during the day over the course of a week before complaining to your ISP about not getting your promised speed.

Troubleshooting Network Problems

What types of problems can I run into when installing wireless networks? The maximum range of wireless devices under the 802.11n standard is

about 350 feet. But as you go farther away from your router, the throughput you achieve will decrease. Obstacles between wireless nodes also decrease throughput. Walls, floors, and large metal objects are the most common sources of interference with wireless signals. For example, placing a computer with a wireless network adapter next to a refrigerator may prevent the signals from reaching the rest of the network. Similarly, a node that has four walls between it and the Internet connection will

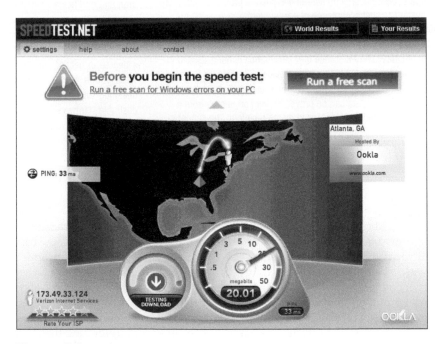

Figure 34

Speed test showing a download speed of 20.01 megabits, which is extremely fast for a home Internet connection.

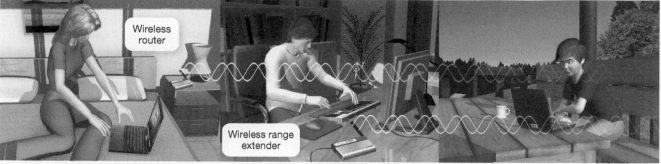

Bedroom　　　　　　　　　　**Den**　　　　　　　　　　**Back porch**

Computer A with
wireless network adapter

Computer B with
wireless range extender

Notebook C with
wireless network adapter

most likely have lower-than-maximum throughput.

What if a node on the network can't get adequate throughput?
Repositioning the node within the same room (sometimes even just a few inches from the original position) can often affect communication between nodes. If this doesn't work, try moving the device closer to the router or to other rooms in your house. If these solutions don't work, you should consider adding a wireless range extender to your network.

A **wireless range extender** is a device that amplifies your wireless signal to get it out to parts of your home that are experiencing poor connectivity. As shown Figure 35, the notebook on the back porch can't connect to the wireless network even though the computer in the den can connect to the network. By placing a range extender in the den, where there is still good connectivity to the wireless network, the wireless signal is amplified and beamed farther out to the back porch. This improves the otherwise poor connectivity on the back porch and allows computer C to make a good connection to the network.

Hopefully, you'll now be able connect all your computing devices to your home network and achieve the throughput you need to move your date efficiently around your home network.

Figure 35

Because a wireless range extender is installed in the den, Notebook C on the back porch can now connect to the wireless network generated by the wireless router in the bedroom.

1. **What is a network, and what are the advantages/disadvantages of setting up one?**

   A computer network is simply two or more computers that are connected using software and hardware so that they can communicate. Advantages of networks include allowing users to (1) share an Internet connection, (2) share peripheral devices, and (3) share files. A disadvantage is that the network must be administered.

2. **What is the difference between a client/server network and a peer-to-peer network?**

   In peer-to-peer networks, each node connected to the network can communicate directly with every other node instead of having a separate device exercise central control over the network. P2P networks are the most common type of network installed in homes. Most networks that have 10 or more nodes are client/server networks. A client/server network contains two types of computers: a client computer on which users perform specific tasks and a server computer that provides resources to the clients and central control for the network.

3. **What are the main components of every network?**

   To function, any network must contain four components: (1) transmission media (cables or radio waves) to connect and establish communication between nodes, (2) network adapters that allow the nodes on the network to communicate, (3) network navigation devices (such as routers and switches) that move data around the network, and (4) software that allows the network to run.

4. **Which type of network is most commonly found in the home?**

   Ethernet networks are the most common networks used in home networking. Most Ethernet networks use a combination of wired and wireless connections depending upon the data throughput required. Wired connections usually achieve higher throughput than wireless connections.

5. **What equipment and software do I need to build a network in my home?**

   All computing equipment that will connect to a network has to contain a network adapter. Network adapters allow computers to communicate (either wired or wirelessly) with network navigation devices such as routers and switches. Wired connections are usually made with Cat 6 twisted pair cable. A router is needed to share an Internet connection as it transmits data between two networks (the home network and the Internet).

6. **Besides computers, what other devices would I connect to a home network?**

   Connecting peripherals such as printers directly to a network allow them to be easily shared by all users on the network. Network-attached storage (NAS) devices allow for the storage and sharing of data files such as movies and music as well as providing a central place for file backups. Connecting digital entertainment devices (such as gaming consoles) provides the ability to stream movies and other entertainment directly from the Internet.

7. **Why are wireless networks more vulnerable than wired networks, and what special precautions are required to ensure my wireless network is secure?**

   Wireless networks are even more susceptible to hacking than wired networks because the signals of most wireless networks extend beyond the walls of your home. Neighbors may unintentionally (or intentionally) connect to the Internet through your wireless connection, and hackers may try to access it. To prevent unwanted intrusions into your network, you should change the default password on your router to make it tougher for hackers to gain access, use a hard-to-guess SSID (network name), turn off SSID broadcasting to make it harder for outsiders to detect your network, and enable security protocols such as WPA or WEP.

Networking: Connecting Computing Devices

8. **How do I configure the software on my computer and set up other devices to get my network up and running?**

Windows features software wizards that facilitate the setup of both wired and wireless networks. Plug in the modem, routers, and all cables, and then switch on the modem, router, and computers (in that order). Run the wizards, which should guide you through the process. Make sure each computer has a distinct name and ensure that all computers are in the same HomeGroup. Devices such as gaming consoles each have their own set-up procedures for connecting to wireless networks but usually require the same information as needed for connecting a computer to a secured wireless network.

9. **What problems might I encounter when setting up a wireless network?**

You may not get the throughput you need through a wireless connection and therefore you may need to consider a wired connection for certain devices. Distance from the router as well as walls, floors, and large metal objects between a device and the router can interfere with wireless connectivity. Wireless range extenders can amplify signals to improve connectivity in areas of poor signal strength.

Networking: Connecting Computing Devices

key terms

802.11 standard (WiFi)
backward compatibility
Cat 6 cable
client
client/server network
coaxial cable
data transfer rate (bandwidth)
Ethernet network
fiber-optic cable
firewall
firmware
gigabit Ethernet
hacker
home area network (HAN)
home network server
Internet appliance
local area network (LAN)
media access control (MAC) address
metropolitan area network (MAN)
Multiple Input Multiple Output (MIMO)
network
network adapter
network administration

network-attached storage (NAS)
  device
network architecture
network interface card (NIC)
network navigation device
network operating system (NOS)
network-ready device
node
packet
peer-to-peer (P2P) network
piggybacking
router
server
service set identifier (SSID)
switch
throughput
transceiver
transmission media
twisted-pair cable
unshielded twisted-pair (UTP) cable
wide area network (WAN)
WiFi
wireless range extender

buzzwords

Word Bank

- Cat 6 cable
- client/server
- data transfer rate
- hacker(s)
- home network server
- LAN
- network adapter(s)
- network-ready
- peer-to-peer (P2P)
- piggybacking
- router
- switch
- throughput
- twisted pair cable
- WAN
- wired
- wireless
- wireless range expander

Instructions: Fill in the blanks using the words from the Word Bank above.

Cathi needed to network three computers for herself and her roommates, Sharon and Emily. She decided that a(n) (1) _____ network was the right type to install in their dorm suite because a(n) (2) _____ network was too complex. Because they all liked to stream digital movies from the Internet, they needed high a(n) (3) _____ but doubted they would achieve the promised (4) _____ in any network they installed. Although they knew using (5) _____ media would provide the fastest Ethernet networks, they decided to use (6) _____ media so that they could use their notebooks wherever they were in their suite. Therefore they needed to buy a(n) (7) _____ with wireless capability that would allow them to share the broadband Internet connection that Sharon already had through a local ISP. This device would also double as a(n) (8) _____, preventing the need to purchase a separate device. Fortunately, all their computers already had (9) _____ installed, making it easy to connect the computers to the network. Cathi knew they would need to purchase some (10) _____ since the Xbox 360 they wanted to share only had a wired Ethernet adapter in it.

Cathi's roommate Emily wanted to know if they could hook into the (11) _____, or small network, that was already deployed for the students in the dorm. This student network was already hooked into the college's (12) _____, or large network, which spanned all three of the college's campuses. She knew they would need to be careful when connecting to the network, because some students from the dorm had accidentally been illegally (13) _____ on a network from the deli across the street. As the connectivity for notebooks in the lounge at the end of the hall was very poor, they needed to consider purchasing a(n) (14) _____ to extend the range of the wireless signal. As a final detail, Emily suggested they get a(n) (15) _____ printer that would plug right into the router and allow them all to print whenever they needed to do so.

becoming computer literate

Your grandmother has moved into a new retirement community. She is sharing a large living space with three other residents. All four retirees have their own notebook computers. Your grandmother has asked you to advise her and her roommates on an appropriate network to install so that they can share an Internet connection, a laser printer, and movies that they want to stream from Netflix via the Internet. And your grandmother is an avid photographer and has thousands of digital photographs on her computer. She is very concerned about forgetting to back up the photographs after she takes new ones and wants her family to be able to access her photos via the Internet.

Instructions: Using the preceding scenario, draft a networking plan for your grandmother and her roommates using as many of the keywords from the chapter as you can. Be sure that your grandmother, who is unfamiliar with many networking terms, can understand your suggestions.

self-test

Instructions: Answer the multiple-choice and true–false questions below for more practice with key terms and concepts from this chapter.

Multiple Choice

1. All of the following are advantages of installing a home network *except* sharing
  a. peripherals.
  b. an Internet connection.
  c. files.
  d. MAC addresses.

2. Which of the following is *not* a reason client/server networks are generally not installed in homes?
  a. Client/server networks can't handle streaming media, which is often required in home networks.
  b. Client/server networks are more difficult to install than peer-to-peer networks.
  c. Client/server networks provide more security than is needed for home networks.
  d. Peer-to-peer networks are less expensive to install than client/sever networks.

3. Which of the following is *not* required on some simple networks?
  a. Network adapters
  b. Networking software
  c. Network navigation devices
  d. Transmission media

4. Which network navigation device is required to move data between two networks?
  a. Repeater   c. Router
  b. Switch   d. Hub

5. If you need very fast throughput in a home network, you should use
  a. an 802.11n wireless Ethernet connection.
  b. a wired power-line network.
  c. a wired gigabit Ethernet connection.
  d. a client/server network.

6. Wireless range expanders
  a. are never used for home networks.
  b. are not needed with 802.11n networks.
  c. improve connectivity in remote areas of a home.
  d. turn devices with wired connections into wireless nodes.

7. Two or more networks connected over long geographic distances to form a single network is usually referred to as a
  a. LAN.   c. HAN.
  b. MAN.   d. WAN.

8. The throughput of a network
  a. is the same on all Ethernet networks.
  b. is usually higher on wireless networks.
  c. is the same in all areas covered by a wireless network.
  d. can vary depending upon the transmission media used.

9. The "name" of a particular wireless network is known as the
  a. NetID.   c. SSID.
  b. HAN-ID.   d. Wifi-ID.

10. The device used to move data around a single network is called a
  a. gateway.
  b. switch.
  c. router.
  d. repeater.

True–False

___ 1. Actual data throughput is usually higher on wireless networks.

___ 2. Ethernet networks require each node on the network to be equipped with its own network adapter.

___ 3. WEP and WPA are popular wired network security protocols.

___ 4. MANs cover a larger geographic area than HANs.

___ 5. 802.11n wireless networks provide faster throughput than wired gigabit Ethernet networks.

1. Dormitory Networking

Mikel, Dylan, Sanjay, and Harrison were sitting in the common room of their campus suite and complaining about their wireless network. They inherited the equipment from the last residents of the suite, and unfortunately their router uses the outdated 802.11g standard. They all have notebooks that have 802.11n network adapters, but their throughput is poor. Since they are often all surfing the Internet at the same time and trying to download movies, their network's performance has become unacceptable.

Since they all just sold last semester's books back to the bookstore for a total of $600, they decided this would be a good time to upgrade their network and peripherals. Dylan has an inkjet printer that gobbles up expensive cartridges, and Phil has a laser printer that just broke. The guys figure one good networked all-in-one printer should meet their needs since it would also provide them with photocopying capabilities. Mikel is concerned about backups for his computer. His external hard drive fell on the floor and no longer works reliably. He has a tremendous amount of photos and schoolwork on his computer that he is concerned about losing if his hard drive fails. Since the guys don't know much about networking, the four roommates have asked for your guidance. Consider the following keeping in mind their $600 budget:

a. Research network-ready laser printers on sites such as **hp.com**, **epson.com**, and **brother.com**. What network-ready all-in-one printer would you recommend? Why?
b. Research 802.11n wireless routers at sites such as **netgear.com**, **linksys.com**, and **dlink.com**. What router do you think will meet the roommates' needs? Why?
c. How would you recommend addressing Dave's backup concerns? Would you recommend a NAS device for the network, or do they have enough money left in their budget for a home network server? Research these devices and make an affordable recommendation. Check sites such as **tigerdirect.com** and **newegg.com** for competitive pricing.

2. Connecting Your Computer to Public Networks

You are working for a local coffee shop that offers free wireless access to customers. Your supervisor has asked you to create a flyer for patrons that warns them of the potential dangers of surfing the Internet in public places. Conduct research on the Internet about using public hot spots to access the Internet. Prepare a flyer that lists specific steps that customers can take to protect their data when surfing on publicly accessible networks.

3. Adding a Home Network Server for Backups to Your Network

You know that adding a home network server to your network would facilitate sharing of your digital media and would make backing up your computers easier. You need to consider the following questions when selecting an appropriate home network server:

1. What is the volume of shared media that you need to store? (In other words, how many music files, movies, and other media files do you have?)
2. What are the sizes of the hard drives of the computers on your network (for backup purposes)? What size hard drive would you need on a home network server to ensure you could back up all your computers as well as store your shared media?
3. Would you need to access files on the home network server when you are away from home or allow others (such as your cousins) to access them?

Research home network servers using sites such as **hp.com**, **acer.com**, and **lenovo.com** or use the term "home server" in a search engine. Select a server that is appropriate for your home network. Prepare a summary of your findings and include the reasons for your selection.

Networking: Connecting Computing Devices

making the
transition to...
the workplace

1. **Wireless LAN for a Small Business**

   You are working for a local coffee shop. The owner of the shop thinks that adding a wireless network and providing free Internet access to customers would be a good way to increase business. The owner has asked you to research this idea and prepare a report of your findings. Consider the following:

   a. Price out business Internet connectivity with local phone and cable providers. Which vendor provides the most cost effective solution for a coffee shop? Are there any limitations on bandwidth or the number of people that can access the Internet at one time through the business account connection?
   b. What potential problems could you foresee with providing unrestricted free access to the Internet? What policies would you suggest to keep people from abusing the free Internet access? (An example of abuse is someone who sits all day and surfs for free without purchasing any coffee.)

2. **Putting Computers to Work on Research Projects**

   Most computer CPUs only use a fraction of their computing power most of the time. Many medical research companies (such as those seeking cures for cancer and AIDS) could benefit from "borrowing" computer CPU time when computers are not being used or are being under utilized. Virtual supercomputers (which are really networks of computers) can be created using software installed on tens of thousands of computers. This type of computing is also known as *grid* or *distributed computing*. These virtual computing nets can be harnessed to solve complex problems when their owners are not using their computers. Assume that you are working for a business that has 100 computers and you would like to participate in a grid computing project. Investigate IBM's Worldwide Community Grid (**worldcommunitygrid.org**). Prepare a report for your boss that:

   a. Describes the Worldwide Community Grid (WCG) and its objectives
   b. Lists current projects that the WCG is working on.
   c. Describes the process for installing the WCG software on the company's computers.
   d. Suggests a strategy for publicizing the company's participation in the WCG project that will encourage your employer's customers to participate.

3. **Testing Your Internet Connection Speed**

   Visit **speedtest.net** and **speakeasy.net/speedtest** and test the speed of your Internet connection at your home and in the computer lab at your school. Try to repeat the test at two different times during the day.

   a. What did you find out about download speeds at your home? Are you getting as much speed as was promised by your ISP? Would this speed be sufficient for a home-based business? What type of business packages does your ISP offer, and what speeds could you expect when paying for a business package?
   b. How does the connection speed at your school compare to the speed at your home? Where do you think you should have a faster connection—at your school or at your home? Why might the connection speed at your school be slower than you think it should be?

Networking: Connecting Computing Devices

Instructions: Albert Einstein used *Gedankenexperiments*, or critical thinking questions, to develop his theory of relativity. Some ideas are best understood by experimenting with them in our own minds. The following critical thinking questions are designed to demand your full attention but require only a comfortable chair—no technology.

1. Protecting Your Wireless Home Network

Many people have installed wireless networks in their homes. Consider the wireless network installed in your home (or in a friend's home if you don't have wireless).

a. Is your network set up to provide adequate protection against hackers? If not, what would you need to do to make it secure?

b. Are there other wireless networks within range of your home? If so, are they set up with an adequate level of security, or can you connect to them easily? How would you go about informing your neighbors that their networks are vulnerable?

2. Adding Devices to Your Network

We discussed adding devices other than computers and computer peripherals to your network in this chapter. Consider the following for your home network:

a. Do you currently stream or download movies from Netflix, Amazon Video on Demand, or another service? If so, is your storage device sufficient or do you need more capacity? If you don't currently download this type of entertainment, would your family do so if you had a device that was attached to your network? What type of device (DVR, home server, etc.) do you think would be most appropriate for the type of media that you enjoy? How much media would you need to download and view in a month to make purchasing equipment worthwhile?

b. Do you have a need for a home security system? Would internal and external cameras be appropriate for monitoring your home? Are their people in your house (babysitters, housekeepers, contractors, etc.) on a regular basis that might need monitoring? Would you monitor these people in real time or make recordings for later review?

3. Evaluating Your Home Networking Needs

You might have a network installed in your home already, or perhaps you are still considering whether it is necessary to install one. Consider these issues:

a. Who uses computing devices in your home? How many computers (notebooks and desktops) are currently in your home? Are the computers networked? If not, should they be networked? What advantages would your family gain by networking its computers?

b. Which computer peripheral devices does your family own? Which family members need to use which peripherals? Are the peripherals network-ready or are they connected to individual computers? How easy is it to share these peripherals? Are there peripherals that your family doesn't own that would be beneficial? (Make sure to explain why.) How would you go about connecting new peripherals to your network?

c. Does your home network have network-attached storage or a home server? Would your family benefit from having this technology on your home network? What types of media do your family members routinely share? What other types would they share if they had the means?

4. Sharing a Home Internet Connection

Perhaps you have considered whether sharing a home Internet connection with your neighbors would save you money. Consider the following issues:

a. How many neighbors would be within range (say, within 350 feet of your router) of an 802.11n signal that came from your house or apartment? Do you think your neighbors would be amenable to sharing the cost of your Internet connection and your bandwidth? Why or why not?

b. Is it permissible to share an Internet connection with neighbors under your ISP's terms of use for the type of connection you purchased? If not, what type of plan would you need to upgrade to in order to share a connection with your neighbors? Would the increased cost of upgrading your connection still make it economically feasible to share a connection?

Networking: Connecting Computing Devices

Creating a Wireless Network

Problem

Wireless technology is being adopted by leaps and bounds, both in the home and in the workplace. Offering easy access free of physical tethers to networks seems to be a solution to many problems. However, wireless computing also has problems, ranging from poor reception to hijackers stealing your bandwidth.

Task

You are volunteering for a charity that installs wireless networks in homes for needy families. Many of these installations are done in older homes, and some recipients of the networks have reported poor connectivity in certain areas of their residences and extremely low bandwidth at other times. You have volunteered to research the potential problems and to suggest solutions to the director of the program.

Process

Break the class into three teams. Each team will be responsible for investigating one of the following issues:

1. **Detecting poor connectivity:** Research methods that can be used to find areas of poor signal strength, including signal sniffing software (**netstumbler.com**) and handheld scanning devices such as WiFi Finder (**kensington.com**). Investigate maximum distances between access points and network nodes and make appropriate recommendations. (Equipment manufacturers such as **netgear.com** and **linksys.com** provide guidelines.)
2. **Signal boosters:** Research ways to increase signal strength in access points, antennae, and wireless cards. Signal boosters are available for access points. You can purchase or construct replacement antennae or antenna enhancements. WiFi cards that offer higher power than conventional cards are now available.
3. **Security:** "War drivers" (people who cruise neighborhoods looking for open wireless networks from which to steal bandwidth) may be the cause of the bandwidth issues. Research appropriate measures to keep wireless network traffic secure from eavesdropping by hackers. In your investigation, look into the WiFi Protected Access (WPA) standard developed by the WiFi Alliance. Check out the security section of the knowledge center on the WiFi Alliance Web site to start (**wi-fi.org**).

Present your findings to your class and discuss possible causes of and ways to prevent the problems encountered at the residences. Provide your instructor with a report suitable for eventual presentation to the CEO of the charity.

Conclusion

As technology improves, wireless connectivity should eventually become the standard method of communication between networks and network devices. As with any other technology, security risks exist. Understanding those risks and how to mitigate them will allow you to participate in the design and deployment of network technology and provide peace of mind for your network users.

Networking: Connecting Computing Devices

In this exercise, you will research and then role-play a complicated ethical situation. The role you play may or may not match your own personal beliefs, but your research and use of logic will enable you to represent whichever view is assigned. An arbitrator will watch and comment on both sides of the arguments, and together the team will agree on an ethical solution.

Topic: Firing Employees for Expressing Views on Social Media Sites

The largest network, the Internet, provides the capability for vast social interaction. Social media sites such as Facebook, YouTube, and MySpace, as well as blogs and wikis, give everyone convenient ways to express their opinions. However, employers often are intolerant of employees who freely express negative opinions or expose inside information about their employers on social media sites. Given that most jurisdictions in the United States use the doctrine of employment at-will (that is, employees can be fired at any time for any reason, or even no reason), many employers are quick to discipline or terminate employees who express opinions with which the company disagrees. When such cases come to court, the courts often find in favor of the employers. It is clear that individual must exercise extreme care when posting work-related content.

Research Areas to Consider

- Ellen Simonetti and Delta Airlines
- Fired for blogging about work
- Free speech
- Joyce Park or Michael Tunison

Process

Divide the class into teams.

1. Research the areas cited above and devise a scenario in which someone has complained about an employee blogging about a sensitive workplace issue such as cleanliness at a food manufacturing facility or employee romances.

2. Team members should write a summary that provides background information for their character—for example: employee, Human Resources manager, or arbitrator — and details their character's behaviors to set the stage for the role-playing event. Then, team members should create an outline to use during the role-playing event.

3. Team members should arrange a mutually convenient time to meet for the exchange, either using the collaboration feature of MyITLab, the discussion board feature of Blackboard, or meeting in person.

4. Team members should present their case to the class, or submit a PowerPoint presentation for review by the rest of the class, along with the summary and resolution they developed.

Conclusion

As technology becomes ever more prevalent and integrated into our lives, more and more ethical dilemmas will present themselves. Being able to understand and evaluate both sides of the argument, while responding in a personally or socially ethical manner, will be an important skill.

802.11 standard A wireless standard established in 1997 by the Institute of Electrical and Electronics Engineers; also known as WiFi (short for Wireless Fidelity), it enables wireless network devices to work seamlessly with other networks and devices.

backward compatibility The accommodation of current devices being able to use previously issued software standards in addition to the current standards.

Cat 6 cable A UTP cable type that provides more than 1 GB of throughput.

client A computer that requests information from a server in a client/server network (such as your computer when you are connected to the Internet).

client/server network A network, consisting of client and server computers, in which the clients make requests of the server and the server returns the response.

coaxial cable A single copper wire surrounded by layers of plastic insulation and sheathing; used mainly in cable television and cable Internet service.

data transfer rate (bandwidth) The maximum speed at which data can be transmitted between two nodes on a network; usually measured in megabits per second (Mbps).

Ethernet network A network that uses the Ethernet protocol as the means (or standard) by which the nodes on the network communicate.

fiber-optic cable A cable that transmits data at close to the speed of light along glass or plastic fibers.

firewall A software program or hardware device designed to prevent unauthorized access to computers or networks.

firmware System software that controls hardware devices.

gigabit Ethernet The most commonly used wired Ethernet standard deployed in devices designed for home networks which provides bandwidth of up to 1 Gbps.

hacker Anyone who unlawfully breaks into a computer system (whether an individual computer or a network).

home area network (HAN) A network located in a home that is used to connect all of its digital devices.

home network server A device designed to store media, share media across the network, and back up files on computers connected to a home network.

local area network (LAN) A network in which the nodes are located within a small geographic area.

media access control (MAC) address A physical address, similar to a serial number on an appliance, that is assigned to each network adapter; it is made up of six 2-digit characters such as 01:40:87:44:79:A5.

metropolitan area network (MAN) A wide area network (WAN) that links users in a specific geographic area (such as within a city or county).

Multiple Input Multiple Output (MIMO) A design in newer routers that provides for faster wireless data transmission by utilizing more than one antenna to transmit and receive data.

network A group of two or more computers (or nodes) that are configured to share information and resources such as printers, files, and databases.

network adapter A device that enables the computer (or peripheral) to communicate with the network using a common data communication language, or protocol.

network administrator Someone who has training in computer and peripheral maintenance and repair, network design, and the installation of network software; installs new equipment, configures computers for users, repairs equipment, and assigns network access to users.

network-attached storage (NAS) device A specialized computing device designed to store and manage network data.

network architecture The design of a computer network; includes both physical and logical design.

network interface card (NIC) An expansion card that enables a computer to connect other computers or to a cable modem to facilitate a high-speed Internet connection.

network navigation device A device on a network such as a router, hub, and switch that moves data signals around the network.

network operating system (NOS) Software that handles requests for information, Internet access, and the use of peripherals for the rest of the network nodes.

network-ready device A device (such as a printer or external hard drive) that can be attached directly to a network instead of needing to attach to a computer on the network.

node A device connected to a network such as a computer, a peripheral (such as a printer), or a communications device (such as a modem).

packet (data packet) A small segment of data that is bundled for sending over transmission media. Each packet contains the address of the computer or peripheral device to which it is being sent.

peer-to-peer (P2P) network A network in which each node connected to the network can communicate directly with every other node on the network.

piggybacking The process of connecting to a wireless network without the permission of the owner of the network.

router A device that routes packets of data between two or more networks.

server A computer that provides resources to other computers on a network.

service set identifier (SSID) A network name that wireless routers use to identify themselves.

switch A device for transmitting data on a network. A switch makes decisions, based on the media access control (MAC) address of the data, as to where the data is to be sent.

throughput The actual speed of data transfer that is achieved. It is usually less than the data transfer rate and is measured in megabits per second (Mbps).

transceiver In a wireless network, a device that translates the electronic data that needs to be sent along the network into radio waves and then broadcasts these radio waves to other network nodes.

transmission media The radio waves or cable that transport data on a network.

twisted pair cable Cables made of copper wires that are twisted around each other and are surrounded by a plastic jacket (such as traditional home phone wire).

unshielded twisted pair (UTP) cable The most popular transmission media option for Ethernet networks. UTP cable is composed of four pairs of wires that are twisted around each other to reduce electrical interference.

wide area network (WAN) A network made up of local area networks (LANs) connected over long distances.

WiFi (Wireless Fidelity) The 802.11 standard for wireless data transmissions established by the Institute of Electrical and Electronics Engineers (IEEE).

wireless range extender A device that amplifies your wireless signal to get it out to parts of your home that are experiencing poor connectivity.

glossary

credits

Chapter opener valdis torms\Shutterstock
Figure 14 Norman Chan \Shutterstock

Networking: Connecting Computing Devices

140

digital lifestyle:

managing digital data and devices

digital lifestyle:

managing digital data and devices

After reading this chapter, you should be able to answer the following questions:

1. What are the changes that have brought us a digital lifestyle?

2. How has the move to digital information affected the communication tools important to both the business world and life outside of work?

3. How do cell phone and smartphone components resemble a traditional computer, and how do they work?

4. Why would I use VoIP, and what does it offer that is unique?

5. How is digital media different from analog?

6. What can I carry in a portable media player, and how does it store data?

7. What ways are there for me to create and to watch digital video?

8. What changes does ubiquitous computing bring to our lifestyles?

Active Helpdesk

- Keeping Your Data on Hand
- Using Portable Media Players

Sound Bytes

- Smartphones Are Really Smart
- Connecting with Bluetooth

Companion Website

The Companion Website includes a variety of additional materials to help you review and learn more about the topics in this chapter. Go to: *pearsonhighered.com/techinaction*

how cool is *this?* TiVo is not the only game in town! PVR (personal video recorder) software is now available, free of charge, for every style of operating system. Using a PVR, you can record standard or HD television broadcasts on your hard drive and then watch them when you have the time. Free programs like **XBMC** Media Center and **MeediOS** let you pause and rewind live TV shows and include features that allow you to automatically detect and **skip commercials**. You even have access to a TV listings guide and can schedule your **PVR** from any location using the Web.

A Digital Lifestyle

Computers today are central to everyday life. Which part of your life isn't touched by some sort of computer or digital technology? Computer-like devices (such as smartphones and iPods) are everywhere. Much of your entertainment—playing games, watching movies and television, and downloading songs—is probably delivered via the Internet.

Do you really understand how all this digital technology works? Do you know all of your options so you can enjoy the digital devices you purchase to the fullest extent? In this chapter, we explore the key aspects of your digital life—digital communication, digital entertainment, and digital mobility—and help you understand how the related technologies work so you can use them to your best advantage.

When did everything go "digital"? It used to be that everything was analog. Today, no matter what you're interested in—music, movies, television, radio, stock prices—digital information is the key. All forms of entertainment have migrated to the digital domain (see Figure 1). MP3 files encode digital forms of music, and digital cameras and video camcorders are now commonplace. In Hollywood, some feature films are now being shot entirely with digital equipment, and many movie theaters use digital projection equipment. Satellite radio systems such as Sirius Satellite Radio and HD Radio are broadcast in digital formats. Phone systems and television signals are now digital streams of data.

What is special about digital? Any kind of information can be digitized (measured and converted to a stream of numeric values). Consider sound. It is carried to your ears by sound waves, which are actually patterns of pressure changes in the air. Images are our interpretation of the changing intensity of light waves around us. These sound and light waves are called **analog** waves or continuous waves. They illustrate the loudness of a sound or the brightness of the colors in an image at a given moment in time. They are continuous signals because you would never have to lift your pencil off the page to draw them; they are just long, continuous lines.

First-generation recording devices such as vinyl records and analog television broadcasts were designed to reproduce these sound and light waves. A needle in the groove of a vinyl record vibrates in the same pattern as the original sound wave. Analog television signals are actually waves that tell an analog TV how to display the same color and brightness as is seen in the production studio. However, it's difficult to describe a wave, even mathematically. The simplest sounds, such as that of middle C on a piano, have the simplest shapes, like the one shown in Figure 2. However, something like the word *hello* generates a highly complex pattern, like the one shown in Figure 2.

What advantages do digital formats have over analog ones? Digital formats describe signals as long strings of numbers. This digital representation gives us a simple way to describe sound and light waves exactly so that sounds and images can be reproduced perfectly each time. In addition, we already have easy ways to distribute digital information (on CDs and DVDs and using e-mail, for example). Thus, digital information can be reproduced exactly and distributed easily. Both give it huge advantages over analog.

How can a sequence of numbers express complicated analog shapes? The answer is provided by something called *analog-to-digital conversion*. In analog-to-digital conversion, the incoming analog signal is measured many times each second. The strength of the signal at each measurement is recorded as a simple number. The series of numbers produced by

Figure 1 | ANALOG VERSUS DIGITAL ENTERTAINMENT

	Analog	Digital
Music	Vinyl record albums and cassette tapes	CDs and MP3 files
Photography	35-mm single lens reflex (SLR) cameras Photos stored on film	Digital cameras, including digital SLRs Photos stored as digital files
Video	8-mm, VHS, and Hi8 camcorders Film stored on tapes	High Definition Digital video (DV) camcorders Film stored as digital files; distributed on DVD and Blu-ray discs and streamed
Radio	AM/FM radio	HD Radio Sirius/XM Radio
Television	Conventional broadcast analog TV	High Definition Digital television (HDTV)

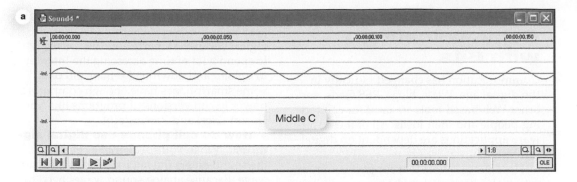

a   Sound4 *

Middle C

b   Sound2 *

"Hello"

the analog-to-digital conversion process gives us the digital form of the wave. Figure 3 shows analog and digital versions of the same wave. In Figure 3a, you see the original, continuous analog wave. You could draw that wave without lifting your pencil from the page. In Figure 3b, the wave has been digitized and is no longer a single line; instead, it is represented as a series of points or numbers.

How has the change from analog to digital technologies affected our lifestyle? When the market for communication devices for entertainment media—like photographs, music, and video—switched over to a digital standard, we began to have products with new and useful capabilities. Small devices can now hold huge collections of a variety of types of information. We can interact with our information any time we like, in ways that, prior to the conversion to digital media, had been too expensive or too difficult to learn. The implications of the shift to digital media are continually evolving. Let's examine the many ways in which digital media has already changed our lifestyles.

Figure 2

(a) This is an analog wave showing the simple, pure sound of a piano playing middle C. (b) This is the complex wave produced when a person says "Hello."

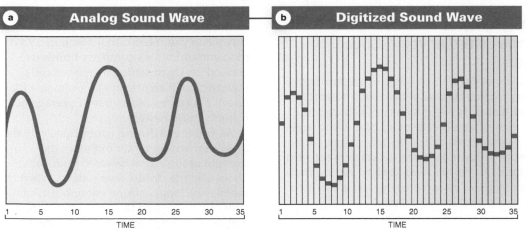

a   **Analog Sound Wave**

b   **Digitized Sound Wave**

TIME

TIME

Figure 3

(a) A simple analog wave.
(b) A digitized version of the same wave.

Digital Lifestyle: Managing Digital Data and Devices

Digital Telephony: Communicating with Bits

Communication has changed radically in the digital age. Wikis, blogs, RSS feeds, and other Web-based tools are used for connecting people and their ideas. All of these software applications are dependent on digital information.

Hardware devices that support communication also have evolved because of digital technologies. **Telephony**, the use of equipment to provide voice communications over a distance, has shifted from an analog science to a digital one. In this section, we examine cell phones, smartphones, and Voice over Internet Protocol (VoIP) devices to see how they are changing to meet modern communication needs.

Cell Phones and Smartphones

What are cell phones and smartphones? The **cellular phone** (or **cell phone**) has evolved from a clunky, boxlike device to a compact, fully featured communication and information storage device. Cell phones offer all of the features available on a traditional telephone system, including automatic redial, call timers, and voice mail capabilities. Most cell phones also feature voice-activated dialing, which is important for hands-free operation. In addition, many cell phones offer Internet access, text messaging, personal information management (PIM) features, voice recording, GPS services, and digital image and video capture. The most fully featured and powerful cellular phones are found in the **smartphone**

category. A smartphone often requires a data plan from the cell phone provider. This is logical because a smartphone user is likely to spend a lot of time accessing the Internet to upload and download e-mail and data. Some smartphones have enough computing power to run versions of programs like Microsoft Excel and PowerPoint.

How do cell phones use digital signals? When you speak into a cell phone, the sound enters the microphone as a sound wave. Because analog sound waves need to be digitized (that is, converted into a sequence of 1s and 0s that the cell phone's processor can understand), an **analog-to-digital converter chip** converts your voice's sound waves into digital signals. Next, the digital data must be compressed, or squeezed, into the smallest possible space so that it will transmit more quickly to another phone. The processor cannot perform the mathematical operations required at this stage quickly enough, so a specialized chip called the **digital signal processor** is included in the cell phone to handle the compression work. Finally, the digital data is transmitted as a radio wave through the cellular network to the destination phone.

When you receive an incoming call, the digital signal processor decompresses the incoming message. An amplifier boosts the signal to make it loud enough, and it is then passed on to the speaker.

What's "cellular" about a cell phone? A set of connected "cells" makes up a cellular network. Each cell is a geographic area centered on a **base transceiver station**, which is a large communications tower with antennas, amplifiers, receivers, and transmitters. When you place a call on a cell phone, a base station picks up the request for service. The station then passes the request to a central location called a **mobile switching center**. (The reverse process occurs when you receive an incoming call.) A telecommunications company builds its network by constructing a series of cells that overlap in an attempt to guarantee that its cell phone customers have coverage no matter where they are.

As you move during your phone call, the mobile switching center monitors the strength of the signal between your cell phone and the closest base station. When the signal is no longer strong enough between your cell phone and the base station, the mobile switching center orders the next base

BITS AND BYTES

Phoning Home—Accessing Your Home Computer from Your Cell Phone

An estimated 1 billion cellular phones that aren't considered smartphones currently are deployed. But don't count your cheap phone out of the running if it doesn't have advanced software capabilities. You can still use it to access your home computer remotely and retrieve that big presentation you need for this afternoon. Remote access services such as GoToMyPC (**gotomypc.com**) and LogMeIn (**logmein.com**) can help and are free of charge. As long as you have a browser on your cell phone and a data plan with your provider, you can access the files on your computer from your phone without installing any software on the cell phone. You may not have to trade in that low-end cell phone yet. Just try getting it to work a little harder!

station to take charge of your call. When your cell phone "drops out," it may be because the distance between base stations was too great to provide an adequate signal.

Are cell phones and smartphones considered computers? Cell phones and smartphones are so advanced that they have many of the same components as a computer: a processor (central processing unit, or CPU); memory; and input and output devices, as shown in Figure 4. Cell/smartphones also require their own operating system (OS) software and have their own application software.

What does the processor inside a cell/smartphone do? Although the processor inside a cell phone is obviously not as fast or as high-powered as a processor in a desktop computer, it is still responsible for a great number of tasks. The processor coordinates sending all of the data among the other electronic components inside the phone. It also runs the cell phone's operating system, which provides a user interface so that you can change phone settings, store information, play games, and so on. Popular processors for cell/smartphones include the Qualcomm Snapdragon, the Texas Instruments OMAP, and the Marvell XScale processor. Some processors use dual-core processing technology, which is also used in some desktop processors.

When shopping for a new phone, be well prepared. Use published smartphone benchmarking results to compare performance. These benchmarks are often published on the *PC Magazine* Web site (**pcmag.com**) or at Wired (**wired.com**).

Is there a standard operating system for cell phones? Each cell phone manufacturer makes its own small changes to the operating system and designs its own user interface. So when moving between different cell phones, you will likely see a different set of commands and icons.

There are a number of operating systems in the cell phone market now. Many smartphones use the Windows Mobile operating system or the newer Windows Phone 7 series. Apple's iPhone uses a version of the OS X operating system that is used in Apple's personal computers, while the Palm Pre uses its own Palm-developed webOS. These operating systems are required to translate the user's commands into instructions for the processor.

There are several free operating systems that a manufacturer can use as a base for its cell/smartphone operating system. One popular OS is the Symbian, from the Symbian Foundation, which transitioned to an open source product in 2010. The Nokia N8 is one device running a Symbian OS. Another open source project to develop a free cell/smartphone operating system is Openmoko. The most successful open OS is the Android collection developed by Google. The goal of open source mobile operating systems is to leverage the creativity of many developers in creating great applications and new phone designs.

Figure 5 illustrates some of the different and creative user interfaces featured among cell phone operating systems.

What does the memory chip inside a cell phone do? The operating system and the information you save in your cell phone (such as phone numbers and addresses) need to be stored in memory. The operating system is stored in read-only memory (ROM) because the phone would be useless without that key piece of software. As you learned earlier, there are two kinds of memory used in computers: volatile memory, which requires power to store data, and nonvolatile memory, which stores data even when the power is turned off. ROM is nonvolatile, or permanent, memory. This means that when you turn off your phone, the data that is stored in ROM

Figure 4

Inside your cell phone, you'll find a CPU, a memory chip, input devices such as a microphone and a keypad, and output devices such as a display screen and a speaker.

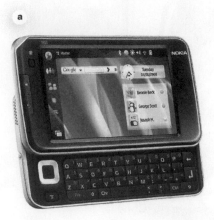

Figure 5

(a) Symbian, (b) Windows Mobile, and (c) Android are all cell/smartphone operating systems.

Figure 6

You can insert additional memory by installing a micro SD flash card in a smartphone.

(including the operating system) remains in memory.

Other phone data, such as ring tones, is stored in separate internal memory chips. Full-featured cell phones have as many as 200 MB of internal memory (with some smartphones carrying 1 GB internally) and support additional memory through micro SD flash cards that can store up to 32 GB. Micro SD cards are easy to install in a phone, as shown in Figure 6, while some models simply have external slots for an SD card. You can use that storage for contact data, ring tones, images, songs, videos, and even software applications such as a language translators or video games. Not every smartphone allows memory upgrades in this way, however. For example, the iPhone series does not allow you to add any memory.

What input and output devices do cell phones use? The primary input devices for a cell phone are a microphone and a keypad. Some phones, such as the Samsung Impression (see Figure 7), feature both a hidden keyboard (to make sending e-mail or text messages more efficient) and a touch-sensitive screen. The Apple iPhone uses its touch-sensitive screen to offer a software-based keyboard (see Figure 7) that supports more than 40 languages.

Cell phones often include a digital camera for capturing photos and video. These cameras are catching up to the quality level of standalone point-and-shoot cameras. For example, the Droid Incredible offers a high-quality 8-megapixel (MP) camera with flash and video capture, and the Nokia N8 sports a 12 MP camera with Carl Zeiss lenses. Most cameras on cell phones can record video as well as take still shots. Picture and video messaging is popular with many smartphone users. They can transmit photos and video files via e-mail, post the files to Web sites such as Facebook, or send them directly to other phones.

Cell phone output devices include a speaker and a liquid crystal display (LCD). Higher-end models include full-color, high-resolution LCD screens. Newer on the market are OLED (organic light-emitting diode) displays, which allow very bright, sharp imaging and draw less power. High-resolution displays are becoming increasingly popular because more people are using their cell phones to send and receive the digital images included in multimedia text messages

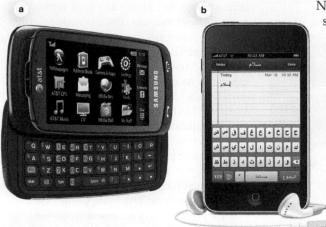

Figure 7

(a) The Samsung Impression includes a touch screen and a built-in QWERTY keyboard. (b) The Apple iPhone has a touch keyboard that supports more than 40 languages and a range of character sets.

NBC, CBS, and PBS are testing this system.

What cell phone and smartphone software is available? Most devices come with a standard collection of software such as a to-do list, contact manager, and calendar. Modified versions of application software such as Microsoft Word, Excel, Outlook, and PowerPoint are available for some high-end smartphones. A variety of games, tools, and reference applications are available from numerous software companies. A good source to locate software applications for your phone is GetJar (**getjar.com**). Many manufacturers have Web-based software stores, like iTunes for the Apple iPhone and the BlackBerry App World for RIM's BlackBerry devices

and e-mail, and even to watch TV (see Figure 8). Cell phone and cable providers are teaming up to deliver broadcast TV programs directly to cell phones through services such as Verizon V Cast and Sprint TV. A developing standard named Mobile DTV allows cell/smartphones to receive free broadcasts from television stations using the Mobile DTV technology. At the time of this writing, affiliates of

SOUND BYTE | **Smartphones Are Really Smart**

In this Sound Byte, you'll learn how to use a smartphone as a powerful tool to communicate, calculate, and organize your workload.

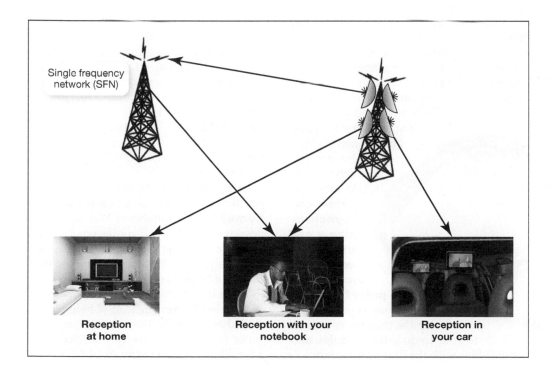

Figure 8

The Mobile DTV system allows local TV stations to broadcast live, digital content to mobile devices.

Single frequency network (SFN)

Reception at home

Reception with your notebook

Reception in your car

Figure 9

The Blackberry App World is one of many online stores delivering software for smartphones.

Figure 10

A USB data synch cable connects your cell phone to your computer for data transfer.

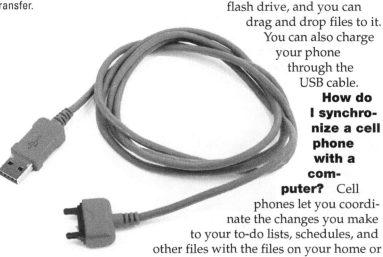

(see Figure 9). The Android developer community has held competitions to spur the creation of new software applications for Android-based phones. Many software applications are available for Android through the Web and the Android Market.

How do I move music from my computer to my smartphone? On the 32 GB micro SD cards available for phones, there is room for thousands of songs, videos, or data files. You can transfer files between your phone and your computer easily. Some phones are designed with a flash card that can be easily removed and slipped directly into a flash card reader on the computer. Almost all phones are designed with a USB port. Some have a mini-USB connector, while other models require a special cable to connect the phone to a standard USB port (see Figure 10). Once connected using a USB data cable, your phone will appear on your computer like an additional flash drive, and you can drag and drop files to it. You can also charge your phone through the USB cable.

How do I synchronize a cell phone with a computer? Cell phones let you coordinate the changes you make to your to-do lists, schedules, and other files with the files on your home or office computer. This process of updating your data so that the files on your cell phone and computer are the same is called **syncing** or **synchronizing**. To synchronize your computer and the device, simply place the cell phone in its cradle (or attach it to the computer via a USB cable) and touch a "sync" button. This begins the process of data transfer that updates both sets of files to the most current version.

Microsoft has recognized the vast increase in portable computing devices by integrating synchronization into the Windows operating system. The Sync Center (see Figure 11), which is accessed from the Control Panel, allows you to set up automatic or manual synchronization. Make sure the device you are trying to set up synchronization parameters for is connected to your computer and then launch the Sync Center. Select the *Set up new sync partnerships* option to view available devices and configure their synchronization options.

Can I transfer files wirelessly?
Bluetooth technology uses radio waves to transmit data signals over short distances (approximately 30 feet for Bluetooth 1 and 60 feet for Bluetooth 2 and 3). Bluetooth 3 devices are expected to hit the market by 2011, with throughput about 8 times faster than Bluetooth 2. Most cell phones on the market today are Bluetooth-enabled, meaning they include a small Bluetooth chip that allows them to transfer data wirelessly to any other Bluetooth-enabled device. One benefit Bluetooth has over infrared, a wireless connection used in the past, is that a direct line of sight does not have to be present between two devices for them to communicate. You also can use Bluetooth to synchronize your device with your computer. Bluetooth accessories such as earpieces, mice, keyboards, and even stereo headsets are now available.

Is there a way to synchronize to my home computer before I get home? Yes, a number of Web services are now available to synchronize your e-mail, files, contacts, and calendars instantly and wirelessly. These Web services follow the model of "cloud computing," where Internet-based services and resources are distributed to users instead of being installed as an application on the user's computer. Some synchronization services charge a fee, like MobileMe from Apple. For a

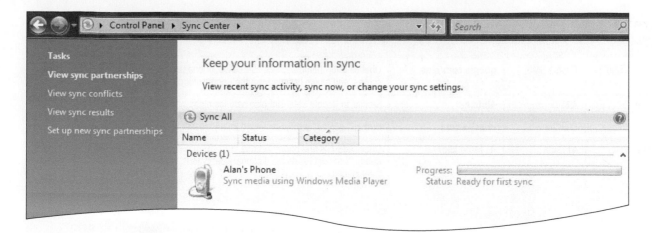

$99 annual fee, you can make sure the same files are always on your iPhone, your iPad, your home desktop, and your notebook computer. As soon as information is changed on one device, it is automatically "pushed" out to all the other devices, updating their files as well. If you lose your iPhone or iPad, MobileMe lets you log in and display its location on a map. You can then set a password and display a message like "Crazy day! Could you please call me and I'll come pick this up?" If you really can't locate the device, you can use MobileMe to remotely wipe all of the data from the device.

There are other providers of wireless synchronization for mobile devices. Google Sync works with iPhones, Blackberry phones, Symbian and Windows Mobile devices, and it's free. All of your Google e-mail, calendar events, and contacts are automatically backed up online instantly on the Google servers. Even the Amazon Kindle uses wireless synchronization so that if you read a bit further in your e-book on your phone, when you get to your office, the Kindle software on your PC will have automatically updated to bookmark to the new page you're on.

SOUND BYTE

Connecting with Bluetooth

In this Sound Byte, you'll learn what freedoms Bluetooth affords you, how to decide whether you want Bluetooth on equipment that you purchase, and how to use Bluetooth devices.

Text Messaging

What is text messaging? Short message service (SMS)—often just called *text messaging*—is a technology that allows you to send short text messages (comprising up to 160 characters) over mobile networks. To send SMS messages from your cell phone, you use the keypad or a pre-saved template and type your message. You can send SMS messages to other mobile devices or to any e-mail address. You also can use SMS to send short text messages from your home computer to mobile devices such as your friend's cell phone.

How does SMS work? SMS uses the cell phone network to transmit messages. When you send an SMS message, an SMS calling center receives the message and delivers it to the appropriate mobile device using something called *store-and-forward* technology. This technology allows users to send SMS messages to any other SMS device in the world.

Many SMS fans like text messaging because it allows the receivers to read messages when it is convenient for them. Companies now support texting in many ways, so for example, your bank may allow you to text commands to request account balances or details about your last transaction, and the bank will text the requested information back to you. As shown in the table in Figure 12, several companies provide useful services based on text messaging.

If you plan to do a lot of texting, check the phone's feature list in advance and look for a phone with a good text prediction algorithm. With such an algorithm, typing a single letter pulls up a list of popular words

Figure 11

The Windows Sync Center makes it easy to arrange for synchronization of all your mobile devices.

>To launch Sync Center, click the **Start** button, select **Control Panel**, and double-click the **Sync Center** icon.

Figure 12 | TEXT MESSAGING SERVICES

SMS Code	Service Name	Web Site	Description
466453 (google)	Google SMS	**google.com/sms**	Obtains information such as addresses, phone numbers, driving directions, sports scores, and movie listings from the Google search engine.
44636 (4Info)	4INFO	**4info.net**	Similar to Google SMS, but also handles flight information and horoscopes.
242 242 (cha cha)	ChaCha	**chacha.com**	Human "guides" provide answers to any question in conversational English.
3109043113	411sms	**411sms.com**	Offers address and phone listings, turn-by-turn directions, movie show times, stock quotes, hot spot locations, dictionary definitions, horoscopes, and foreign language translations.

beginning with that letter, saving you typing time. For example, the T9 (Text on 9 keys) algorithm also "learns" from your usage patterns and displays the most-used word first.

Can I send and receive multimedia files using a cell phone? SMS technology allows you to send only text messages. However, an extension of SMS called **multimedia message service (MMS)** allows you to send messages that include text, sound, images, and video clips to other phones or e-mail addresses. MMS messages actually arrive as a series of messages; you view the text, then the image, and then the sound, and so on. You can then choose to save just one part of the message (such as the image), all of it, or none of it. MMS users can subscribe to financial, sports, and weather services that will "push" information to them, sending it automatically to their phones in MMS format.

411 for Answers

Most phone services charge as much as $2.00 for a 411 call for information on a phone listing or address. Now there is competition. The Google 411 service is a free way to find out the address of, directions to, or phone number of a business or person. A call to 1-800-GOOG-411 gets you this information at no charge. If you say "text" into the phone, it kicks back a text message with the address and a map.

If you are looking for a different kind of information, try the ChaCha service. You can either call (1-800-2chacha) or text (242 242) with any kind of question, and real human "guides" will find the answer and send it back to you. So, answers to questions like the following are just a free call or text away!

- How many calories are there in a slice of pizza?
- When is *American Idol* on tonight?
- Is there a way to get acrylic paint out of jeans?

Internet Connectivity

How do I get Internet service for my smartphone? Just as you have an Internet service provider (ISP) for Internet access for your desktop or notebook computer, you must have a **wireless Internet service provider** (or **wireless ISP**) to connect your smartphone to the Internet. Phone companies that provide phone calling plans (such as T-Mobile, Verizon, and AT&T) usually double as wireless ISPs. An Internet connectivity plan or text messaging plan is usually known as a **data plan**. Data charges are separate from phone calling charges and are provided at rates different from voice calls. Most carriers provide separate plans for different levels of texting usage and for various levels of data transfer to and from Internet sites. Before subscribing to a data plan, you should assess your needs: How often do you download new wallpaper, ring tones, or games? Do you use your smartphone's Internet access to download files from e-mails or from your company Web site? Begin by estimating how many kilobytes of data you transfer up and down from the Internet each month. Then select a plan that provides adequate service at a good price.

At what speed is digital information transferred to my smartphone? A smartphone connection often is slower than the one you have at your home. Although broadband speeds of 50 megabits per second (Mbps) are achievable at home using a cable or fiber-optic connection, your smartphone will connect at a much lower speed (see Figure 13).

Providers have introduced many smartphones based on two standards that support faster data transfer technologies: EDGE (short for enhanced data rate for global evolution) and 3G. EDGE and 3G have brought mobile devices much faster data transfer—as high as 1.4 Mbps (or more) under ideal conditions. If you use a smartphone that supports EDGE or 3G, and have a phone plan that allows data transfer, both uploading information (such as e-mail messages that include photos) and downloading information (such as from a company intranet or the Internet) can take place much more quickly. Of course if you are in range of a WiFi signal, that is going to be a much faster transfer option. EDGE and 3G have advantages over WiFi, however. They are more reliable and less susceptible to interference. Moreover, you won't have to hunt for a WiFi hot spot, because these technologies are used to blanket major urban areas with connectivity.

4G networks are beginning to be rolled out across the United States. The promise of 4G is incredible: mobile connection speeds of up to 100 Mbps. Currently, most providers can deliver speeds of 3 Mbps to 6 Mbps. The expansion of 4G will usher in a new generation of mobile devices and applications that will continue to expand how we think of mobile computing.

How can I survive when I find I have no WiFi signal? There are devices available that will instantly create a mobile hot spot for you. MiFi (pronounced "my fi") devices, like the Verizon model shown in Figure 14, are often available free with a new account from major Internet providers like Verizon and Sprint. The MiFi can fit in a shirt pocket and run for up to four hours on a single charge. It connects to the Internet through the 3G wireless phone network and then distributes the WiFi signal over an area of 30 feet. These personal hot spots can then support up to five WiFi-enabled devices.

An iPhone 3G has a similar capability. It can connect to your notebook computer through wireless Bluetooth, and then provide Internet access through the 3G network signal. This "Bluetooth tethering" makes sure your computer can access the Internet even when it

Figure 13	CELLULAR CONNECTION SPEEDS	
Network	Availability	Connection Speed (Mbps)
Edge	13,000 cities	0.1
3G	300 major markets	0.6–2.3
WiFi	WiFi hot spots	4–5
4G	Major cities	5–12

Note: Speeds will vary depending on provider and location.

tells you there are no available wireless networks as long as you have 3G signal.

How do smartphones display content from the Internet? On smartphones that have a limited amount of screen space, it is difficult to view Web pages without a great deal of horizontal scrolling. This is because most Web sites are designed for viewing on desktop monitors, which have much wider pixel widths than mobile screens. To enhance your Internet browsing experience on mobile devices, special micro-browser software runs on your phone. **Microbrowser** software provides a Web browser that is optimized to display Web content effectively on the smaller screen (see Figure 15). Popular versions of micro-browser software include Internet Explorer Mobile (included with

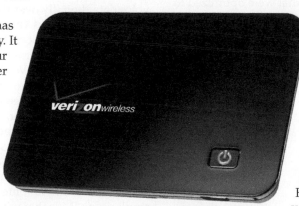

Figure 14

A MiFi device turns your 3G phone signal into a WiFi connection for you and four of your friends.

Make Your Cell Phone Deliver

Carriers offer many additional services for your cell phone. MusicID, for example, allows you to identify a song easily. Just hold your phone close to the radio's speaker for 15 seconds. You will then receive a text message with the name of the artist and the song. MusicID has a database of more than 3 million songs, so you can be the first to grab those new titles.

Other services can be added to your cell phone plan. For example, you can subscribe to high-definition radio stations over your cell phone. The extra fee allows you to stream more than 50 channels of commercial-free digital radio through your phone. Many phones are equipped for navigation services such as TeleNav Navigator. TeleNav delivers turn-by-turn instructions to you over your phone and displays real-time traffic information.

the Windows Mobile OS), Safari on the iPhone, and Opera Mobile. Opera Mobile uses special small-screen rendering technology to reformat the Web images to fit on your smartphone screen, then zooms in with a simple tap. For the best Web experience, consider a phone that has a large screen, such as the HTC HD2, which boasts a 4.3-inch HD touch screen.

More and more Web sites are being created with content specifically designed for wireless devices. This specially designed content, which is text based and contains no graphics, is written in a format called **Wireless Markup Language (WML)**. Content is designed so that it fits the smaller display screens of handheld mobile devices.

Can I keep my e-mail up to date using my cell phone? A popular feature of cell phones with Internet access lets users check e-mail. BlackBerry handhelds were the first devices that were optimized to check e-mail. BlackBerry pioneered the

"push" technology that delivers your e-mail automatically to your phone, whether you want it or not. Now many other systems also offer "push" technology. BlackBerry devices are still an excellent option, but they aren't the only option. With Internet access, users can always e-mail through Web-based e-mail accounts like Gmail or Yahoo!

If checking and sending e-mail while on the go is mission critical for you, check out smartphones with larger displays and integrated keyboards that make it easier to read and respond to messages.

Voice over Internet Protocol

Cell phone service is still not 100 percent reliable. Dropped calls and poor reception are a problem in many areas. In addition, the call quality of landline phone service is often superior to cell phone call quality. Therefore, many people who run home businesses or make business calls from their home maintain a landline to ensure high voice quality of calls. In many instances, landline phone plans can be cheaper than cell phone plans, especially for international calls. Therefore, you may want to consider a style of landline phone service called VoIP (Voice over Internet Protocol).

How is VoIP different from regular telephone service? Voice over Internet Protocol (VoIP) is a form of voice-based Internet communication that turns a standard Internet connection into a means to place phone calls, including long-distance calls. Traditional telephone communications use analog voice data and telephone connections. In contrast, VoIP uses technology similar to that used in e-mail to send your voice data digitally over the Internet.

What do I need to use VoIP? For the simplest and least costly VoIP service, you need speakers, a microphone, an Internet connection, and a VoIP provider (see Figure 16). Depending on the provider you choose, you also may need to install software or a special adapter. Creating a VoIP account with Skype (**skype.com**) is similar to creating an instant messaging (IM) account. Skype requires that both callers and receivers have the company's free software installed on their computers. Another similarity to IM is that with Skype you can change your online status, look at your contact list, and decide whom you want to talk to. Other VoIP services, such as Vonage

Figure 15

Microbrowser software for phones like Opera lets you quickly switch between open browser windows.

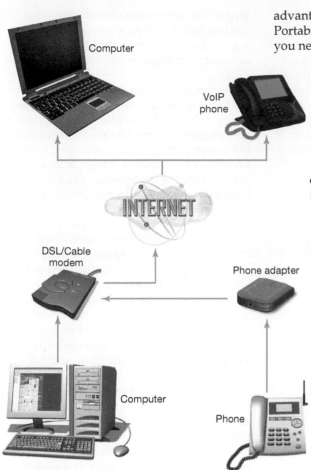

Computer

VoIP phone

INTERNET

DSL/Cable modem

Phone adapter

Computer

Phone

Figure 16

Depending on your VoIP service, you can hold conversations through a computer, a special VoIP telephone, or a regular telephone with an adapter.

(**vonage.com**), are a bit more complicated to set up and are not free. You can use your own telephone by connecting your phone to a special adapter that the company provides, or you can buy a special IP phone that connects to your broadband Internet connection or to a USB port on your computer.

One limitation of VoIP used to be that when you made a call, you had to be at your computer. WiFi (wireless Internet) IP phones, however, make it possible to place VoIP calls from any WiFi hot spot location. And there are Skype applications available for many mobile devices, like the iPhone and the Sony PSP. You can use these devices from any WiFi spot to make free calls to other Skype users or make low-cost calls to non-Skype users.

What are the advantages and disadvantages of VoIP? For people who make many long-distance phone calls, the

advantage of VoIP is it's free or low cost. Portability is another advantage because all you need is an Internet connection. With Internet accessibility so abundant, you can keep in touch with friends and family no matter where you are. As long as you are covered by a WiFi signal, you can plug in your headset or IP phone, sign on to your VoIP service, and make your call.

Although VoIP is affordable and convenient, it does have drawbacks. Some people regard sound quality and reliability issues as VoIP's primary disadvantages. Another drawback is the loss of service if power is interrupted. Although many traditional phones do not depend on electricity, your Internet connection and IP phone do. One serious drawback when VoIP service was first offered to the public was the inability for 911 calls to be traced back to the caller, unlike with a traditional phone. The FCC now requires all VoIP providers to provide traceable 911 services.

Another issue with VoIP is security. Security risks are similar to the risks associated with e-mail (such as spam) and fraud (such as when a hacker breaks into a VoIP system to

BITS AND BYTES

How Do You Find Your WiFi?

Detecting a nearby WiFi signal is important if you are looking for Internet connectivity while you are on the move. Some notebooks have a built-in WiFi scanner that displays a row of lights on the case whenever a WiFi signal is available. Keychain fobs that light up when they detect WiFi signals in the vicinity are also available.

If you are running Windows 7, the Connect to a Network dialog box (accessible from the Network and Sharing Center) shows the strength of all wireless networks within range of your computer.

At ThinkGeek (**thinkgeek.com**), you may find the most easy-to-use WiFi detector ever. The WiFi Detector t-shirt has a logo that lights up to indicate the signal strength of a nearby WiFi network (see Figure 17). Find your WiFi and look . . . well, look geeky while doing so!

Figure 17

The WiFi Detector T-shirt makes a statement—a geeky statement.

make unauthorized calls). These are real risks but they are avoidable if you take proper precautions. In addition, encryption services (similar to those used with e-mail) that convert data into a form that is not easily understood by unauthorized people are being deployed to help protect the very nature of calls made over the Internet. Despite these concerns, VoIP continues to enjoy explosive growth, and the technology will continue to improve.

What new features come with having an Internet-based digital phone at home? Once you are using an Internet-based digital phone system, new features become possible. You can have your telephone messages automatically bundled up as e-mails and sent to your account. If you are watching television and a call comes in, it can be displayed on the screen with caller ID information. Many cable delivery companies are bundling digital phone services in for free if you already purchase cable and television through them, so the price may be attractive.

"How do I keep my cell/ smartphone number private?"

Cell Phone/Smartphone Security

Can I get a virus on my cell/ smartphone? Although viruses can already infect cell phones, manufacturers and software engineers are bracing themselves for a tidal wave of viruses targeted to cell/smartphones. With half of users reporting that they send confidential e-mails using their phones and one-third of users indicating that they access bank account or credit card information, cell/smartphones are the next most likely realm of attack by cybercriminals. The potential of cell/smartphone

ACTIVE HELP-DESK **Keeping Your Data on Hand**

In this Active Helpdesk call, you'll play the role of a helpdesk staffer, fielding calls about smartphones—what you can use them for, what internal components and features they have, and how you can synchronize these mobile devices with your computer.

viruses ranges from the mildly annoying (certain features of your phone stop working) to the expensive (your phone is used without your knowledge to make expensive calls).

Symantec, McAfee, and F-Secure are the leading companies currently providing antivirus software for mobile devices. Products are designed for specific cell phone operating systems; for example, Symantec Mobile Security for Symbian is designed for cell phones running the Symbian OS. Often businesses will have their information technology department install and configure an antivirus solution like this for all the phones used in the organization. Although viruses plaguing cell phones have not yet reached the volume of viruses attacking PC operating systems, with the proliferation of mobile devices it is expected that such virus attacks will increase. If no antivirus program is available for your phone's operating system, the best precautions are common sense ones. Check the phone manufacturer's Web site frequently to see whether your cell/smartphone needs any software upgrades that could patch security holes. In addition, remember that you should not download ring tones, games, or other software from unfamiliar Web sites.

How do I keep my cell/smartphone number private? It seems that every time you fill out a Web form someone is asking for your phone number. If you are concerned about widely distributing your cell/smartphone number and potentially inviting lots of unwanted solicitation calls, you should consider using a virtual phone number. A virtual phone number is a phone number you create that can be assigned to ring on existing phone numbers (such as your cell phone). Companies such as Telusion (**tossabledigits.com**) provide these virtual numbers. Then, when you are filling out a registration form for some Web service, you can input your virtual phone number in the Web form instead of giving out your number. When you set up the virtual account, you can restrict the hours that you will receive calls from that number (no more 2 a.m. telemarketing calls), and if you are receiving many unwanted calls, you can disable the virtual number without affecting your cell/smartphone service.

Digital Media and Information

The entertainment industry has become an all-digital field. Today, videos, music, and photographs are created using digital recording devices, processed using digital software systems, and delivered over digital distribution channels. What does this mean for you and your use of music, photography, and video?

How is digital media created? All digital media, whether an image, a song, or a video, has the same basis— digitized information. Figure 18 shows the process of creating digital information for a musical selection. This process is described below:

1. Playing music creates analog waves.

2. A microphone feeds the sound waves into a chip called an *analog-to-digital converter (ADC)* inside the recording device.

3. The ADC digitizes the waves into a series of numbers.

4. This series of numbers can be recorded onto CDs and DVDs or sent electronically.

5. On the receiving end, a playback device such as a CD player or DVD player is fed that same series of numbers. Inside the playback device is a digital-to-analog converter (DAC), a chip that converts the digital numbers to a continuous analog wave.

6. That analog wave tells the receiver how to move the speaker cones to reproduce the original waves, resulting in the same sound as the original.

More precisely, the digital wave will be *close* to exact. How accurate it is, or how close the digitized wave is in shape to the original analog wave, depends on the sampling rate of the ADC. The **sampling rate** specifies the number of times the analog wave is measured each second. The higher the sampling rate, the more accurately the original wave can be re-created. However, higher sampling rates also produce much more data, and therefore result in bigger files. For example, sound waves on CDs are sampled at a rate of approximately 44,000 times a second. This produces a huge list of numbers for even a single minute of a song!

When sounds or image waves are digitized, it means that analog data is changed into digital data—from a wave into a series of numbers. The digital data is perfectly reproducible and can be distributed easily on CDs and DVDs or through the airwaves. The data also can be easily processed by a computer.

Digital Music

How can I carry music files easily? **Portable media players (PMPs)** are small portable devices (such as an iPod) that enable you to carry your MP3 files around with you. Many PMPs handle video and still images, as well as music files. Many smartphones are capable of storing and playing media files, but for the best experience, a dedicated media player, such as a portable media player, is often the optimal choice because PMPs tend to offer more features and storage.

Depending on the player, you can carry several hours of music or video—or possibly your entire CD collection—in an incredibly small device. For example, an Apple iPod classic with a 160 GB hard drive is 4.1 inches by 2.4 inches (and only 0.41 inch thick), yet it can hold as many as 40,000 songs, or 200 hours of video. The most compact players are slightly larger than a flash drive

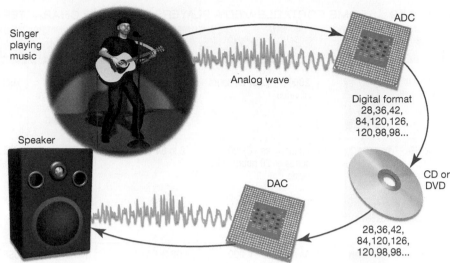

Singer playing music

Speaker

Analog wave

ADC

Digital format
28,36,42,
84,120,126,
120,98,98...

CD or DVD

DAC

28,36,42,
84,120,126,
120,98,98...

Figure 18

During the complete recording process, information changes from analog form to digital data and then back again to analog sound waves.

Figure 19 | SOME PORTABLE MEDIA PLAYERS AND THEIR CHARACTERISTICS

	Media Capacity	Built-In Flash Memory	Hard Drive Capacity	Connection to Computer	Other Features
Sansa Fuze Player 	2000 songs or 24 hours of video	2 GB to 8 GB	None but 16 GB micro SD card supported	USB 2.0 port	FM radio, voice recorder and available "radio" cards prefilled with 1000 songs.
Zune HD 	As many as 16,000 songs or 20 hours of HD video	16 to 64 GB	None	USB 2.0 port or wireless	Has HD radio, OLED screen, multitouch navigation.
Apple iPod touch 	As many as 14,000 songs or 80 hours of video	8 GB to 64 GB	None	USB 2.0 port	Weighs only 4.05 ounces; flash memory enables skip-free playback.
Apple iPod classic 	As many as 40,000 songs or 200 hours of video	None	160 GB	USB 2.0 port	Has calendar feature that syncs with Outlook; can serve as a small, portable hard drive.
Archos 7 	As many as 2,000 songs or 24 hours of video	2 GB to 8 GB	None but 32 GB SDHC card supported	USB 2.0 port	Includes 7″ screen display, WiFi, and touch screen.

(although they hold far less music than the iPod). Figure 19 shows several models of PMPs, all of which connect to computers via USB 2.0 ports.

Are all music files MP3 files? The letters at the end of a file name (the file extension) indicate how the data in the file is organized. MP3 is the name of just one type of file format used to store digital music, but many others exist, such as AAC and WMA. There are also many video formats such as DivX, MPEG-4 (which usually has an .mp4 extension), WMV, and XviD. All file formats compete on sound and video quality and *compression*, which relates to how small the file can be and still provide high-quality playback. If you buy a song from the iTunes Music Store, for example, you receive an .aac format file. AAC files can be played only on iPods but can be converted to the more widely used MP3 or Windows Media Audio (WMA) formats. WMA files can be played on a wide variety of MP3 players. Most PMPs that support video playback can play a wide range of video formats.

Are PMP devices the only choice for portable media management? PMP devices are not the only choice for portable media management. A number of electronic devices now incorporate the capability to carry electronic files and play music and video files. Some models of digital cameras, such as the Samsung NV3, have support for playing both music and videos. Gaming devices such as the Sony PlayStation Portable (PSP) allow you to play video games, play music and videos, and browse the Internet.

How do I know how much digital media a PMP can hold? The number of songs or hours of video a portable media player can hold depends on how much storage space it has. Most PMPs use built-in **flash memory**, a type of nonvolatile memory, to store files. Most PMPs that support video use a hard drive instead of flash memory and can store a much greater amount of music and video. Less expensive PMPs use flash memory (ranging from 1 GB to 32 GB), whereas models that are more expensive use built-in hard drives, which provide as much as 160 GB of storage. Some of the PMPs that use flash memory allow you to add storage capacity by purchasing removable flash memory cards.

Another factor that determines how much music a player can hold is the quality of the MP3 music files. The size of an MP3 file depends on the digital sampling of the song. The same song could be sampled at 320 kbps or 64 kbps. The size of the song file will be five times larger if it is sampled at 320 kbps rather than the lower sampling rate of 64 kbps. The higher the sampling rate, the better quality the sound—but the larger the file size.

How do you control the size of an MP3 file? If you are *ripping*, or converting, a song from a CD into a digital MP3 file, you can select the sampling rate yourself. You decide by considering what quality sound you want, as well as how many songs you want to fit onto your MP3 player. For example, if your player had 1 GB of storage and you have ripped songs at 192 kbps, you could fit about 694 minutes of music onto the player. The same 1 GB could store 2,083 minutes of music if it were sampled at 64 kbps. Whenever you are near your computer, you can connect your player and download a different set of songs, but you always are limited by the amount of storage your player has.

What if I want to store more music or video than the memory on my PMP allows? Some PMPs allow you to add memory by inserting removable flash memory cards. Flash memory cards are quiet and light, use tiny amounts of power, and slide into a special slot in the player. If you've ever played a video game on PlayStation or Xbox and saved your progress to a memory card, then you have used flash memory. Because flash memory is nonvolatile, when you store data on a flash memory card, you won't lose it when you turn off the player. In addition, flash memory can be erased and rewritten with new data. PMPs use a variety of different types of flash cards.

How do I transfer media files to my portable media player? All portable media players come with software that enables you to transfer audio and video files from your computer to the player. As noted earlier, players that hold thousands of songs and hours of video use internal hard drives to store the files. For example, devices such as Apple iPods can hold several gigabytes of data. To move large volumes of data between your computer and your PMP, you want a high-speed port. Most PMPs use a USB 2.0 port, but some players may use FireWire ports, which provide comparable throughput. Using a USB 2.0 port, you can transfer two dozen MP3 files to the iPod in less than 10 seconds.

> **Audio receivers now come with a port to connect a PMP device directly.**

What if I want a lot of people to listen to my digital music? PMPs are great for individual listening, but to share music from a PMP, you have to connect it to an alternative device. Many audio receivers now come with a port or a dock so that you can connect a PMP device directly to them as another audio input source, like a CD player or a television. Most new cars are equipped with at least an auxiliary input to the speaker system to support connecting a PMP; others have a fully integrated software system that displays and runs the PMP playlists. There are alarm clocks and home speaker docks that can mate with a PMP and broadcast brilliant sound.

How did the shift to digital music impact the music industry? The initial MP3 craze was fueled by sites such as MP3.com, which originally stored its song

files on a public server with the permission of the original artists or recording companies. Therefore, you were not infringing on a copyright by downloading songs from sites such as MP3.com (which still exists and now provides free music in streaming format).

Napster was a file exchange site created to correct some of the annoyances found by users of MP3.com. One such annoyance was the limited availability of popular music in MP3 format. With the MP3 sites, if you found a song you wanted to download, the link to the site on which the file was found often no longer worked. Napster differed from MP3.com because songs or locations of songs were not stored in a central public server, but instead were "borrowed" directly from other users' computers. This process of users transferring files between computers is referred to as **peer-to-peer (P2P) sharing**. Napster also provided a search engine dedicated to finding specific MP3 files. This direct search and sharing eliminated the inconvenience of searching links only to find them unavailable.

The problem with Napster was that it was so good at what it did. Napster's convenient and reliable mechanism to find and download popular songs in MP3 format became a huge success. The rapid acceptance and use of Napster—at one point, it had nearly 60 million users—led the music

industry to sue the site for copyright infringement, and Napster was closed in June 2002. Napster has since reopened as a music site that sells music downloads and is sanctioned by the recording industry.

The reaction of the recording industry was to continue to enforce its absolute ownership over digital forms of its music. The industry even filed legal actions against individuals who had downloaded large amounts of music from Internet sites. This heavy-handed reaction to the new era of digital music ultimately backfired and left the music industry scrambling. Overall music sales in 2009 were about half what they were at the industry's peak. The record industry is still trying to counter losing CD sales to digital forms of music. The approach they took early on did not allow them to adapt quickly enough to the new business models required by the shift to digital technologies.

So if I don't pay for a music download, is it illegal? Although you need to pay for most music you download, some artists post songs for free. Business models are still evolving as artists and recording companies try to meet audience needs while also protecting their own intellectual property rights. Several different approaches exist. One is to deliver something called *tethered downloads* in which you pay for the music and own it, but are subject to restrictions on its use.

Another approach is to offer *DRM-free* music, which is music without any digital rights management. These song files can be moved freely from system to system. For example, Apple's iTunes store currently sells only DRM-free types of music. A DRM-free song can be placed on as many computers or players as you wish. Other sites offer subscription services. For a monthly fee, Napster to Go allows you to download as many songs as you like to your MP3 player. These songs will be usable, however, only as long as you are paying the monthly subscription fee.

Why buy any music if peer-to-peer (P2P) sharing sites are still operating? When Napster was going through its legal turmoil, other P2P Web sites were quick to take advantage of a huge opportunity. Napster was "easy" to shut down because it used a central index server that queried other Napster computers for requested songs. Current P2P protocols (such as LimeWire and BearShare) differ

Digital Lifestyle: Managing Digital Data and Devices

from Napster in that they do not limit themselves to sharing only MP3 files. Video files are obtainable easily on P2P sites. More importantly, these sites don't have a central index server. Instead, they operate in a true P2P sharing environment in which computers connect directly to other computers. This makes them a prime source of unwanted viruses and spyware.

The argument these P2P networks make to defend their legality is that they do not run a central server like the original Napster, but only facilitate connections between users. Therefore, they have no control over what the users choose to trade. Note that not all P2P file sharing is illegal. For example, it is legal to trade photos or movies you have created with other folks over a P2P site.

People who oppose such file-sharing sites contend that the sites know their users are distributing files illegally and breaking copyright laws. Be aware that having illegal content on your computer, deliberately or by accident, is a criminal offense in many jurisdictions.

Will PMPs eliminate radio stations? Radio stations have always had certain advantages: early access to new music, and personalities and conversations that add to the listening experience. However, the Internet allows artists to release new songs to their fans immediately (on sites such as mp3.com) and without relying on radio airtime. This opens up new channels for artists to reach an audience and changes the amount of power radio stations have in the promotion of music. Many radio stations have increased listenership by making their stations available through Internet

sites and by broadcasting in high-definition quality.

Another development that competes with radio (and television) is *podcasting*, which allows users to download audio and video content and then listen to those broadcasts on their PMPs whenever they want. Podcasting is paving the way for anyone to create a radio or television show at home and distribute it easily to an audience. Using free software such as Audacity (**audacity.sourceforge.net**) and a microphone, you can record voice-overs, sequence songs, and generate special effects for your recordings. Loyal fans can use podcasting software such as Juice (**juicereceiver.sourceforge.net**) or iTunes (for Windows or Mac) to find a podcast's latest episode and automatically transfer it to their portable media players. Plugging your iPod into a data port on your computer causes the iPod to search iTunes for new content from the podcasters you subscribe to and then automatically transfers the new files to your iPod. Podcasts are easy to subscribe to and download using iTunes (see Figure 20).

Digital Navigation

How has digitized information impacted navigation? In the last few years, stand-alone **GPS (global positioning system)** devices have dropped dramatically in price and size. Small, handheld units deliver turn-by-turn instructions and real-time traffic information. GPS units are available with a wide range of features.

Garmin, for example, offers a wide range of services on its line of GPS units. A Map

Figure 20

iTunes makes it easy to subscribe to and manage podcasts.

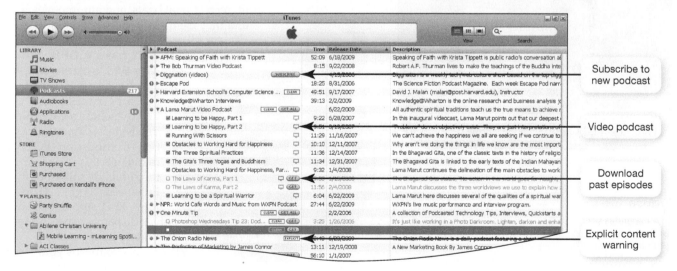

Figure 21

In addition to the driving applications shown, the Garmin Nuvi series GPS devices are also able to provide Internet services.

mode displays your location and the current speed limit on a map that is updated in real time as you drive. When you enter a series of destinations, an optimal route is developed for you. A voice warns you of lane changes and approaching turns, giving you directions using the actual street name (such as "Turn right on Hancock Avenue"). Lane Assist flips into a 3D display mode and shows you how to navigate through lane changes in highway merges. If you miss a turn, the unit automatically recalculates the required route and gives you directions to get back on course. Flip to another screen, and it shows you how far you have to drive to the next gas station, restaurant, or hospital. Some models automatically mark the location of your car when you remove them from the vehicle, and can give you step-by-step directions back to your car.

How do I get GPS in my car? Most automotive companies now offer GPS systems as installed options in their vehicles. Of course, GPS navigation can be added to any vehicle using a portable GPS device or a PDA/smartphone equipped with GPS (see Figure 21), or by adding GPS software and accessories to your notebook.

How does the GPS system work? Built and operated by the U.S. Department of Defense, the global positioning system is a network of 21 satellites (plus 3 working spares) that constantly orbits the Earth. GPS devices use an antenna to pick up the signals from these satellites and use special software to transform those signals into latitude and longitude. Using the information obtained from the satellites, GPS devices determine the geographical location anywhere on the planet to within 3 feet (see Figure 22). The exact accuracy depends on such things as atmospheric conditions, and interference from obstacles like mountains or buildings. Because they provide such detailed positioning information, GPS devices are now used as navigational aids for aircraft, recreational boats, and automobiles, and they even come in handheld models for hikers.

If I don't have a GPS, how does the 911 system know where I am? By the end of 2005, every cell phone had to include a GPS chip. The Federal Communications Commission (FCC) mandated this to enable the complete rollout of the Enhanced 911 (E911) program. E911 automatically gives dispatchers precise location information for any 911 call. It also means your

Figure 22

GPS computes your location anywhere on Earth from a system of orbiting satellites.

phone records may include this precise tracking information, which indicates where you are when you make a call.

Can I use the GPS chip on a child's cell phone? Cellular phone providers offer plans (for a monthly fee) that allow you to track where a phone is at any given time via a Web site. For example, AT&T's service Family Maps allows parents to track all of the phones on their family plan in real time. Locations of all phones are displayed over the Web on a map, or the service will send an automatic text message alert with the phone's location at a specific time each day. So a parent could have a text or e-mail sent with their daughter's phone location each day at 3 p.m. to be sure the she made it home from school. The person being tracked cannot turn off the service.

Do GPS devices carry other information? Full-featured GPS models such as the Garmin Nuvi 705 series include MP3 players, audio book players, and the capability to display photos and connect to the Internet. Using Internet services such as MSN Direct, your GPS can keep you informed about the weather, traffic backups, local movie times, and even local gas prices.

Digital Photography

What is "analog" photography?
Before digital cameras hit the market, most people used some form of 35-mm single-lens reflex (SLR) camera. When you take a picture using a traditional SLR camera, a shutter opens, creating an aperture (a small window in the camera) that allows light to hit the 35-mm film inside. Chemicals coating the film react when exposed to light. Later, additional chemicals develop the image on the film, and the image is printed on special light-sensitive paper. A variety of lenses and processing techniques, special equipment, and filters are needed to create printed photos from traditional SLR cameras.

What is different about digital photography? Digital cameras do not use film. Instead, they capture images on electronic sensors called *charge-coupled device (CCD) arrays* and then convert those images to digital data, long series of numbers that represent the color and brightness of millions of points in the image. Unlike traditional cameras, digital cameras allow you to see your images the instant you shoot them. Most camera models can now record digital video as well as digital photos.

How do I select a digital camera?
With hundreds of models to choose from, where do you begin? The first question to answer is whether you want a compact "point-and-shoot" model camera or a more serious digital SLR. The larger digital SLR cameras allow you to switch among different lenses and offer features important to serious amateur and professional photographers (such as depth-of-field previewing). Although having such flexibility in moving up to a larger zoom lens is a great advantage, these cameras are also larger, heavier, and use more battery power than the tiny point-and-shoot models. Think about how you will be using your camera and decide which model will serve you best in the long run.

"**What is smile shutter?**"

Next, you'll want to evaluate the quality of the camera on a number of levels. One great resource to use is Digital Photography Review (**dpreview.com**). The site's camera reviews evaluate a camera's construction as well as its features, image quality, ease of use, and value for the cost. In addition, the site provides comparisons to similar camera models by other manufacturers and feedback from owners of those models. Links are provided to several resellers, making it easy to compare prices as well.

Why not just use the camera on my cell/smartphone? Many cell/smartphones include a digital camera. These cameras often provide lower resolutions than stand-alone models and inferior lenses. Many features that photographers rely on are not often available in the cameras included on phones, such as different types of autofocus, image stabilization algorithms, and *smile shutter*, which waits to take a shot until your subject is smiling.

What determines the image quality of a digital camera? The overall image quality is determined by many factors: the quality of the lenses used, the file format and compression used, and the color management software. Another part of what determines the image quality of a digital camera is its **resolution**, or the number of data points it records for each image captured. A digital camera's resolution is measured in megapixels (MP). The prefix *mega* is short for millions. The word *pixel* is short for picture element, which is a single dot in a digital image. Point-and-shoot models typically offer resolutions from 10 MP to 15 MP. Professional digital SLR cameras, such as the Canon EOS-5D Mark II, can take photos at resolutions as high as 21.1 MP, but they sell for thousands of dollars. Figure 23 shows some popular digital camera models and the number of pixels they record at their maximum resolution.

If you're interested in making only 5″ × 7″ or 8″ × 10″ prints, a lower-resolution camera is fine. However, low-resolution images become grainy and pixelated when pushed to make larger-size prints. For example, if you tried to print an 11″ × 14″ enlargement from a 2 MP image taken using your cell phone's camera, the image would look grainy; you would see individual dots of color instead of a clear, sharp image. The 10 MP to 15 MP cameras on the market now have plenty of resolution to guarantee sharp, detailed images even with enlargements as big as 11″ × 14″.

What file formats are used for digital images? To fit more photos on the same size of flash memory card, digital cameras allow you to choose from several different file types in order to compress, or squeeze, the image data into less memory space. When you choose to compress your images, you will lose some of the detail, but in return, you'll be able to fit more images on your flash card. The most common file types supported by digital cameras are raw uncompressed data (RAW) and Joint Photographic Experts Group (JPEG). Raw files have different formats and extensions depending on the manufacturer of a particular camera. The raw file records all of the original image information, so it is larger than a compressed JPEG file. JPEG files can be compressed just a bit, keeping most of the details, or compressed a great deal, losing some detail. Most cameras allow you to select from a few different JPEG compression levels.

Often cameras also support a very low-resolution storage option, enabling you to create files that you can easily attach to e-mail messages. This low-resolution setting typically provides images that are not useful for printing but are so small in size that they are easily e-mailed. Even people who have slow Internet connections are able to quickly download and view such images on-screen.

How do I move photos to my computer? If you just want to print your photos, you may not need to transfer them to your computer. Many photo printers can make prints directly from your camera or from a flash memory card, and many retailers, like CVS and Walmart, provide photo printing machines that can read directly from your memory card. However, transferring the photos to your computer does allow you to store them and frees your flash card for reuse.

Digital cameras have a built-in USB 2.0 port. Using a USB 2.0 cable, you can connect the camera to your computer and copy the converted images as uncompressed files or in a compressed format as JPEG files. Another option is to transfer the flash card from your camera directly to the built-in memory card reader on your computer. Some camera

Figure 23

Digital camera resolutions.

Panasonic Lumix G2 (12.1 MP)

Kodak V1273 (12 MP)

Canon EOS 5D Mark II (21.1 MP)

Sony Cybershot DSC-T1 (10.2 MP)

Samsung TL225 DualView (12.2 MP)

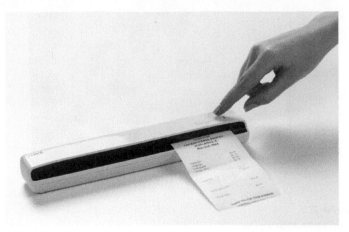

models support wireless network connections so that you can transfer the images without the fuss of putting a cable in place. If your model doesn't, you can purchase a memory card with built-in WiFi: the Eye-Fi. Eye-Fi will wirelessly transfer your photos to Google Picasa, Facebook, or one of 30 other Web destinations. It will also back up the photos and videos you take with your camera to your home computer. And when you are away from home, Eye-Fi comes with hot spot access so you can upload for free from any McDonald's, Starbucks, hotel, or airport.

Can I make my old photos digital? Obviously, not every document or image you have is in an electronic form. What about all the photographs you have already taken? What about an article from a magazine or a hand-drawn sketch? How can these be converted into digital format?

Digital scanners such as the ones shown in Figure 24 convert paper text and images into digital formats. You can place any flat material on the glass surface of the scanner and convert it into a digital file. Most scanner software allows you to store the converted images as TIFF files or in compressed form as JPEG files. Some scanners include hardware that allows you to scan film negatives or slides as well or even insert a stack of photos to be scanned in sequence.

Scanner quality is measured by its resolution, which is given in dots per inch (dpi). Most modern scanners can digitize a document at resolutions as high as 4,800 × 9,600 dpi, in either color or grayscale mode. You can easily connect a scanner to your computer using USB 2.0 or FireWire ports. Scanners also typically come with software that supports optical character recognition (OCR). OCR software converts pages of

handwritten or typed text into electronic files. You can then open and edit these converted documents with traditional word processing programs such as Microsoft Word. In addition, many scanners have a copy function that allows you to scan and print documents, taking the place of a copy machine.

How do I print a digital image? You can print a digital image using a professional service or your own printer. Most photo printing labs, including the film processing departments at stores such as Walmart and Target, offer digital printing services, as do many high-end online processing labs. The paper and ink used at processing labs are higher quality than what is available for home use and produce heavier, glossier prints that won't fade. You can send your digital photos directly to local merchants such as CVS and Walgreens for printing using Windows Live Photo Gallery. Online services, such as Flickr (**flickr.com**) and Shutterfly (**shutterfly.com**), store your images and allow you to organize them into photo albums or to create hard-copy prints, mugs, T-shirts, or calendars.

Photo printers for home use are available in two technologies: inkjet and dye sublimation (see Figure 25). The most popular and inexpensive ones are inkjet printers. Some inkjet printers are capable of printing high-quality color photos, although they vary in speed and quality. Some include a display window so that you can review the image as you stand at the printer, whereas others are portable, allowing you to print your photos wherever you are. Some printers even allow you to crop the image right at the printer without having to use special image editing software.

Figure 24

Scanners are available in a variety of shapes, but all of them can convert paper documents, photo prints, and strips of film negatives into digital data.

Digital Lifestyle: Managing Digital Data and Devices

Figure 25

The Sony DPP-F700 is both a 7-inch digital frame and a dye sublimation printer. With a click of the remote, you can print the image in 45 seconds.

Unlike inkjet printers, which use an inkjet nozzle, dye-sublimation printers produce images using a heating element. The heating element passes over a ribbon of translucent film that has been dyed with bands of colors. Depending on the temperature of the element, dyes are vaporized from a solid into a gas. The gas vapors penetrate the photo paper before they cool and return to solid form, producing glossy, high-quality images. If you're interested in a printer to use for printing only photographs, a dye-sublimation printer is a good choice. However, some models print only specific photo sizes, such as 4″ × 6″ prints, so be sure the printer you buy will fit your long-term needs.

Transferring images to a printer is similar to transferring them to your computer. If you have a direct-connection camera, you can plug the camera directly into the printer with a cable. Some printers have slots that accept different types of flash memory cards. Of course, you also can transfer your images to the printer from your computer if you have stored them there.

Do I need to print out my photos?
You may decide not to print your photos at all. As noted earlier, online albums let you share your photos without having to print them. There are a number of digital scrapbooking sites that let you electronically design scrapbooks. Portable devices, such as Apple's iPod and cell phones, also enable you to carry and display your photos. The iPod, for example, can be connected to a TV and deliver slide shows of your photographs, complete with musical soundtracks you have selected. If you have networked your home, a television connected to your network (or to a network-enabled device like a PlayStation 3 or a networked Blu-ray player) can display all the photos and videos stored on your computer.

Digital Video

Where does digital video come from?
Digital video that you watch comes from several sources, but now people often create their own digital videos. As a video creator, you may purchase dedicated digital camcorders to record digital video. Most cell phones can record video, and digital cameras take video as well as digital still shots. Webcams also work as inexpensive devices for creating digital video.

There are many other sources of digital video available to you now. Television is broadcasting in digitally formatted signals. The Internet delivers a huge amount of digital video through Google Video, YouTube, communities like Vimeo (**vimeo.com**), and webcasting sites like Ustream (**ustream.tv**). Sites like Hulu (**hulu.com**) rebroadcast many current television shows as well as films and movie trailers. Many pay services are available to deliver digital video to you. These include on-demand streaming from cable providers, iTunes, Netflix's Instant Watch films, and Amazon's Video On Demand download service.

How do I record my own digital video? Video equipment for home use stores information in a digital video (DV) format. This allows the cameras to be incredibly small and light. Such cameras don't require any tapes at all; they store hours of video on built-in hard drives or flash cards. Some models even record directly to DVD discs.

You can easily transfer video files to your computer and, using video editing software, edit the video at home, cutting out sections, resequencing segments, and adding titles. To do the same with analog videotape would require expensive and complex audio/video equipment available only in video production studios. You can save (or *write*) your final product on a CD or DVD and play it in your home DVD system or on your computer. For true videophiles, cameras and burners are now available for high-definition video format.

What if I decide to add some special effects and a sound track? Video editing software presents a storyboard or *timeline* with which you can manipulate your video file, as shown in Figure 26. You can review your clips frame by frame or trim them at any point. You can order each segment on the timeline in whichever sequence you like and correct segments for color balance, brightness, or contrast.

In addition, you can add transitions to your video such as those you're used to seeing on TV—fades to black, dissolves, and so on. Just select the type of transition you want from the drop-down list and drag that icon into the timeline where you want the transition to occur.

Video editing software also lets you add titles, animations, and audio tracks to your video, including background music, sound effects, and additional narration. You can adjust the volume of each audio track to switch from one to the other or have both playing together. Finally, you can preview all of these effects in real time.

There is a lot to learn about digital video editing, and with the number of choices available, it is easy to be overwhelmed. Examine online tutorial resources such as Izzy Video podcasts (**izzyvideo.com**) to learn how to make the most impact with the editing and effects you apply to your raw video footage.

What kinds of files will I end up with? Once you're done editing your video file, you can save (or export) it in a variety of formats. Figure 27 shows some of the popular video file formats in use today, along with the file extensions they use.

Figure 26

Adobe Premiere Elements allows you to build a movie from video clips and add sound tracks and special effects.

Figure 27	TYPICAL FILE FORMATS FOR DIGITAL VIDEO	
Format	**File Extension**	**Notes**
QuickTime	.mov .qt	You can download QuickTime player without charge from **apple.com/quicktime**. The pro version allows you to build your own QuickTime files.
Moving Picture Experts Group (MPEG)	.mpg .mpeg .mp4	MPEG-4 video standard adopted internationally in 2000; recognized by most video player software.
Windows Media Video	.wmv	Microsoft file format recognized by Windows Media Player (included with the Windows OS).
Microsoft Video for Windows	.avi	Microsoft file format recognized by Windows Media Player (included with the Windows OS).
RealMedia	.rm	Format from RealNetworks; popular for streaming video. You can download the player for free at **real.com**.
Adobe Flash Video	.flv	Adobe Flash video format, sometimes embedded in Shockwave files (*.swf).

So you just returned from your trip to the Grand Canyon and all your friends are raving about the quality of the photographs you took. You decide to put the photographs out on Flickr so your friends can see them. You also think that maybe someone might see your photos and want to use them in a commercial publication such as a magazine. Because you own the copyright to your photos, you control how they can be used—and you want to protect your rights. You add a disclaimer to Flickr indicating that all rights are reserved on your photos. Anyone who wants to use them will need to contact you and request permission.

All of a sudden, you are bombarded by dozens of requests for permission to use your photographs for all sorts of purposes. A high school student in Illinois wants to feature one of your photos on her travel blog. A church in Georgia wants to use a photo for their newsletter to illustrate a story about a church member's trip to Arizona. An advertising agency in Seattle wants to modify your sunrise photo by inserting a family on a camping trip into the photo. You want to be ethical and protect your ownership rights as well (maybe the ad agency might even pay you!), but how are you going to manage all these photo permission requests?

Copyleft, a play on the word copyright, is designed for this situation. Copyleft is a term for various licensing plans that enables copyright holders to grant certain rights to the work while retaining other rights. The GNU General Public License is a popular copyleft license that is used for software. For other works, the Creative Commons, a nonprofit organization, has developed a range of licenses that can be used to control rights to works.

Creative Commons has various types of licenses available based on the rights you wish to grant. The company provides a simple form to assist you with selecting the proper license for your work. Creative Commons provides two licenses at **creativecommons.org/about/licenses** that could simplify your life. An *attribution license* permits others to copy, distribute, and display your copyrighted work, but only if they give you credit in the way you specify. Under this license, the high school student could use one of your photos as long as he or she gave you credit.

A *noncommercial license* allows anyone to copy, distribute, and display your work, but only for noncommercial purposes. The church in Georgia could use one of your photos under this license because it is not profiting from its use.

Both of these licenses can also be used to cover **derivative works**. A derivative work is based on the original work (one of your photos) but is modified in some way. The ad agency that wants to modify one of your photos is seeking permission to create a derivative work. If you had used an attribution license, the ad agency could use your work for a derivative purpose, but only if it attributed the original work to you as the author. If you had used a noncommercial license, the ad agency could not use your work to make a profit for itself.

The obvious advantage to using these Creative Commons licenses is that people won't constantly annoy you with permission requests to use your work. These licenses explain exactly how you are willing to have your work be used. Also, many advocates of copyleft policies feel that creativity is encouraged when people are free to modify other people's work instead of worrying about infringing on copyright.

Opponents of Creative Commons licenses often complain that these licenses have affected their livelihoods. If millions of images are out on Flickr with Creative Commons licenses that permit free commercial use, professional photographers might have a tougher time selling their work. Furthermore, Creative Commons licenses are irrevocable. If you make a mistake and select the wrong license for your work, or you later find out a work is valuable and you've already selected a license that allows commercial use, you're out of luck.

Many people find listings of Creative Commons licenses confusing. If there is a Creative Commons disclaimer at the bottom of a group of photos, does that mean all the photos are available under that license, or just some of them? What actually constitutes commercial use? Is displaying Google Adsense ads on your blog commercial use?

Each of us needs to carefully consider the value of our intellectual property and decide how best to conduct our digital livelihood. Understanding the meaning of copyright, and copyleft, is important both so that you respect the rights of others and so that you can simplify your life in granting permission rights to the works you create.

Your choice of file format for your finished video will depend on what you want to do with your video. For example, the QuickTime streaming file format is a great choice if your file is really large and you plan to post it on the Web. The Microsoft AVI format is a good choice if you're sending your file to a wide range of users, because it's extremely popular and is commonly accepted as the standard video format for the Windows Media Player.

You also can try different compression choices to see which one does a better job of compressing your particular file. A **codec** (*compression/decompression*) is a rule, implemented in either software or hardware, that squeezes the same audio and video information into less space. Some information will be lost using compression, and there are several different codecs to choose from, each claiming better performance than its competitors. Commonly used codecs include MPEG-4, H.264, and DivX. There is no one codec that is always superior—a codec that works well for a simple interview may not do a good job compressing a live-action scene.

What if I want a DVD with a menuing system? If you want a DVD with a menuing system, you can use special DVD authoring software such as Pinnacle Studio or Adobe Encore DVD. These DVD software packages often include preset selections for producing video for mobile devices (like the Apple iPod or the Sony PSP). These programs can also create final DVDs that have animated menu systems and easy navigation controls, allowing the viewer to move quickly from one movie or scene to another. Home DVD players as well as gaming systems such as PlayStation and Xbox can read these DVDs.

What is the quickest way to get my video out to viewers? Because of the popularity of videos on the Web, products and services are now available that let you quickly upload your videos. One such product is the Flip SlideHD video camcorder, shown in Figure 28.

Flip camcorders, which are priced from $150, can record 1–4 hours of video depending on the model. After recording, simply flip out the USB connector and plug it into your computer. Flip has built-in software that lets you transfer the video file directly to YouTube or several other sites or e-mail the file. It's a simple solution that takes advantage of the easy Web-based distribution of video.

YouTube has a special Mobile Upload Profile that you can set up for your account. Once your unique e-mail address has been assigned, you can submit a video that you have on your phone to YouTube by e-mailing the file to the account address. Of course, it is illegal for you to upload videos you do not own. You also cannot take a piece of a copyrighted video and post it publicly. The Ethics in IT section in this chapter presents several legal and ethical situations that it is important for you to be aware of as a content creator in the digital age.

Webcasting, or broadcasting your video live to an audience, is another option that has become simpler. Inexpensive webcams (costing from $25 to $100) can be easily attached to your desktop or notebook computer. Many models of monitors have built-in webcams. Webcam models that are more expensive have motors that allow you to automatically rotate to track the sound, so you are always in the frame even if you are moving around the room. Services such as YouTube offer Quick Capture buttons, so with one click, your video can be recorded through your webcam and delivered to the Internet.

How can I distribute my video to the greatest number of viewers?
Sites like justin.tv or ustream.tv let you quickly set up to webcast your video as it is captured to a live Internet audience. You can also display an interactive chat next to the video feed. Both the chat and the video are captured and archived for viewers who missed the live broadcast. iTunes offers free distribution of video podcasts, so you can build a following there for your video work.

Are the television shows and movies I watch digital? There are a number of ways you can create video content yourself; but probably most of the video you consume in a typical week was created by someone else—movie studios, television studios, or other students. The number of sources we have for video has increased dramatically since digital video appeared. Because the hardware for capturing video and the software for doing professional-level editing have become so inexpensive, there are few barriers to anyone making video. Further, because the opportunities for distributing video have broadened so much and become so instantaneous, there is an ever-growing market for more video.

Is all video digital video now? The switch to digital video as a broadcasting medium has happened over the past few years. In June 2009, all television stations were required to make the move to digital signal broadcasting. **DTV.gov** is a site that keeps consumers current on using conversion boxes to allow older television sets to operate with the new digital signal.

Movie production studios have also been moving toward digital video for many years. George Lucas, a great proponent of digital technology, filmed *Star Wars Episode II: Attack of the Clones* completely in digital format way back in 2002. It played in a special digital release at digital-ready theaters.

Figure 28
The Flip SlideHD video camcorder can capture up to 4 hours HD video and quickly post it on Facebook or YouTube.

And in January 2005, the digital film *Rize*, by David LaChapelle, premiered at the Sundance Film Festival. It was streamed from computers in Oregon to a full-size cinema screen in Park City, Utah, beginning a new age of movie distribution.

Since the conversion to digital TV signals, are there any more "free" television signals? Digital television signals now flood the air around you and can be picked up by a digital antenna. If you live in an area with good "over-the-air" (OTA) reception, you can pick up crisp, high-quality digital versions of all the shows on local network affiliates for free.

How is HD different from "plain" digital? HD stands for *high definition*. It is a standard of digital television signal that guarantees a specific level of resolution and a specific *aspect ratio*, which is the rectangular shape of the image. A 1080 HD TV displays 1,920 vertical lines and 1,080 horizontal lines of video on the screen,

which is over six times as many pixels as standard definition. The aspect ratio used is 16:9, which makes the screen wider, giving it the same proportions as the rectangular shape of a movie theater screen (see Figure 29). This allows televisions to play movies in the widescreen format that they were created for, instead of "letterboxing" the film with black bars on the top and the bottom of the screen.

What types of connectivity are provided on modern television sets? As video sources have increased, so have the number and types of connectors on a television. A typical HD set has at least three HDMI connectors, allowing game consoles, Blu-ray players, and cable boxes to be connected and produce the highest-quality output. HDMI is a single cable, with just one plug, that carries all of the video and all of the audio information. That means there is one connector, not three for different parts of the video signal and another two for the stereo sound signals!

Many sets have a built-in SD card reader. This allows users to display slide shows of photographs captured by their digital cameras. A PC VGA port is also included on most sets. This allows you to feed your computer's output video signal directly to the television so you can display an Internet browser or work on your files on the big screen. Some sets are now incorporating a wireless network adapter so the set can stream video from the Internet without having a separate computer connected. Several manufacturers are offering TV sets that stream Internet content. Sony Bravia Internet Video link can deliver content on demand from a number of free sources (see Figure 30), and the Panasonic Viera Cast feature works in a similar fashion. Google announced that it is working with Sony and Logitech to offer Google TV. Google TV is built into some sets and also available as a set top box add-on. It allows a single search utility to check for content on the Internet, on your stored recorded programs, and on the TV guide listing.

What advantages are there to watching digital video? Because the signal can be stored into computer memory as it is delivered, a digital video

Figure 29

(a) Standard definition television has a more "square" aspect ratio, while (b) high-definition television matches the 16:9 ratio used in the motion picture industry without resorting to (c) letterboxing.

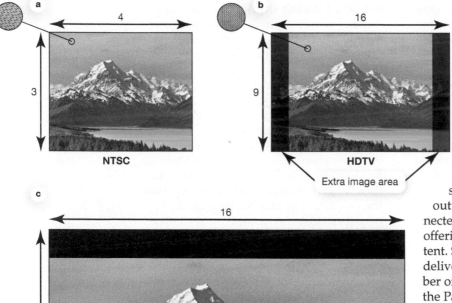

NTSC

HDTV

Extra image area

Letterbox

television show can be paused, or can be rewound in real time. Other information services can be integrated with the broadcast; so if a telephone call came through during the show, a pop-up could appear identifying the caller. The Sony Bravia series of televisions, for example, has Internet video capabilities that let you select "widgets" you can position on the screen to display the latest news, weather, sports, or other Internet downloads. In the future, there will be more interactivity integrated so you can participate in live polls or chats on-screen as the show is broadcast.

In movie studios, digital video is ushering in the age of "remixable" films. The components of these feature films—from production footage to soundtrack, dialogue, and sound effects—are available to the audience online, and each person is able to interact with and modify the film, creating a new plotline or a different ending. The MOD Films site (**modfilms.com**) is one place where remixers gather.

Can I record the digital video that comes over my television? There are a variety of digital video recorders (DVRs) available to record the digital video from your television. These can record in either standard or HD quality and store the information on a hard drive. Useful features include being able to record two shows at once, being able to download movie purchases or rentals from the Internet directly to the DVR unit, and easily moving stored content to a mobile device like an iPod or a notebook. Using a DVR, you can pause live TV or set up a schedule to capture every episode of a series, no matter when it airs. Models like TiVo even recommend new shows you might like based on what you have been watching. If you don't want to purchase a DVR or pay the monthly subscription fee for DVR service, you can install PVR (personal video recording) software on your computer. When connected to your cable signal, programs like BeyondTV (**snapstream.com**) and SageTV (**sagetv.com**) turn your computer itself into a DVR.

How else can I get digital video to my TV? In addition to the broadcast content coming in to your TV, there are a number of streaming sources of digital video. Cable providers offer a wide range of on-demand video services. Many older films, as well as shows such as exercise classes, are offered free of charge. Other

premium content, like new-release movies, is offered for a fee. Just one click and you can instantly watch any offered movie for 24 hours, with full control—stopping, starting, and rewinding. Other providers, like Netflix, also offer streaming video content. While Netflix's basic business model is to ship members DVDs physically in the mail, they now also offer Watch Instantly. Thousands of movies and TV series are available with just a click. You can view these shows on a television through any gaming console, a PC, an iPad, or a specialized device like the Roku digital video player.

Can I get digital video to watch on my portable device? Yes. Many DVR units, like TiVo, support software that allows you to transfer recorded shows to files on your PC and format them for viewing on an iPod, a PlayStation Portable, or another mobile device. There are also devices like Slingbox that take the video from your television and broadcast it to you over the Internet. With Slingbox, you can be in another room, or another country, and control and watch your home television on your notebook or your smartphone (see Figure 31).

Figure 30
Sony Bravia televisions use a wireless network adapter to stream digital video from a number of online sources.

Figure 31
Slingbox can send your digital television content to your notebook or phone, wherever you may be.

Digital Mobility and Access

Once you are comfortable with digital communication and digital media, you'll want to be able to communicate and to access your music, files, and videos whether you are in front of a desktop at home or in an airport while traveling. Access to your digital assets is required in a modern business environment and is a great benefit in your personal life. Earlier chapters discussed expensive solutions like notebook computers; but now there is a much wider range of devices that grant you access to your media and data wherever you are.

Selecting the Right Device

How do I select the right device for my needs? There are a wide range of computing devices on the market today that give you varying access to digital communication and digital media. A **netbook** runs a fully featured operating system but weighs in at 2 pounds or less. An **Internet tablet** is another type of very light, very portable device. Internet tablets do not offer full-size keyboards. Netbooks and Internet tablets can carry files, music, and videos as well as provide specialized services. Then there is the full range of notebooks and tablet computers, and new blends of various features are appearing in new devices all the time. Figure 32 lists the main features of several different mobile devices.

What if I don't need a phone but do need Internet access? Tiny, lightweight Internet-enabled devices are appearing that don't bother to include cell phone features at all. The Nokia N810 Internet tablet series (see Figure 33), for example, uses Skype or Gizmo for voice communications instead of a cell phone service. It has a high-resolution screen and WiFi connectivity so you can stream audio and video, use Web e-mail clients, and access Web sites. It features an RSS reader so you can peruse the latest from the sites you are following. Memory expands with SD expansion cards.

The Sony PlayStation Portable (PSP) can play video games but also includes a Web browser, Skype, and an RSS reader. It uses Sony Memory Sticks to store data

Figure 32 | MOBILE DEVICES: PRICE, SIZE, WEIGHT, AND CAPABILITIES

Device	Relative Price	Approximate Size	Approximate Weight	Standard Capabilities
Cell phone	$$ (Includes cost for the phone, a monthly plan, and Internet access)	5" × 2" × 0.5"	0.25 lb.	Voice, e-mail, some application software, and Internet connectivity
PMP	$$–$$$	4" × 2" × 0.5"	0.25 lb. or more	Storage of digital music, video, and other digital files
Smartphone	$$–$$$	4.5" × 2" × .75"	0.25 lb.	PIM capabilities, access to application software, and access to the Internet
Internet tablet	$$	6" × 3" × 0.5"	0.5 lb	Webcam, GPS, phone calls using Skype, sharp resolution, and widescreen display
Netbook	$$$$	10" × 7"	1–2 lbs.	8" to 10" screens and run full-featured operating systems and applications
Tablet PC	$$$$$	10" × 8" × 1"	3 lbs.	PIM capabilities, access to application software, access to the Internet, and special handwriting- and speech-recognition capabilities
Notebook	$$$$–$$$$$	10" × 13" × 2"	5 to 8 lbs.	All the capabilities of a desktop computer plus portability

files, videos, music, and images. The screen is a 4.3″ widescreen design with great clarity and brightness. The PSP can even connect over the Internet to your PlayStation 3 system at home and display the videos or music stored there for you wherever you are.

What if I need a larger screen and keyboard? If you require a larger screen and more processing power, then look at a category of emerging computer systems known as *netbooks*. Examples include the Asus Eee PC and the Dell Inspiron Mini 10 (see Figure 34). Netbooks pack major computing power into a tiny package, and manufacturers try to extend battery life as long as possible. Screen sizes are typically between 8″ to 10″, and keyboards are less than full sized. No optical drive is integrated but one can be connected as a separate peripheral via the USB port. Netbooks often come with a Windows operating system. Some users opt to install a flavor of Linux, however, because Linux requires fewer resources than Windows. Solid-state hard drives are a good choice for netbooks because they use less power and produce less heat. Many models include integrated webcams as well as Bluetooth, so while netbooks are small and light, they still can serve many functions.

New tablet entries also fall into this category. The Apple iPad has a touch keyboard that is almost full size in landscape mode. It has a 9.7″ multitouch screen and weighs in at only 1.5 pounds. Although the iPad

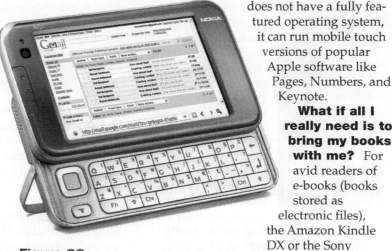

Figure 33

The Nokia N810 series Internet tablet features a touch screen and keypad and is designed primarily for Web surfing and sending e-mail.

does not have a fully featured operating system, it can run mobile touch versions of popular Apple software like Pages, Numbers, and Keynote.

What if all I really need is to bring my books with me? For avid readers of e-books (books stored as electronic files), the Amazon Kindle DX or the Sony Reader Digital Book could be what you are looking for. These feature internal RAM, but also support flash memory cards for more storage. You can get approximately 7,500 turned pages on one charge, so on long plane flights this may be the device you use most. The Apple iPad supports reading e-books as well, with the Amazon Kindle software app and with Apple's own iBooks bookstore. The iPad is full color, however, whereas both of the other readers display content in shades of gray. The iPad also supports video viewing, music, Internet browsing and thousands of apps on its 9.7″ multitouch screen (see Figure 35).

Ubiquitous Computing

What is in the future for our digital lifestyles? Mark Weiser, a researcher at Xerox's PARC laboratories, has predicted that "computing will be woven into the fabric of everyday life until it is indistinguishable from it." This concept is called **ubiquitous computing** (or *ubicom*). More and more styles of digital devices are being

Figure 34

Subnotebooks like the Asus Eee PC weigh in at less than two pounds but run fully featured operating systems.

Figure 35

The Apple iPad has a color 9.7" screen and lasts more than 10 hours on a single battery charge.

introduced, but there is a second force at work. Digital computing devices are increasingly embedded in appliances, clothing, cars—all the items we physically interact with in our day. The era of "smart things" is just beginning.

How will our lifestyles change as computing becomes everywhere and invisible? While we can't predict the future, there are trends in design that give us hints. Researchers and inventors like Mike Kuniavsky of ThingM are creating devices that exploit the new digital nature of our world to make tasks easier. The WineM product from ThingM is a good example (see Figure 36). WineM is a "smart" wine rack. Each bottle is labeled with a radio frequency identification (RFID) tag when it is stored by the owner. When it is time to pick the perfect bottle for dinner, the owner can ask the wine rack to show just the Chardonnay, and LEDs light up just those

bottles. WineM can also display which wines are ready to drink, or if any of your friends has a similar wine collection, or if the winery is having a sale. It updates information automatically and will e-mail or text you an alert when a bottle of wine is removed from the rack.

How is shopping changing with increased access to digital information? Recent studies show that 93% of adults in the U.S. ages 18–29 now have a cell phone. Combined with the explosion in popularity of social networking sites, consumers' experiences are changing. Shopping now begins with price comparison tools like ShopSavvy and RedLaser. These "location aware" tools compare prices between nearby stores and then also compare the prices with the best prices available online. Once you've selected a store, many different mobile apps let you take advantage of mobile coupons, called *mobicoupons*. A smartphone can simply read the barcode on the item, and then will display a barcode for a coupon. The cashier scans the mobicoupon right at the register. More and more sites are appearing that offer some type of mobile coupon, including Zavers, Yowza, mobiOpons, and Cell Fire. Future trends in this area include a tighter integration with the information customer loyalty programs already store about you. Based on location and your past buying preferences, specialized coupons could be designed and delivered through the mobicoupon system.

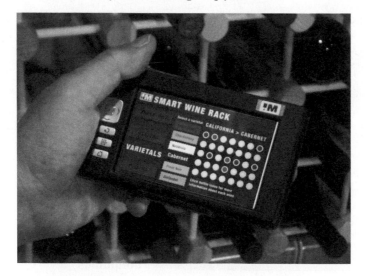

Figure 36

The smart wine rack uses WineM technology and answers queries from its controller, (a) like "Show me all of the California wines I have that are ready to drink and under $50 in value." (b) In response WineM lights up the bottles that fit the criteria.

How is marketing changing because of ubiquitous computing?

New strategies in marketing and communications are counting on the fact that so many people have a cell phone with a camera and Internet access. A new technology from Microsoft called Microsoft Tag transforms everyday things in the real world into live links to online information and entertainment. From your smartphone, simply snap a Tag image (see Figure 37) anywhere you see it—on a product, in an advertisement, on a sign or storefronts—and your phone takes you directly to a display of information. It might be a Web site, video, or a schedule, or a social network. To use Tag just download the free Tag reader on your Web-enabled camera phone.

Marketers also have to be aware of the phenomenon of "crowdsourcing"—checking in with the voice of the crowd. Consumers are using apps like MobileVoice to let you check in on what the verdict of the crowd is on the quality of an item. Forward-thinking companies are using this input to improve their products and services. TaxiHack, for example, allows phone users to comment on NYC cab drivers, and AT&T has an app to let customers report locations of coverage gaps.

How will our "ownership" of objects change with the new access to information?

The evolution of information to a digital form is allowing us to change our relationship to objects. Items like bicycles and cars can become "subscriptions" instead of large one-time purchases. Call a Bike is a program run in Germany. At most major street corners, there is a rack of Call a Bikes (see Figure 38). Place a call to the phone number printed on the bike, and it texts you a code you can use to unlock the bike lock. Ride the bike to where you're going. When you arrive, re-lock it. The amount of time you rode it automatically is billed (by the minute) to your phone.

City CarShare is another system using the digital communication of information to change our lifestyle habits. Many cities, like San Francisco and Philadelphia, now offer a City CarShare program. Residents sign up for the program and receive a key that has an RFID chip in it. All cars are connected to a central network. You can open a City CarShare car and start the engine only when your specific key is scheduled to open and start it. GPS technology is used to track

When you photograph this tag, the image on the right displays on your phone.

where the car is, whether it has been dropped off at the right location, and how far it has been driven. The entire process is transparent to City CarShare members. Members have 24/7 access to a vehicle—a truck, a hybrid, a convertible—when they need it, with very little advance notice, for a cost of about $6.00 an hour (gas and insurance included!).

Could ubiquitous computing technology improve the world?

The notion of an instantly connected population is an

Figure 37

In print advertising, Microsoft Tag technology can quickly take a reader to a display on their cell phone that includes more information and a mobile coupon.

Figure 38

Call a Bike uses digital technology to change our lifestyle from one of ownership to one of "subscription."

Computers in Society: "Ecosystem" of New Tools—Augmented Reality

We are familiar with digital data—comfortable with carrying around music, some files, contact lists, and calendars. But where is your data when you need it? Today, your information is locked in your cell phone, your iPad, or your notebook computer. This mobility is revolutionary compared to the access of any prior generations, but it still requires you to take out your notebook, open it up, boot it up, and initiate a request for information. What lies ahead?

The Media Lab of MIT provides some great clues. The Fluid Interfaces group works to develop new tools to bring our data more directly into the physical world. One of the most promising of these new tools is called Sixth Sense. It is a wearable device hanging around your neck consisting of a camera, a projector, and a mirror that can communicate with the Internet over wireless Bluetooth via the cell phone in your pocket. What Sixth Sense can do is augment your experience of reality by adding the information you need as you need it.

Say you are on your way to the airport and pull out your boarding pass. Sixth Sense uses pattern recognition to realize you are holding an airline ticket. It then goes out to the Internet to check if the flight is on time or if a gate change has been issued. If it has, the words *Delayed: 20 Minutes* suddenly appear on the top of the boarding pass (see Figure 39a). The information is no longer trapped in your mobile device—it is part of your environment. Or say you are in a bookstore and select the title *Ambient Findability*. As you hold the book, its Amazon rating appears on the cover (see Figure 39b). You open to the inside sleeve, and the comments from readers at Amazon begin to scroll over the page. Then you can tap any one of those comments for more detail.

Sixth Sense is the product of work by Pranav Mistry and his advisor Patti Maes. The product can also respond to gestures, so when you make a rectangle with your fingers, it takes a photograph. When you reach your destination, any flat surface such as a wall or table can be used to "dump" your photos into a "pile." Using your hands, you can shuffle the images, or resize or rotate an image. Or draw a watch-sized circle on your wrist, and Sixth Sense displays an analog watch face on your arm.

a

b

Figure 39

Sixth Sense recognizes what information you need added to your environment and displays it automatically.

idea that has appealed to futurists throughout time. Writer and futurist Jamais Cascio has presented ideas of how such a setting might bring all citizens into a more engaged role in changing the world. In his TED talk "The Future We Will Create" (**ted.com**), Cascio discusses how a smartphone-carrying population can work to create a better world—more sustainable, more secure, and more desirable.

Having an international population armed with cameras and a means to quickly distribute their video allows the invisible to become visible in many ways (see Figure 42). This transparency can be used to let us see the consequences of our behavior directly—and make changes. The Witness Project, founded by Peter Gabriel, uses this strategy to stop human rights abuses throughout the world (**witness.org**). Their slogan is "See it. Film it. Change it." Similar efforts are aimed at documenting the environmental state of the world. Environmental successes can be collected together along with evidence to document ecological crimes.

What if each of the cell phones distributed around the world had integrated atmospheric sensors? Then millions of points around the world would be "reporting" in on quality of air and water. And what if these sensors could monitor for flu viruses? Tagged with geographical information, the data could be combined with maps for easy viewing and analysis. Ideas like these are being explored by UCLA researcher Dr. Deborah Estrin, the

Figure 40

Any surface can become an input device using Sixth Sense.

In fact your hand is as good a flat surface as any to Sixth Sense (see Figure 40). Need to make a phone call? Sixth Sense will display a keypad on your palm. Tap out the number on the virtual keypad, and one touch of the red CALL button that appears on your palm places your call.

The shirt of the person walking toward you will also work as a projection surface. When a person walks up to us, we don't often pull out our cell phone and Google them before speaking, but as a person approaches a Sixth Sense wearer, it recognizes their face, heads off to their Facebook page or blog, and scans the most recent entries. It then projects the keywords that describe the person and their interests on their clothing as you watch them approach. Currently the Sixth Sense is small but not very stylish. The product is constructed from off-the-shelf components costing about $350. Within a few years its inventors believe it can be produced as a button-sized device, costing less than a cell phone costs now. You can monitor the progress of this device at **pranavmistry.com/projects/sixthsense**.

There are a number of iPhone apps available right now that use the integrated compass and camera of iPhone to add information to your environment. BionicEye is a $1 app that "augments" reality. When you point the camera's lens at a building, it shows you the nearest subway lines or restaurants, along with which direction you need to go in to get there (see Figure 41).

This kind of direct integration of digital information with the physical world around us is a hallmark of our digital future. Augmented reality combines the digital information we have accumulated in an immediate and spontaneous manner. So where will your new reality take you?

Figure 41

Augmented reality apps let you look through your phone's camera and see the world with extra information superimposed.

director of the Center for Embedded Network Sensing.

There is no exaggerating the range and severity of problems facing us, from environmental threats to dangers brought on by how we treat each other. Technological advances, like cell phones equipped with cameras and Internet access, could provide the means to change the course of our future. It will be our job to focus the direction of that change, using it as a response to the challenging problems facing us.

Figure 42

Using mobile devices we could document the environmental dangers and successes around the world.

1. What are the changes that have brought us a digital lifestyle?

The increased use of digital information has led to a period of greater creativity and control of our data. In a digital format, information is easy to carry, manipulate, and exchange. This has led to revolutionary changes in communication, entertainment media, and mobile computing.

2. How has the move to digital information affected the communication tools important to both the business world and life outside of work?

The age of digital information has brought new opportunities and challenges to businesses. Some have had to struggle to shift their business models to the new style of information. Because information can be shared so easily, issues of copyright and intellectual property have become critical. In our personal lives, we see products that allow us to interact with information in ways that had been too expensive or difficult before.

3. How do cell/smartphone components resemble a traditional computer, and how do they work?

Like a traditional computer, a cell/smartphone has a central processor, memory, and an operating system. These components work in the same way as in a computer to process information and support communications, software applications, and other services.

4. Why would I use VoIP, and what does it offer that is unique?

VoIP allows inexpensive communication using a computer or a WiFi-enabled phone. Because it is based on a digital format for information, it can support services like automatic delivery of phone messages to an e-mail account or texts to a mobile device.

5. How is digital media different from analog?

Digital media is based on a series of numeric data comprising number values that were measured from the original analog waveform. As a string of numbers, a digital photo or video file can be easily processed by modern computers.

6. What can I carry in a portable media player, and how does it store data?

Most PMPs can store any kind of digital information—photos, videos, or music files for example. Some PMPs store data on a hard drive, while others use flash memory. Some also allow the amount of memory to be upgraded, while others have a fixed amount of memory.

7. What ways are there for me to create and to watch digital video?

You can create digital video using any digital camera, webcam, or digital camcorder. Digital editing software allows you to add transitions, effects, and sound tracks. There are a great many sources of digital video, including free sources like YouTube and JustIn, as well as pay-per-view services like Amazon Video On Demand or cable providers' streaming video options.

8. What changes does ubiquitous computing bring to our lifestyles?

As computers become smaller and less obvious, they will begin to integrate into our lifelike appliances rather than be complicated tools. Ubiquitous computing is beginning to allow us to move some objects from an ownership model to a subscription service model.

Digital Lifestyle: Managing Digital Data and Devices

key terms

analog
analog-to-digital converter chip
base transceiver station
Bluetooth
cellular phone (cell phone)
codec
copyleft
data plan
derivative work
digital signal processor
flash memory
global positioning system (GPS)
Internet tablet
microbrowser
mobile switching center

multimedia message service (MMS)
netbook
peer-to-peer (P2P) sharing
portable media player (PMP)
resolution
sampling rate
short message service (SMS)
smartphone
syncing (or synchronizing)
telephony
ubiquitous computing
VoIP (Voice over Internet Protocol)
wireless Internet service provider
   (wireless ISP)
Wireless Markup Language (WML)

Word Bank

- analog-to-digital converter
- Bluetooth
- cell phone
- GPS
- Internet tablet
- microbrowser
- MMS
- netbook
- P2P
- PMP
- sampling rate
- smartphone
- SMS
- synchronize
- telephony
- ubiquitous computing
- VoIP
- WML

Instructions: Fill in the blanks using the words from the Word Bank above.

Elizabeth knows that everything seems to be "digital" these days. In the past, she carried a traditional SLR camera but now she uses her simple (1) _____ to take photos. She can connect wirelessly to the computer to transfer the images because the phone supports (2) _____. Sometimes she doesn't bother to do that because she has already sent a(n) (3) _____ message to a friend with the image. Her old phone couldn't do that because it only supported (4) _____. If she upgraded to a(n) (5) _____, she could actually make many refinements and edits to the image without transferring it to the computer at all.

Pete is a real fan of technology, and so he has selected a(n) (6) _____ instead of a cell phone. He's always near a WiFi signal, so he doesn't need an actual phone. He doesn't even pay for traditional phone service at home, where he uses (7) _____ instead of a landline. He's fallen in love with his new device for many reasons. It can give him driving directions with its built-in (8) _____. The (9) _____ software displays full HTML Web pages right on the device. To keep this device coordinated with the data on his computer, he makes sure to (10) _____ the data each night.

Niti can't quite decide what device will work best for his new life. He's moving to California and plans to be outside a lot, so he wants something very light. He thinks the two-pound (11) _____ might be ideal because he doesn't really need a full keyboard or a huge screen. When he's out biking, he'll just wear his (12) _____ on his arm to keep the tunes flowing. He downloads free songs offered by bands that are just starting out from a(n) (13) _____ site. The songs have a much lower (14) _____ than he usually demands, but at least they don't take up much space on his hard drive. He's heard that electronics are merging with clothing more and more, so maybe soon (15) _____ will lead to a T-shirt that can take care of his mobile music needs!

Instructions: Write a report providing answers to the question posed below, using as many of the key terms from the chapter as you can. Be sure the sentences are grammatically and technically correct.

You have a limited budget to spend on technology tools and toys in the years you will be a student. You are considering communication, entertainment media, and your need to be able to work and connect with your information when you are not at home. Which digital media services and products would you definitely invest in? How would you justify their value? What kinds of services and products would you use that are free or low cost? Has the migration to a digital lifestyle given you more freedom and creativity or just caused you more annoyance and expense?

Digital Lifestyle: Managing Digital Data and Devices

Instructions: Answer the multiple-choice and true–false questions below for more practice with key terms and concepts from this chapter.

Multiple Choice

1. Which is *not* a factor that determines the quality of images taken with a digital camera?
a. Lens quality
b. File format
c. Resolution
d. EyeFi

2. Which is the process of ensuring that two computer devices have the same data?
a. Mapping
b. Standardizing
c. Synchronizing
d. Transferring

3. The operating system of your cell phone is stored in
a. read-only memory.
b. the display.
c. the digital signal processor.
d. random-access memory.

4. If you want the lightest, most portable computing solution, you would purchase
a. a netbook.
b. a tablet PC.
c. an Internet tablet.
d. a notebook.

5. P2P is an acronym for
a. packet-to-packet networking.
b. peer-to-peer sharing.
c. person-to-person texting.
d. power-to-power delivery.

6. What software makes it possible to view Web pages on a cell phone?
a. Microbrowser
b. Extension

c. Push technology
d. 3G standard

7. Flash memory is a type of
a. nonvolatile memory.
b. hard drive memory.
c. SSD memory.
d. volatile memory.

8. VoIP is phone service that
a. works even when the electricity goes out.
b. works over an Internet connection.
c. requires no special setup for a secure connection.
d. has extremely high quality and is very reliable.

9. Which of the following is *not* true about modern televisions?
a. They incorporate wireless connectivity.
b. They allow other services, like caller ID, to be integrated.
c. They can use widgets to display sports and news updates.
d. They run word processing and slide presentation software.

10. Which service allows you use your cell phone to send messages that contain images?
a. MMS
b. ISP
c. SMS
d. MiFI

True–False

___F___ 1. All smartphones allow you to add more memory.

___T___ 2. Digital music files must be converted to the MP3 format if they are transferred to a mobile device.

___T___ 3. A codec is the algorithm that compresses and decompresses video files.

___F___ 4. If your digital camera doesn't support wireless connectivity, you can use a memory card with built-in WiFi.

___T___ 5. Some Internet-enabled devices like the Nokia N810 Internet tablet use Skype for voice communications instead of cell phone service.

Digital Lifestyle: Managing Digital Data and Devices

1. Choosing Mobile Devices to Fit Your Needs

As a student, which devices discussed in this chapter would have the most immediate impact on the work you do each day? Which would provide the best value (that is, the greatest increase in productivity and organization per dollar spent)? Consider the full range of devices, from cell phones to notebook systems.

2. Ready... Set... Act!

As a student, you often give presentations or take on student teaching assignments. What would be the steps for creating a digital video recording of one of your presentations? What tools would you need to record? What kind of file would you end up producing? How would you make a DVD from that? How would you distribute the video to a live Internet audience?

3. Do You Still Need a Phone?

Explore Skype (**skype.com**) as an alternative to paid telephone service. What equipment would you need to use Skype as your everyday communication medium? When would this be useful? What telephone services and features would you lose if you went to Skype?

4. Choosing the Best Phone

Your friend wants to trim down the number of different devices that she carries. Visit the most popular cellular providers' Web sites and research options. Which phone would you recommend to your friend, and why? Compare at least three different models of phones and list their price, music storage capacity, built-in memory, and expandability options.

a. Which of the three models you compared is the best value for your friend?
b. What special features does the phone you chose have? What accessories would you recommend your friend buy to make the phone more useful?
c. Would you suggest buying a refurbished phone? Why or why not?

5. iTunes U

Download a free copy of iTunes software. In the iTunes Store, explore the iTunes U podcast directory, which contains free audio and video lectures published by major universities.

a. Look for the MIT Open Courseware video podcasts. How many lectures are available from MIT (Massachusetts Institute of Technology)?
b. If each lecture were 90 minutes on average and approximately 200 MB in size, how much storage would it take to save all of the video lectures in every course published by MIT?
c. Is there a mobile device that can store and play that much content? What devices could store the lectures from all of the courses in mathematics offered by MIT Open Courseware?

Digital Lifestyle: Managing Digital Data and Devices

1. Corporate Mobile Communications Needs

Imagine your company is boosting its sales force and looking to the future of mobile technology. Your manager has asked you to research the following issues surrounding mobile communications for the company:

a. Do mobile communication devices present increased security risks? What would happen if you left a cell phone at a meeting and a competitor picked it up? Are there ways to protect your data on mobile devices?

b. Can viruses attack cell phones? Is there any special software on the market to protect mobile devices from viruses? How much would it cost to equip 20 devices with virus protection?

c. Is there a role for mobile communication devices even if employees don't leave the building? Which devices would be important for a company to consider for use within corporate offices? Are there software solutions that would work as well?

d. Should employees be allowed to use smartphones provided by the company for personal use even though files related to personal use might eat up potentially valuable memory and space? What restrictions should be put on personal use to protect the privacy of proprietary company information contained on the devices?

2. 4G Communications

The most recent generation of telecommunications (nicknamed "4G" for fourth generation) allows the speed of cellular network transmissions to hit 3-6 Mbps. How does that compare to dial-up and broadband access over wired networks? What implications does it have for information access and e-commerce? What download speed would be ideal? Upload speed? How would it change how you communicate?

3. Subscription versus Ownership

Consider the examples of Call-a-Bike and CarShare. Are there other businesses you can identify that would be able to take advantage of digital information and become subscription services instead of vendors of a physical product? What are the advantages to the consumer of subscription over ownership? What are the drawbacks?

4. Too Much Media?

Imagine you are a manager of 18 employees, all of whom work with constant Internet access. As a manager, what concerns might you have about their use of corporate bandwidth to download and view media files? Do you think it would benefit your business to block any MP3 file transfers? Should you put in place a block to prevent access to sites that store huge numbers of streaming videos? As a manager, are there concerns you might have if employees have digital cameras on their cell phones? Would your answers be different in an academic setting?

5. Mobile Devices on the Highway

Mobile devices used in vehicles are becoming the norm in today's society. Consider the following:

a. Several car manufacturers provide Bluetooth option packages for their vehicles. What advantages are there to having Bluetooth connectivity in your car? Are there any disadvantages?

b. Examine the Microsoft Sync software package. List the features and services it provides. If you were a salesperson with a territory that you covered by car, how would Sync help you?

Digital Lifestyle: Managing Digital Data and Devices

Instructions: Albert Einstein used *Gedankenexperiments*, or critical thinking questions, to develop his theory of relativity. Some ideas are best understood by experimenting with them in our own minds. The following critical thinking questions are designed to demand your full attention but require only a comfortable chair—no technology.

1. Digital Entertainment

Can you name a style of media that has not made the shift to digital? What advantages does digital photography offer? Digital video? What disadvantages come along with a digital format for entertainment media? Has the growth in digital media promoted an increased understanding between people or has it created more isolation?

2. The Ultimate Style

As ubiquitous computing continues to evolve, devices become lighter and smaller, and we are beginning to see a convergence of computing and clothing.

a. What would the ultimate convergent mobile clothing be for you? Is there a limit in weight, size, or complexity?

b. Can you imagine uses for technology in fashion that would support better health? Better social relationships? A richer intellectual life?

c. What other applications can you think of for a device like Sixth Sense? What kind of information needs to be displayed in our environment to be helpful?

3. Ubiquitous Means Everywhere

As we continue to see computing power distributed throughout all of our environment, there are shifts happening in how we relate to objects, how we shop, and how marketing is done. Consider three other areas of our lives—professional sports, buying a house, and staying healthy. How will ubiquitous computing change those activities? How would just knowing that every participant has a smartphone change the activity?

4. Too Much Information?

Consider the following questions:

a. Your rent a car that has a GPS installed. After you return it, the rental company uses the GPS data to determine whether you have driven the car at speeds above the speed limit. They then issue fines for violations of the rental contract. Does this lead to safer highways? Is it an infringement of your privacy?

b. Would you agree to insert a GPS-enabled tracking chip into your pet? Your child? What legislation do you think should be required regarding use of the tracking data from your phone records? Would you be willing to sell that information to marketing agencies? Should that data be available to the government if you were suspected of a crime?

5. Electronic Publishing

Explore the specifications of the Sony Portable Reader, the Barnes & Noble NOOK, the Amazon Kindle, and the Apple iPad. How would your study habits change if your textbooks were only delivered to you in electronic format on one of these devices? What unique advantages would there be? What disadvantages would there be? How would using such a device compare with just receiving the book as an electronic file, such as a PDF document, to your notebook computer?

Digital Lifestyle: Managing Digital Data and Devices

Convergence? Any Time Soon?

Problem

There are so many different mobile devices saturating the market that many people are left in a state of confusion. Either they are buying too many devices and not using them, or they are refusing to buy anything because of the dilemma of too many choices.

Task

Each team will assign a member to become the expert resource in one of the digital areas presented in this chapter: digital communication, digital media, or digital mobility. For each scenario described by a client, the group will select the minimum set of devices that would support and enhance the client's life.

Process

1. Consider the following three clients:
   - A retired couple who now travel for pleasure a great deal. They want to be involved in their grandchildren's lives and will need support for their health and personal care as they age.
   - A young family with two children, two working parents, and a tight budget.
   - A couple in which each individual is a physician and both adore technology.
2. Make two recommendations for your client in terms of digital technologies that will enhance their business or their lifestyle. Discuss the advantages and disadvantages of each technology. Consider value, reliability, computing needs, training needed and communication needs, as well as expandability for the future.
3. As a group, prepare a final report that considers the costs, availability, and unique features of the recommendations you have made for each client.
4. Bring the research materials from the individual team meetings to class. Looking at the clients' needs, make final decisions as to which digital technologies are best suited for each client.

Conclusion

Digital information has allowed the development of a new style of living, both at home and at work. With so many digital solutions on the market today, recommending digital communication, media management, and mobility options needs to focus on converging to the minimum set of tools that will enhance life without adding complication to it.

In this exercise, you will research and then role-play a complicated ethical situation. The role you play might or might not match your own personal beliefs; in either case, your research and use of logic will enable you to represent the view assigned. An arbitrator will watch and comment on both sides of the arguments, and together the team will agree on an ethical solution.

Topic: When Everyone Has a Voice

In the near future much of the world's population could be equipped with Internet-ready camera phones. Sensors on these phones could report location, measure for viruses, and compute pollution indexes, while the cameras could be used to document a range of human behavior. This could create changes in political movements, art, and culture as everyone's experience is documented and shared.

Research Areas to Consider

- Ted.com

- Mobilebehavior.com

- Witness project

- Center for Embedded Network Sensing

Process

Divide the class into teams.

1. Research the sources cited above and devise a scenario in which mobile access could make an impact politically or environmentally.
2. Team members should write a summary that provides background information for their character—for example: business owner, politician, reporter, and arbitrator—and details their character's behaviors to set the stage for the role-playing event. Then, team members should create an outline to use during the role-playing event.
3. Team members should arrange a mutually convenient time to meet for the exchange, either using the collaboration feature of MyITLab, the discussion board feature of Blackboard, or meeting in person.
4. Team members should present their case to the class, or submit a PowerPoint presentation for review by the rest of the class, along with the summary and resolution they developed.

Conclusion

As technology becomes ever more prevalent and integrated into our lives, more and more ethical dilemmas will present themselves. Being able to understand and evaluate both sides of the argument, while responding in a personally or socially ethical manner, will be an important skill.

Digital Lifestyle: Managing Digital Data and Devices

analog Waves that illustrate the loudness of a sound or the brightness of the colors in an image at a given moment in time.

analog-to-digital converter chip Converts analog signals into digital signals.

base transceiver station A large communications tower with antennas, amplifiers, and receivers/transmitters.

Bluetooth technology A type of wireless technology that uses radio waves to transmit data over short distances (approximately 30 feet for Bluetooth 1 and 60 feet for Bluetooth 2). Often used to connect peripherals such as printers and keyboards to computers or headsets to cell phones.

cellular phone (cell phone) A telephone that operates over a wireless network. Cell phones can also offer Internet access, text messaging, personal information management (PIM) features, and more.

codec A rule, implemented in either software or hardware, which squeezes a given amount of audio and video information into less space.

copyleft A simplified licensing scheme that enables copyright holders to grant certain rights to a work while retaining other rights.

data plan A connectivity plan or text messaging plan in which data charges are separate from cell phone calling charges and are provided at rates different from those for voice calls.

derivative work Intellectual property that is based on an original work but is modified in some way.

digital signal processor A specialized chip that processes digital information and transmits signals very quickly.

flash memory Portable, nonvolatile memory.

Global Positioning System (GPS) A system of 21 satellites (plus 3 working spares), built and operated by the U.S. military, that constantly orbit the earth. They provide information to GPS-capable devices to pinpoint locations on the earth.

Internet tablet A very light, portable computing device without a keyboard.

microbrowser Software that makes it possible to access the Internet from a PDA/smartphone.

mobile switching center A central location that receives cell phone requests for service from a base station.

multimedia message service (MMS) An extension of short message service (SMS) that enables messages that include text, sound, images, and video clips to be sent from a cell phone or PDA to other phones or e-mail addresses.

netbook A computing device that runs a full-featured operating system but weighs two pounds or less.

peer-to-peer (P2P) sharing The process of users transferring files between computers.

portable media player (PMP) A small portable device (such as an iPod) that enables you to carry your MP3s or other media files around with you.

resolution The clearness or sharpness of an image, which is controlled by the number of pixels displayed on the screen.

sampling rate The number of times per second a signal is measured and converted to a digital value. Sampling rates are measured in kilobits per second.

short message service (SMS) Technology that enables short text messages (up to 160 characters) to be sent over mobile networks.

smartphone A device that combines the functionality of a cell phone, a PMP, and a PDA into one unit.

syncing (or synchronizing) The process of updating data on portable devices (such as a cell phone or iPod) and computer so that they contain the same data.

telephony The use of equipment to provide voice communications over a distance.

ubiquitous computing The condition in which computing is so woven into the fabric of everyday life that it becomes indistinguishable from it.

VoIP (Voice over Internet Protocol) The transmission of phone calls over the same data lines and networks that make up the Internet. Also called *Internet telephony*.

wireless Internet service provider (wireless ISP) An ISP that provides service to wireless devices such as PDA/smartphones.

Wireless Markup Language (WML) A format for writing content viewed on a cellular phone or personal digital assistant (PDA) that is text-based and contains no graphics.

Chapter opener	grzym\Shutterstock	**Figure 19d**	Apple Computer, Inc.
		Figure 19e	Archos, Inc.
Figure 6	David Young-Wolff\PhotoEdit Inc.	**Figure 24**	NeatReceipts®
		Figure 28	Pure Digital Technologies Inc
Figure 7b	MWW Group	**Figure 31**	Sling Media, Inc.
Figure 8a	Koksharov Dmitry\Shutterstock	**Figure 33**	Nokia
		Figure 38	Superbass\Wikipedia, The Free Encyclopedia
Figure 17	ThinkGeek Inc.		
Figure 19a	SanDisk and Sanza FUZE are trademarks of SANDISK Corporation	**Figure 42a**	Len Green\Shutterstock
		Figure 42b	Pedro Salaverria\Shutterstock
Figure 19c	Courtesy of Apple		

190

securing your system:

protecting your digital data and devices

From Chapter 9 of *Technology in Action Complete,* Eighth Edition, Alan Evans, Kendall Martin, Mary Anne Poatsy.

securing your system

protecting your digital data and devices

securing your system

objectives

After reading this chapter, you should be able to answer the following questions:

1. From which types of viruses do I need to protect my computer?

2. What can I do to protect my computer from viruses?

3. How can hackers attack my computing devices, and what harm can they cause?

4. What is a firewall, and how does it keep my computer safe from hackers?

5. How do I create secure passwords and manage all of my passwords?

6. How can I surf the Internet anonymously and use biometric authentication devices to protect my data?

7. How do I manage online annoyances such as spyware and spam?

8. What data do I need to back up, and what are the best methods for doing so?

9. What is social engineering, and how do I avoid falling prey to phishing and hoaxes?

10. How do I protect my physical computing assets from environmental hazards, power surges, and theft?

multimedia resources

 Active Helpdesk

- Avoiding Computer Viruses
- Understanding Firewalls

 Sound Bytes

- Protecting Your Computer
- Installing a Personal Firewall
- Surge Protectors

 Companion Website

The Companion Website includes a variety of additional materials to help you review and learn more about the topics in this chapter. Go to: *pearsonhighered.com/techinaction*

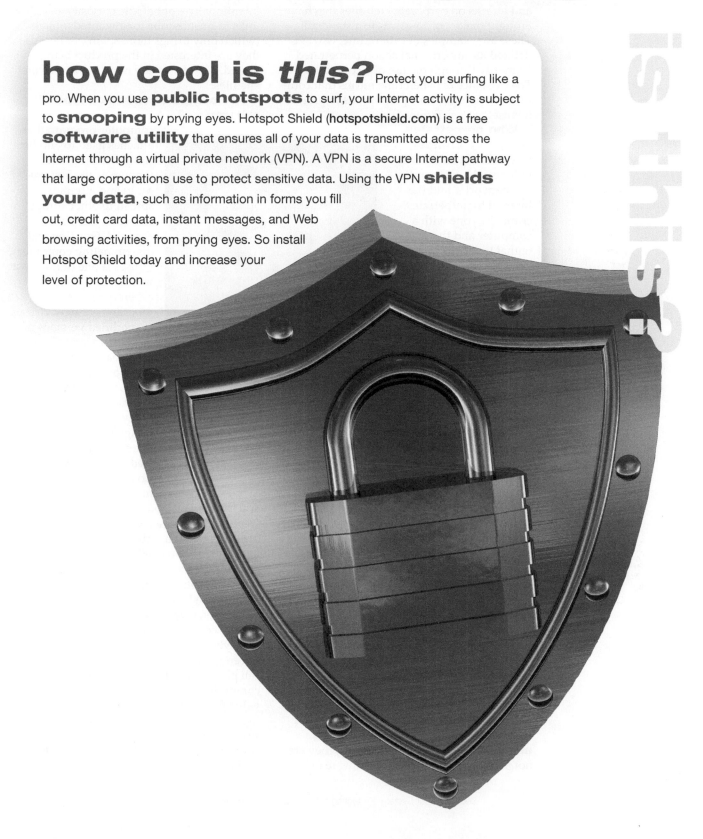

how cool is *this?*

Protect your surfing like a pro. When you use **public hotspots** to surf, your Internet activity is subject to **snooping** by prying eyes. Hotspot Shield (**hotspotshield.com**) is a free **software utility** that ensures all of your data is transmitted across the Internet through a virtual private network (VPN). A VPN is a secure Internet pathway that large corporations use to protect sensitive data. Using the VPN **shields your data**, such as information in forms you fill out, credit card data, instant messages, and Web browsing activities, from prying eyes. So install Hotspot Shield today and increase your level of protection.

Keeping Your Data Safe

The media is full of stories about malicious computer programs damaging computers, criminals stealing people's identities online, and attacks on corporate Web sites that have brought major corporations to a standstill. These are examples of **cybercrime**, which is defined as any criminal action perpetrated primarily through the use of a computer. The existence of cybercrime means that computer users must take precautions to protect themselves (see Figure 1).

Who perpetrates computer crimes? **Cybercriminals** are individuals who use computers, networks, and the Internet to perpetrate crime. Anyone with a computer and the wherewithal to arm him- or herself with the appropriate knowledge can be a cybercriminal.

What kinds of cybercrimes are conducted over the Internet? The Internet Crime Complaint Center (IC3) is a partnership between the Federal Bureau of Investigation (FBI) and the National White Collar Crime Center (NW3C). In 2009, the latest year for which data is available, IC3 processed more than 336,000 complaints related to Internet crime, an increase of 22 percent over 2008. Many complaints were fraud related, such as auction fraud, nondelivery of ordered items, credit and debit card fraud, and advanced fee scams. Complaints not related to fraud still pertained to serious issues such as computer intrusions, unsolicited e-mail, and child pornography. Much of the credit card fraud was perpetrated when credit card numbers were stolen by criminals tricking people into revealing sensitive information or by computer programs that gather credit card data.

With all the news coverage about cybercrimes, aren't people being more cautious? Unfortunately, they are not. Although most people are aware of spam, a recent survey by the Messaging Anti-Abuse Working Group (MAAWG) found that half of e-mail users in North American and Europe have opened spam. And the MAAWG discovered that 46 percent of people who opened spam did so intentionally—out of idle curiosity, to follow links to unsubscribe to unwanted e-mails (which only brings more spam), or because they are interested in the product being touted. Clearly, we are often our own worst enemies!

Are computer viruses a type of cybercrime? A computer **virus** is a computer program that attaches itself to another computer program (known as the *host program*) and attempts to spread to other computers when files are exchanged. Creating and disseminating computer viruses is one of the most widespread types of cybercrimes. Tens of thousands of new viruses or modified versions of old viruses are released each year. Some viruses cause only minor annoyances, while others cause destruction of data. Many viruses are now designed to gather sensitive information such as credit card numbers. The Conficker virus was the most widespread in 2009 and infected millions of computers in a few weeks of its release, which illustrates how serious a threat a virus can pose to your digital security. You need to make sure your data is protected from viruses and other malicious software attacks.

Does cybercrime include the theft of computing devices? Although theft of computer equipment is not classified as a cybercrime (rather, it is considered larceny), the theft of notebook computers, cell phones, iPods, and other portable computing devices is on the rise. The resale value for used electronic equipment is high, which contributes to demand for stolen merchandise. The ease with which equipment can be sold online also fuels this problem.

Figure 1

Cybercrimes, including virus attacks, are a serious problem for Web surfers.

In this chapter, we discuss serious threats to your digital security (such as computer viruses and other activities of cybercriminals), less serious annoyances (such as spyware and spam), and good security practices to keep yourself from undermining your digital security. We also discuss methods for protecting your digital assets from attacks and damage.

Computer Threats: Computer Viruses

Computer viruses are threatening because they are engineered to evade detection. Viruses normally attempt to hide within the code of a host program to avoid detection. And viruses are not just limited to computers. Any computing device such as a smartphone, notebook, netbook, or iPad can be infected with a virus. Even your car, which now contains embedded computer systems, could catch a virus, especially if it connects to the Internet for software updates.

What do computer viruses do? A computer virus's main purpose is to replicate itself and copy its code into as many other files as possible. Although virus replication can slow down networks, it is not usually the main threat. The majority of viruses have secondary objectives or side effects, ranging from displaying annoying messages on the computer screen to destroying files or the contents of entire hard drives. Because computer viruses cause disruption to computer systems, including data destruction and information theft, virus creation and deployment is a form of cybercrime.

How does my computer catch a virus? If your computer is exposed to a file infected with a virus, the virus will try to copy itself and infect a file on your computer. If you never expose your computer to new files, then it will not become infected. However, this would be the equivalent of a human being living in a bubble to avoid catching viruses from other people—quite impractical.

Downloading infected audio and video files from peer-to-peer file sharing sites is a major source of virus infections. Shared flash drives are also a common source of

> **"Viruses are not just limited to computers."**

virus infection, as is e-mail, although many people have misconceptions about how e-mail infection occurs. Just opening an e-mail message will not usually infect your computer with a virus, although some new viruses are launched when viewed in the preview pane of your e-mail software. Downloading or running a file that is attached to the e-mail is a common way that your computer becomes infected. Thus, be extremely wary of e-mail attachments, especially if you don't know the sender. Figure 2 illustrates the steps by which computer viruses are often passed from one computer to the next:

1. An individual writes a virus program disguised as a music file of a popular music group's new hit song and posts it to a file sharing site.

2. Unsuspecting Bill downloads the "music file" and infects his computer.

3. Bill sends his cousin Fred an e-mail with the infected "music file" and contaminates Fred's computer.

4. Fred saves the MP3 file to a flash drive and then copies it to his work computer and infects that machine as well.

5. Everyone who copies files from Fred's infected computer at work, or whose computer is networked to Fred's computer, risks spreading the virus.

Types of Viruses

Although thousands of computer viruses and variants exist, they can be grouped into six broad categories based on their behavior and method of transmission.

Boot-Sector Viruses

What are boot-sector viruses? A **boot-sector virus** replicates itself into a hard drive's master boot record. The **master boot record** is a program that executes whenever a computer boots up, ensuring that the virus will be loaded into memory immediately, even before some virus protection programs can load. Boot-sector viruses are often transmitted by a flash drive left in a USB port. When the computer boots up with the flash drive

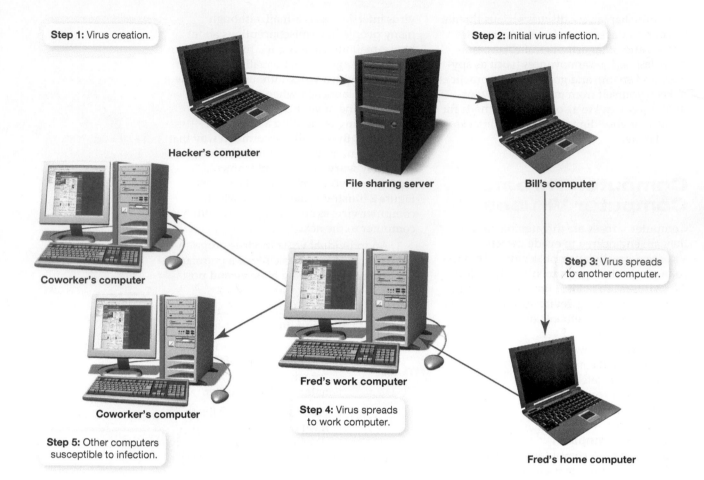

Step 1: Virus creation.

Hacker's computer

Step 2: Initial virus infection.

File sharing server

Bill's computer

Coworker's computer

Fred's work computer

Step 3: Virus spreads to another computer.

Step 4: Virus spreads to work computer.

Coworker's computer

Step 5: Other computers susceptible to infection.

Fred's home computer

Figure 2

Computer viruses are passed from one unsuspecting user to the next.

connected, the computer tries to launch a master boot record from the flash drive, which is usually the trigger for the virus to infect the hard drive.

Logic Bombs and Time Bombs

What is a logic bomb? A logic bomb is a virus that is triggered when certain logical conditions are met—such as opening a file or starting a program a certain number of times. A **time bomb** is a virus that is triggered by the passage of time or on a certain date. For example, the Michelangelo virus was a famous time bomb that was set to trigger every year on March 6, Michelangelo's birthday. The BlackWorm virus (otherwise known as Kama Sutra, Mywife, or CME-24), another time bomb, spreads through e-mail attachments. Opening the attachment infects the computer, and on the third day of every month, the virus seeks out and deletes certain file types (such as executable or .EXE files) on Windows

computers. The effects of logic bombs and time bombs range from the display of annoying messages on the screen to reformatting of the hard drive, which causes complete data loss.

Worms

What is a worm? A **worm** is slightly different from a virus in that a worm attempts to travel between systems through network connections to spread an infection. A virus infects a host file and waits until that file is executed on another computer to replicate. A worm, however, works independently of host file execution and is much more active in spreading itself. When the Conficker worm broke out, it quickly infected an estimated 9 million to 15 million individual computers. This worm spread through vulnerabilities in the Windows code and compromised computers by disabling certain software services and utility programs (such as Windows Update). Fortunately, it is easy to protect yourself from most worms.

Installing **antivirus software**, which is software specifically designed to detect viruses and protect your computer and files from harm, is a good start. You also should apply software patches (updates issued by the manufacturers of software such as Windows that repairs known security problems) to your computer whenever they are issued. We discuss protective measures later in the chapter.

Script and Macro Viruses

What are script and macro viruses?
Some viruses are hidden on Web sites in the form of scripts. A **script** is a series of commands—actually, a miniprogram—that is executed without your knowledge. Scripts are often used to perform useful, legitimate functions on Web sites such as collecting name and address information from customers. However, some scripts are malicious. For example, say you receive an e-mail encouraging you to visit a Web site full of useful programs and information. When you click a link to display a video on the Web site you were directed to, a script runs that infects your computer with a virus without your knowledge

A **macro virus** is a virus that attaches itself to a document (such as a Word or Excel file) that uses macros. A macro is a short series of commands that usually automates repetitive tasks. However, macro languages are now so sophisticated that viruses can be written with them. The Melissa virus became the first major macro virus to cause problems worldwide.

The Melissa virus was also the first practical example of an e-mail virus. **E-mail viruses** use the address book in the victim's e-mail system to distribute the virus. Anyone opening an infected document triggered the virus, which infected other Word documents on the victim's computer. Once triggered, the Melissa virus sent itself to the first 50 people in the address book on the infected computer. This helped ensure that Melissa became one of the most widely distributed viruses ever released.

Encryption Viruses

What are encryption viruses? When **encryption viruses** infect your computer, they run a program that searches for common types of data files (such as Microsoft Word and Excel files) and compresses them using a complex encryption key that renders

CAPTCHA: Keeping Web Sites Safe From Bots

Automated programs called *bots* (or *Web robots*) are used to make tasks easier on the Internet. Search engines use bots in a technique called *spidering* to search and index Web pages. Unfortunately, bots can also be used for malicious or illegal purposes because these bots can perform some computing tasks much faster than humans. For example, bots can be used on ticket ordering sites to try to buy large blocks of high-demand concert tickets or to make repeated entries into contests in attempts to increase the chances of winning sweepstakes or prizes. Frequently, bots are used to post spam in the comments sections of blogs. Fortunately, Web site owners can easily deploy software known as a *CAPTCHA program* (see Figure 3) to prevent such bot activities.

CAPTCHA (Completely Automated Public Turing Test to Tell Computers and Humans Apart) programs generate distorted text and require that it be typed into a box. Because bots can't yet be programmed to read distorted text, which most people usually can, the CAPTCHA program is used to verify that a human is performing whatever task is being tested. The program helps Web site owners defend against all types of automated scams. If you want to try integrating a CAPTCHA program into your Web site (to protect your e-mail address), go to **recaptcha.net**, which offers free CAPTCHA tools to help you protect your data.

Figure 3
CAPTCHA programs like this one verify that a human, not a bot being used for malicious purposes, is performing the requested task.

your files unusable. You then receive a message that asks you to send money to an account if you want to receive the program to decrypt your files. The flaw with this type of virus, which keeps it from being widespread, is that law enforcement officials can trace the payments to an account and may possibly be able to catch the perpetrators. Still, we see these types of viruses from time to time.

Virus Classifications

How else are viruses classified?
Viruses can also be classified by the methods they take to avoid detection by antivirus software:

- A **polymorphic virus** changes its own code (or periodically rewrites itself) to avoid detection. Most polymorphic

Computer Safeguard: Antivirus Software and Software Updates

Certain viruses merely present minor annoyances, such as randomly sending an ambulance graphic across the bottom of the screen, as is the case with the Red Cross virus. Other viruses can significantly slow down a computer or network, or destroy key files or the contents of entire hard drives. The best defense against viruses is to install antivirus software. Symantec, Kaspersky, AVG, and McAfee are among the companies that offer highly rated antivirus software packages.

Although you can buy stand-alone antivirus software, antivirus protection is included in comprehensive Internet security packages such as Norton Internet Security, Kaspersky Internet Security, or McAfee Total Protection. These software packages will help protect you from other threats as well as from computer viruses.

viruses infect a particular type of file (.EXE files, for example).

- A **multipartite virus** is designed to infect multiple file types in an effort to fool the antivirus software that is looking for it.
- **Stealth viruses** temporarily erase their code from the files where they reside and then hide in the active memory of the computer. This helps them avoid detection if only the hard drive is being searched for viruses. Fortunately, current antivirus software scans memory as well as the hard drive.

Given the creativity of virus programmers, you can be sure we'll see other types of viruses emerge in the future. In the next section, we discuss preventing virus infections.

Avoiding Computer Viruses

In this Active Helpdesk call, you'll play the role of a helpdesk staffer, fielding calls about different types of viruses and what users should do to protect their computer from them.

Antivirus Software

How often do I need to run antivirus software? Although antivirus software is designed to detect suspicious activity on your computer at all times, you should run an active virus scan on your entire system at least once a week. By doing so, all files on your computer will be checked for undetected viruses. Because these checks take time, you can configure the software to run them automatically when you aren't using your system—for example, late at night (see Figure 4). Alternatively, if you suspect a problem, you can launch a scan and have it run immediately.

How does antivirus software work? Most antivirus software looks for virus signatures in files. A **virus signature** is a portion of the virus code that is unique to a particular computer virus. Antivirus software scans files for these signatures and thereby identifies infected files and the type of virus that is infecting them.

The antivirus software scans files when they're opened or executed. If it detects a virus signature or suspicious activity (such as the launch of an unknown macro), it stops the execution of the file and virus and notifies you that it has detected a virus. It also places the virus in a secure area on your hard drive so that it won't spread infection to other files. This procedure is known as **quarantining**. Usually the antivirus software then gives you the choice of deleting or repairing the infected file. Unfortunately, antivirus programs can't always fix infected files to make them usable again. You should keep backup copies of critical files so that you can restore them in case a virus damages them irreparably.

Most antivirus software will also attempt to prevent infection by inoculating key files on your computer. In **inoculation**, the antivirus software records key attributes about files on your computer (such as file size and date created) and keeps these statistics in a safe place on your hard drive. When scanning for viruses, the antivirus software compares the files to the attributes it previously recorded to help detect attempts by virus programs to modify your files.

Does antivirus software always stop viruses? Antivirus software catches known viruses effectively. Unfortunately, new viruses are written all the time. To combat unknown viruses, modern antivirus programs search for suspicious virus-like activities as well as virus signatures. However, virus authors know how antivirus software works. They take special measures to disguise their virus code and hide the effects of a virus until just the right moment. This helps ensure that the virus spreads faster and farther. Thus, your computer can be attacked by a virus that your antivirus software doesn't recognize. To minimize this risk, you should keep your antivirus software up to date.

How do I make sure my antivirus software is up to date? Most antivirus programs have an automatic update feature that downloads updates for virus signature files every time you go online (see Figure 5).

What should I do if I think my computer is infected with a virus? Boot up your computer using the antivirus installation disc. (*Note:* If you download your antivirus software from the Internet, it is a good idea to copy your antivirus software to a DVD in case you have problems in the future.) This should prevent most virus

programs from loading and will allow you to run the antivirus software directly from your disk drive. If the software does detect viruses, you may want to research them further to determine whether your antivirus software will eradicate them completely or whether you will need to take additional manual steps to eliminate the virus. Most antivirus company Web sites, such as the Symantec site (**symantec.com**), contain archives of information on viruses and provide step-by-step solutions for removing viruses.

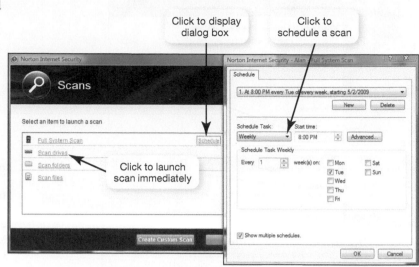

Figure 4

In Norton Internet Security, complete virus scans can be set up to run automatically. This computer will be scanned every Tuesday at 8 P.M.

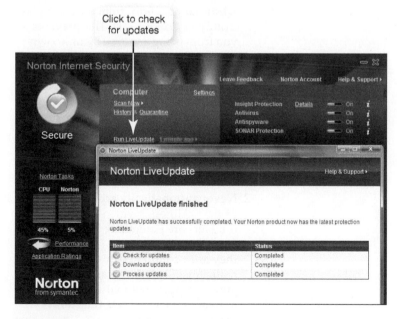

Figure 5

Antivirus software, such as Norton Internet Security, provides for automatic updates to the software installed on the computer.

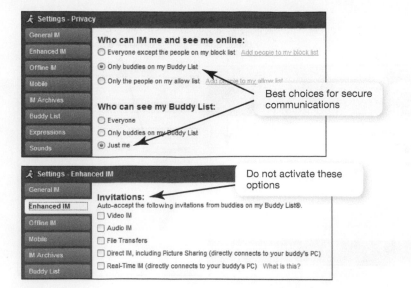

Best choices for secure communications

Do not activate these options

Figure 6

When you use instant messenger programs, check all of the preference screens for appropriate settings.

Are instant messenger programs safe from virus attacks? Virus attacks and other forms of malicious hacking can be perpetrated via instant messenger (IM) programs such as Google Talk, Skype, Facebook Chat, and iChat. Even if you have antivirus protection installed, people still could contact you for the purposes of trying to trick you into revealing sensitive information. Therefore, you should try to hide your instant messaging activity from everyone except people you know. To keep your IM sessions safe, follow these precautions:

1. **Allow contact only from users on your Buddy or Friends List.** This prevents you from being annoyed by unknown parties. On Facebook, you should restrict your profile information to be viewed only by friends and only accept friend requests from people you know and trust. On the settings screen for your IM program (Figure 6), select Allow only users on my Buddy List. And, of course, don't put anyone you don't know and trust on your buddy list.

2. **Never automatically accept transfers of data.** Although video IMs and file transfers are potentially useful for swapping files over IM (see Figure 6), they are a common way of transmitting malicious files, which can then infect your computer with viruses. Enabling auto-acceptance of data transfers is never a good idea.

3. **Avoid using instant messaging programs on public computers.** If you use

a shared computer, such as one in a computer lab at school, be sure you don't select any features that remember your password or connect you automatically. The next person who uses the computer might be able to connect to the instant messaging service with your screen name (or your Facebook account) and impersonate you.

Software Updates

Is there anything else I should do to protect my system? Many viruses exploit weaknesses in operating systems. Malicious Web sites can be set up to attack your computer by downloading harmful software onto your computer. According to research conducted by Google, this type of attack, known as a **drive-by download**, is common and affects almost 1 in 1,000 Web pages. To combat these threats, make sure your antivirus software and your operating system are up to date and contain the latest security patches. You can update your Windows operating system with an automatic update utility called *Windows Update*. When you enable automatic updates, your computer searches for updates on the Microsoft Web site every time it connects to the Internet. OS X has a similar utility for gathering updates.

Do updates only happen automatically? Although many people decide to receive updates automatically, there are several options you can choose from in Windows, as shown in Figure 7. The following options are noteworthy.

- Option 1: **Install updates automatically.** Selecting this option will automatically download and install updates at a time you have specified. We strongly recommend that you select this option.

- Option 2: **Download updates but let me choose whether to install them.** Although this option automatically

  Protecting Your Computer

In this Sound Byte, you'll learn how to use a variety of tools to protect your computer, including antivirus software and Windows utilities.

Securing Your System: Protecting Your Digital Data and Devices

downloads updates, they are not installed until you instruct Windows to install them. We don't usually recommend this option because you may forget to install important updates.

- Option 3: **Check for updates but let me choose whether to download and install them**. This is an appropriate choice if you have low bandwidth Internet access. Because downloads over dial-up can take a long time due to low bandwidth, you need to control when downloads will occur so they don't interrupt your workflow.
- Option 4: **Give me recommended updates**. This option ensures you receive recommended (optional) updates as well as critical (necessary) updates.
- Option 5: **Microsoft Update**, This option ensures you receive updates for other Microsoft products besides Windows (such as Microsoft Office).

In the next section, we explore another major threat to your digital security—hackers.

Computer Threats: Hackers

Although there is a great deal of disagreement as to what a hacker actually is (especially among hackers themselves), a **hacker** is most commonly defined as anyone who unlawfully breaks into a computer system—either an individual computer or a network (see Figure 8).

Are there different kinds of hackers? Some hackers are offended by being labeled as criminals and therefore attempt to classify different types of hackers. A hacker who breaks into systems just for the challenge of it (and who doesn't wish to steal or wreak havoc on the systems) may refer to him- or herself as a **white-hat hacker**. These individuals tout themselves as experts who are performing a needed service for society by helping companies uncover the vulnerabilities in their systems.

White-hat hackers look down on those hackers who use their knowledge to destroy information or for illegal gain. A term for these more villainous hackers is **black-hat hacker**. (The terms *white hat* and *black hat* are references to old Western movies in which the heroes wore white hats and the outlaws wore

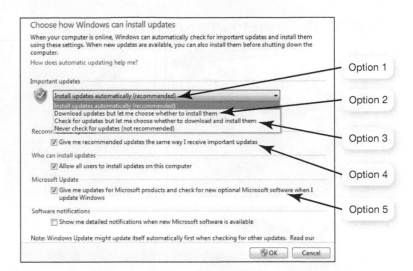

black hats.) Regardless of the hackers' opinions, the laws in the United States and in many other countries consider any unauthorized access to computer systems a crime.

What about the teenage hackers who are caught every so often? These amateur hackers are often referred to as **script kiddies**. Script kiddies don't create the programs they use to hack into computer systems; instead, they use tools created by skilled hackers that enable unskilled novices to wreak the same havoc as professional hackers.

Fortunately, because the users of these programs are amateurs, they're usually not proficient at covering their electronic tracks. Therefore, it's relatively easy for law enforcement officials to track them down and prosecute them. Script kiddies nevertheless can cause a lot of disruption and damage to computers, networks, and Web sites.

Why would a hacker be interested in breaking into my home computer? Some hackers just like to snoop. They enjoy the challenge of breaking into systems and seeing what information they can find. Other hackers are hobbyists seeking information about a particular topic wherever they can find it. Because many people keep proprietary business information on their home computers, hackers bent on industrial espionage may break into home computers. For other hackers, hacking is a way to pass time.

What Hackers Steal

Could a hacker steal my credit card number? If you perform financial transactions online, such as banking or buying

Figure 7

The Windows Update screen makes it easy for users to configure Windows to update itself.

>To enable automatic updates, click **Start**, select **Control Panel**, select **System and Security**, click the **Windows Update** link, and then click the **Change Settings** link.

BRINGING CIVILIZATION TO ITS KNEES...

Goths

Vandals

Huns

Geeks

Figure 8

Although they do not necessarily destroy civilization, hackers can cause problems for corporations and individuals alike.

goods and services, then you probably do so using a credit (or debit) card. Credit card and bank account information can thus reside on your hard drive and may be detectable by a hacker. Also, many sites require you to provide a login ID and password to gain access. Even if this data is not stored on your computer, a hacker may be able to capture it when you're online by using a packet sniffer or a keylogger (a program that captures all keystrokes made on a computer).

What's a packet sniffer? Data travels through the Internet in small pieces, each called a **packet**. The packets are identified with an IP address, in part to help identify the computer to which they are being sent. Once the packets reach their destination, they are reassembled into cohesive messages. A **packet sniffer** is a computer program deployed by hackers that looks at (or sniffs) each packet as it travels on the Internet—not just those that are addressed to a particular computer, but all packets. Some packet sniffers are configured to capture all the packets into memory, whereas others capture only packets that contain specific content (such as credit card numbers). Wireless networks can be particularly vulnerable to this type of exploitation because many people do not enable encryption of data when they set up their wireless

networks. A hacker might sit in a coffee shop connected to a wireless network and run a packet sniffer to capture data from other patrons who are using the wireless network. This makes it easy for hackers to intercept and read sensitive information transmitted without encryption, such as credit card numbers or the contents of e-mails.

What do hackers do with the information they "sniff"? Once a hacker has your credit card information, he or she can either use it to purchase items illegally or sell the number to someone who will. If a hacker steals the login ID and password to an account where you have your credit card information stored (such as eBay or Amazon), he or she can also use your account to purchase items and have them shipped to him- or herself instead of to you. If hackers can gather enough information in conjunction with your credit card information, they may be able to commit identity theft. **Identity theft** is characterized by someone using personal information about you (such as your name, address, or Social Security number) to assume your identity for the purpose of defrauding others.

Although this sounds scary, you can easily protect yourself from packet sniffing by installing a firewall (which we discuss later in this chapter) and using data encryption on a wireless network.

Trojan Horses

Besides stealing information, what other problems can hackers cause if they break into my computer? Hackers often use individuals' computers as a staging area for mischief. To commit widespread computer attacks, for example, hackers need to control many computers at the same time. To this end, hackers often use Trojan horses to install other programs on computers. A **Trojan**

horse is a program that appears to be something useful or desirable (like a game or a screen saver), but while it runs does something malicious in the background without your knowledge. The term *Trojan horse* derives from Greek mythology and refers to the wooden horse that the Greeks used to sneak into the city of Troy and conquer it. Therefore, computer programs that contain a hidden (and usually dreadful) "surprise" are referred to as Trojan horses.

What damage can Trojan horses do? Often, the malicious activity perpetrated by a Trojan horse program is the installation of a **backdoor program** that allows hackers to take almost complete control of your computer without your knowledge. Using a backdoor program, hackers can access and delete all the files on your computer, send e-mail, run programs, and do just about anything else you can do with your computer. A computer that a hacker controls in this manner is referred to as a **zombie**. Zombies are often used to launch denial-of-service attacks on other computers.

Denial of Service Attacks

What are denial-of-service attacks?
In a **denial-of-service (DoS) attack**, legitimate users are denied access to a computer system because a hacker is repeatedly making requests of that computer system through a computer he or she has taken over as a zombie. A computer can handle only a certain number of requests for information at one time. When it is flooded with requests in a denial-of-service attack, it shuts down and refuses to answer any requests for information, even if the requests are from a legitimate user. Thus, the computer is so busy responding to the bogus requests for information that authorized users can't gain access.

Couldn't a DoS attack be traced by to the computer that launched it?
Launching a DoS attack on a computer system from a single computer is easy to trace. Therefore, most savvy hackers use a **distributed denial-of-service (DDoS) attack**, which launches DoS attacks from more than one zombie (sometimes thousands of zombies) at the same time. Figure 9 illustrates how a DDoS attack

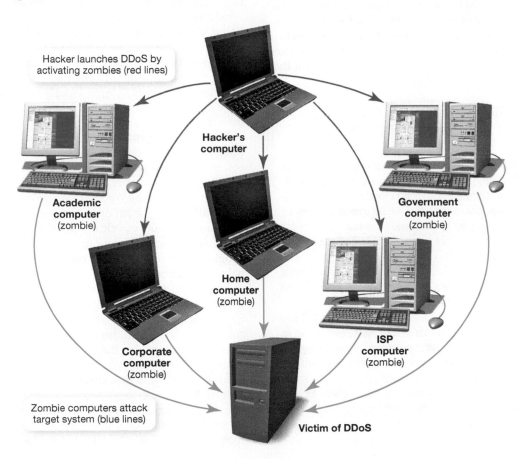

Figure 9

Zombie computers are used to facilitate a distributed denial-of-service (DDoS) attack.

Hacker launches DDoS by activating zombies (red lines)

Hacker's computer

Academic computer (zombie)

Government computer (zombie)

Home computer (zombie)

ISP computer (zombie)

Corporate computer (zombie)

Zombie computers attack target system (blue lines)

Victim of DDoS

works. A hacker creates many zombies and coordinates them so that they begin sending bogus requests to the same computer at the same time. Administrators of the victim computer often have a great deal of difficulty stopping the attack because it comes from so many computers. Often the attacks are coordinated automatically by botnets. A **botnet** is a large group of software programs (called *robots* or *bots*) that runs autonomously on zombie computers. Some botnets have been known to span 1.5 million computers.

DDoS attacks are a serious problem. In April 2009, the International Federation of the Phonographic Industry (IFPI) and Motion Picture Association of America (MPAA) Web sites were subjected to DDoS attacks in protest of the conviction of the owners of The Pirate Bay (a notorious file-sharing site) on charges of assisting in copyright infringement. In August 2009, social networking sites including Twitter and Facebook were subjected to a DDoS attack that was apparently aimed at a blogger. Twitter and Facebook users experienced problems accessing the sites for hours during the attack. Because many Web sites receive revenue from users, either directly (such as via subscriptions to online games) or indirectly (such as when Web surfers click on advertisements), DDoS attacks can be financially distressing for the owners of the affected Web sites.

Prevention of Identity Theft . . . Don't Overlook Photocopiers!

We are constantly bombarded with identity theft warnings regarding suspicious e-mail, phishing sites, and telephone scams. Many people are unaware that photocopiers, too, present a risk of identity theft. This is because most photocopiers manufactured today contain hard drives, just as computers do. Documents are scanned, stored on the hard drive, and then printed by the copier. So, unless the copier has been specially configured to have the hard drive overwritten to destroy data or to use encryption, copies of your tax return may be lurking on the public copier at your local library or copy shop that you used before you mailed your return to the Internal Revenue Service. A clever hacker could retrieve a wealth of potential information off just one public copy machine.

So what should you do to protect yourself? Ask the local copy shop or public library, or the IT department at your office, about the security measures it has set up on its copiers before you use them to copy sensitive documents. If you are buying a copier for your business, investigate security options that are available to protect your employees. For small copying jobs (such as your tax return), consider buying an all-in-one device (combining a printer, copier, scanner, and fax machine) for your home office because you can more easily keep that machine protected from wily hackers.

How Hackers Gain Access

How exactly does a hacker gain access to a computer? Hackers can gain access to computers directly or indirectly. Direct access involves sitting down at a computer and installing hacking software. It is unlikely that such an attack would occur in your home. However, to deter unauthorized use, you may want to lock the room that your computer is in or remove key components (such as the power cord) when strangers such as repair personnel are in your house and may be unobserved for periods of time. You might also set up your computer so that it requires a password for a user to gain access to your desktop.

The most likely method a hacker will use to access a computer is to enter indirectly through its Internet connection. When connected to the Internet, your computer is potentially open to attack by hackers. Many people forget that their Internet connection is a two-way street. Not only can you access the Internet but also people on the Internet can access your computer.

Think of the computer as a house. Common sense tells you to lock your doors and windows to deter theft when you aren't home. Hooking your computer up to the Internet is like leaving the front door to your house wide open. Anyone passing by can access your computer and poke around for valuables. Your computer obviously doesn't have doors and windows like a house, but it does have logical ports.

What are logical ports? Logical ports are virtual—that is, not physical—communications gateways or paths that allow a computer to organize requests for information (such as Web page downloads or e-mail routing) from other networks or computers. Unlike physical ports (USB, FireWire, and so on), you can't see or touch a logical port; it is part of a computer's internal organization.

Logical ports are numbered and assigned to specific services. For instance, logical port 80 is designated for hypertext transfer protocol (HTTP), the main communications protocol (or standard) for the World Wide Web. Thus, all requests for information from your browser to the Web flow through logical port 80. E-mail messages sent by simple mail transfer protocol (SMTP), the protocol used for sending e-mail on the Internet, are routed through logical port 25. Open logical ports, like open windows in a home, invite intruders, as illustrated in Figure 10. Unless you take precautions to restrict access to your logical ports, other people on the Internet may be able to access your computer through them.

Fortunately, you can thwart most hacking problems by installing a firewall.

Restricting Access to Your Digital Assets

Keeping hackers at bay is often just a matter of keeping them out. This can be achieved either by preventing them from accessing your computer (usually through your Internet connection), by protecting your digital information in such a way that it can't be accessed (with passwords, for example), or by hiding your activities from prying eyes. In the next section, we explore strategies for protecting access to your digital assets and keeping your Internet surfing activities from being seen by the wrong people.

Firewalls

A **firewall** is a program or hardware device designed to protect computers from hackers. A firewall specifically designed for home networks is called a **personal firewall**. Personal firewalls are made to be easy to install. By using a personal firewall, you can close open logical ports to invaders and potentially make your computer invisible to other computers on the Internet.

Firewalls are named after a housing construction feature. When houses were first being packed densely into cities, they were attached to each other with common walls. Fire was a huge hazard because wood burns readily. An entire neighborhood could be lost in a single fire. Thus, builders started building common walls of nonflammable or slow-burning material to stop, or at least slow, the spread of fire. These came to be known as *firewalls*.

Types of Firewalls

What kinds of firewalls are there? As noted earlier, firewalls can be configured using either software or hardware devices. Although installing either a software or a hardware firewall on your home network is

probably sufficient, you should consider installing both for maximum protection.

What software firewalls are there? Most current operating systems include reliable firewalls. Many security suites such as Norton Internet Security, McAfee Internet Security, and ZoneAlarm Internet Security Suite also include firewall software. Although the firewalls that come with Windows 7 and OS X will protect your computer, firewalls included in security suites often come with additional features such as monitoring systems that alert you if your computer is under attack.

If you are using a security suite (say, for virus protection and parental controls) that includes a firewall, you should disable the firewall that came with your operating system. Two firewalls running at the same time can conflict with each other and can cause your computer to slow down or freeze up.

What are hardware firewalls? You can also buy and configure hardware firewall devices. Many routers sold for home networks include firewall protection. Just like software firewalls, the setup for hardware firewalls is designed for novices, and the default configuration on most routers keeps unused logical ports closed. Documentation accompanying routers can assist users with more experience in adjusting the settings to allow access to specific ports if needed.

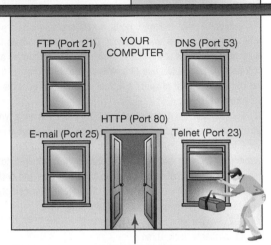

FTP (Port 21) YOUR COMPUTER DNS (Port 53)

HTTP (Port 80)

E-mail (Port 25) Telnet (Port 23)

WEB SITE REQUEST

Figure 10

Open logical ports are an invitation to hackers.

ACTIVE HELP-DESK Understanding Firewalls

In this Active Helpdesk call, you'll play the role of a helpdesk staffer, fielding calls about how hackers can attack networks and what harm they can cause, as well as what a firewall does to keep a computer safe from hackers.

Firewalls are designed to restrict access to a network and its computers. Firewalls protect you in two major ways: by blocking access to logical ports and by keeping your computer's network address secure.

To block access to logical ports, firewalls examine data packets that your computer sends and receives. Data packets contain information such as the address of the sending and receiving computers and the logical port the packet will use. Firewalls can be configured so that they filter out packets sent to specific logical ports. This process is referred to as **packet filtering**.

For example, file transfer protocol (FTP) programs are a typical way in which hackers access a computer. Hackers can disguise their requests for information as legitimate packets that appear to be FTP requests authorized by your computer. If a firewall is configured to ignore *all* incoming packets that request access to port 21 (the port designated for FTP traffic), no FTP requests will get through to your computer. This process is referred to as **logical port blocking**. If port 21 were a window at your home, you would probably lock it so that a burglar couldn't get in. If you needed port 21 for a legitimate purpose, you could instruct the firewall to allow access to that port for a specified period of time or by a certain user.

For the Internet to share information seamlessly, data packets must have a way of getting to their correct locations. Therefore, every computer connected to the Internet has a unique address called an **Internet Protocol address** (or **IP address**). As noted earlier, data packets contain the IP address of the computer to which they are being sent. Routing servers on the Internet make sure the packets get to the correct address. This is similar to the way addresses work on a conventional letter. A unique street address (such as 123 Main St., Anywhere, CA 99999) is placed on the envelope, and the postal service routes it to its correct destination. Without such addressing, data packets, like letters, would not reach their intended recipients.

IP addresses are assigned in a procedure known as **dynamic addressing** when users log on to their Internet service provider (ISP), as shown in Figure 11). The dynamic host configuration protocol (DHCP) server assigns IP addresses out of a pool of available IP addresses licensed to the ISP in this manner:

1. When you connect to your ISP, your computer requests an IP address.
2. The ISP's DHCP server consults its list of available IP addresses and selects one.
3. The selected IP address is communicated to your computer. The address remains in force for as long as you are connected to the ISP.
4. Once on the Internet, your Web browser requests access to ABC Company's Web site.
5. The ABC Company server consults an IP address listing and determines that the IP address of your computer is assigned to your ISP. It then forwards the requested information to the ISP's router.
6. The ISP knows to whom it assigned the IP address and, therefore, routes the requested information to your computer.

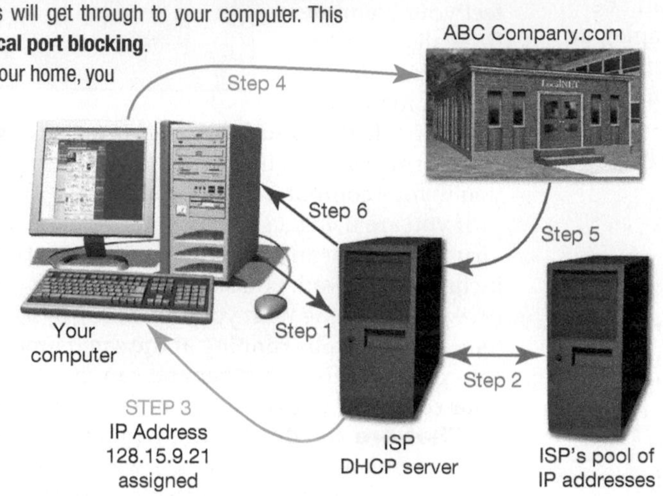

Because hackers use IP addresses to find victims and come back to their computers for more mischief, frequently switching IP addresses helps make users less vulnerable to attacks. Periodically switching off your modem and rebooting it will cause a different IP address to be assigned dynamically

Figure 11

How dynamic addressing works.

Knowing Your Computer Is Secure

How can I tell if my computer is at risk? For peace of mind (and to ensure that your firewall setup was successful), you can visit several Web sites that offer free services that test your computer's vulnerability. One popular site is Gibson Research (**grc.com**). The company's ShieldsUP and LeakTest programs are free, easy to run, and can pinpoint security vulnerabilities in a system that is connected to the Internet. If you get a clean report from these programs, your system is probably not vulnerable to attack. Figure 13 shows the results screen from a ShieldsUP port probe test, which checks which logical ports in your computer are vulnerable. This test was run on a computer connected to the Internet with no firewall installed. Ports reported as closed or in stealth mode are safe from attack. Ports reported as open (such as port 1025) are subject to exploitation by hackers. Installation of a hardware or software firewall should close any open ports.

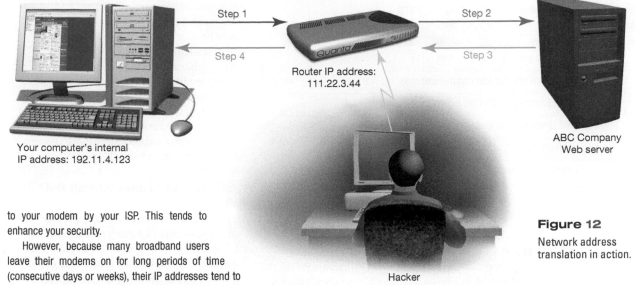

Step 1
Step 2
Step 4
Step 3

Router IP address:
111.22.3.44

Your computer's internal
IP address: 192.11.4.123

ABC Company
Web server

Hacker

Figure 12

Network address
translation in action.

to your modem by your ISP. This tends to enhance your security.

However, because many broadband users leave their modems on for long periods of time (consecutive days or weeks), their IP addresses tend to change less frequently than those of dial-up users. This is similar to having an IP address assigned by **static addressing**. In static addressing, your IP address is always the same and is assigned by your ISP. This process is often used by businesses who are hosting a Web site. When a broadband user has a static address, the user is more vulnerable to hackers because the hackers have a more permanent IP address with which to locate the computer. It also makes it easier for hackers to make repeated visits to a computer.

To combat the problems associated with static addressing, firewalls use a process called **network address translation (NAT)** to assign internal IP addresses on a network. These internal IP addresses are only shared with devices that are part of the network, so the addresses are safe from hackers. Figure 12 shows how NAT works. Your computer's internal IP address is assigned to your computer by the router. This IP address is used only on the internal network and therefore cannot be detected by other Internet users. Here's how it works:

1. Your computer's Web browser requests access to the ABC Company's Web site. This request travels through the router, which is configured as a firewall.

2. The router forwards the browser request to the ABC Company Web server and directs that server to send the data back to the router's

external IP address (in this example, 111.22.3.44). The internal IP address of your computer (assigned by NAT) is not revealed to computers outside your network.

3. The ABC Company Web server processes the request and sends the data back to the router's external IP address (111.22.3.44). This is the IP address the ISP assigned to your router, and it can be detected by other users on the Internet.

4. The router then passes the requested data to the IP address of the computer that requested it (in this example, 192.11.4.123).

The router's IP address is assigned by your ISP. Only the router's external IP address can be detected by other users on the Internet. For hackers to access your computer, they must know your computer's internal IP address. With a NAT-capable router/firewall installed on your network, hackers are unable to access the internal IP address assigned to your computer, so your computer is safe.

You can use NAT in your home by purchasing a hardware firewall with NAT capabilities. As noted earlier, many routers sold for home use are also configured as firewalls, and many feature NAT as well.

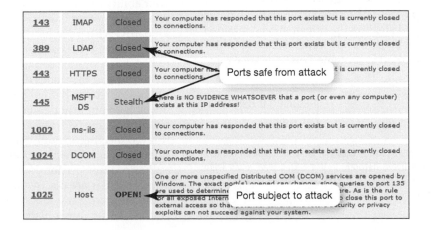

143	IMAP	Closed	Your computer has responded that this port exists but is currently closed to connections.
389	LDAP	Closed	Your computer has responded that this port exists but is currently closed to connections.
443	HTTPS	Closed	Your computer has responded that this port exists but is currently closed to connections.
445	MSFT DS	Stealth	There is NO EVIDENCE WHATSOEVER that a port (or even any computer) exists at this IP address!
1002	ms-ils	Closed	Your computer has responded that this port exists but is currently closed to connections.
1024	DCOM	Closed	Your computer has responded that this port exists but is currently closed to connections.
1025	Host	OPEN!	One or more unspecified Distributed COM (DCOM) services are opened by Windows. The exact port(s) opened can change, since queries to port 135 are used to determine ... As is the rule for all exposed Intern... close this port to external access so tha... ...curity or privacy exploits can not succeed against your system.

Ports safe from attack

Port subject to attack

Figure 13

ShieldsUP common ports test results.

Securing Your System: Protecting Your Digital Data and Devices

Figure 14 | COMMON LOGICAL PORTS

Port Number	Protocol Using the Port
21	FTP (file transfer protocol) control
23	Telnet (unencrypted text communications)
25	SMTP (simple mail transfer protocol)
53	DNS (domain name system)
80	HTTP (hypertext transfer protocol)
443	HTTPS [HTTP protocol with transport layer security (TLS) encryption]

What if I don't get a clean report from the testing program? If the testing program detects potential vulnerabilities and you don't have a firewall, you should install one as soon as possible. If the firewall is already configured and common ports (such as those shown in Figure 14) are identified as being vulnerable, consult your firewall documentation for instructions on how to close or restrict access to those ports.

Preventing Bluetooth Attacks

What are the security vulnerabilities of Bluetooth devices? Bluetooth is a transmission medium for exchanging data wirelessly over short distances. Most smartphones are Bluetooth enabled. Although progress is being made, Bluetooth hardware and software still are riddled with security holes, especially on smartphones. If you have a Bluetooth-enabled device, you are susceptible to two severe types of mischief: bluesnarfing and bluebugging.

- Bluesnarfing involves exploiting a flaw in the Bluetooth access software for the purpose of accessing a Bluetooth device and stealing the information contained on it. Think how much valuable information is contained on your smartphone

SOUND BYTE | Installing a Personal Firewall

Firewalls provide excellent protection against hackers on a home network. In this Sound Byte, you'll learn how to install and configure software firewalls to protect your computer.

(names, contact information, and meeting notes) that might be valuable to a business competitor. Unfortunately, Bluesnarfing is relatively easy (and cheap) because a lot of Bluesnarfing software is available on the Internet. A twist on this attack is Car Whisperer software, which is specifically designed to eavesdrop on conversations taking place in your car when you are using a hands-free device (such as a cell phone or GPS).

- Although much more difficult and expensive to execute, Bluebugging presents more serious dangers. The process involves a hacker actually taking control of a Bluetooth-enabled device. Once a hacker gains control of the device, he or she can make phone calls, establish Internet connections, read phonebook entries, set call forwarding, or send, receive, and read short message service (SMS) messages.

Bluebugging is a major risk in Europe because Bluetooth and SMS are wildly popular there, but the rise of Bluetooth usage in the United States is making it a risk here as well. Many Europeans use their phones to make micropayments (small purchases from merchants that eventually appear on their cell phone bill) by a process known as *reverse* SMS. If a hacker Bluebugs your phone, he or she could potentially send payments to fake accounts he or she controls, using reverse SMS.

How can I protect myself from Bluetooth attacks? Most devices with Bluetooth capability give you the option of making your device invisible to unauthorized Bluetooth devices. This does not affect your ability to use two Bluetooth devices you own together (such as a wireless headset paired with a phone). When you pair your headset with your phone, the headset (which has a unique serial number) becomes an authorized Bluetooth device for your phone. Moreover, by making your device invisible to unauthorized devices (such as hackers' headsets), you prevent hackers from connecting to your equipment (your phone) because their headsets are not authorized devices for your phone. When vulnerabilities are discovered, cell phone manufacturers issue software patches. Antivirus software is also available for mobile devices, so you may wish to purchase this for your phone. You must ensure that you update the software in your mobile devices just as you do your computer's OS and antivirus software. For more information on securing your Bluetooth devices, go to the Bluetooth technology Web site (**bluetomorrow.com**).

Password Protection and Password Management

Passwords, used in conjunction with login IDs, are the major way we restrict access to computers, networks, and online accounts. You no doubt have many passwords that you need to remember to access your digital life. However, creating strong passwords—ones that are difficult for hackers to guess—is an essential piece of security that individuals sometimes overlook. Password cracking programs have become more sophisticated lately. In fact, some commonly available programs, such as John the Ripper, can test more than 1 million password combinations per second! Creating a secure password is therefore more important than ever.

Many people use extremely weak passwords. The Imperva Application Defense Center (a computer security research organization) conducted a review of 32 million passwords that were used at the Web site **rockyou.com**. More than 345,000 people were using "12345," "123456," or "123456789" as their password. And almost 62,000 people were using "password"! Passwords such as these are extremely easy for hackers to crack.

Creating Passwords

What constitutes a strong password?
Strong passwords are difficult for someone to guess. They should not contain easily deduced components related to your life such as parts of your name, your pet's name, your street address, or your telephone number. To create strong passwords, follow the basic guidelines shown here:

- Your password should contain at least 14 characters and include numbers, symbols, and upper- and lowercase letters.
- Your password should not be a single word or any word found in the dictionary.

- Ideally, it should be a combination of several words with strategically placed uppercase characters.
- Your password should not be easily associated with you (such as your birth date, the name of your pet, or your nickname).
- Use a different password for each system or Web site you need to access. This prevents access to other accounts you maintain if one of your passwords is discovered.
- Never tell anyone your password or write it down in a place where others might see it.
- Change your password on a regular basis (say, every month) and change it sooner if you think someone may know it.

Figure 15 shows some possible passwords and explains why they are strong or weak candidates.

How can I check the strength of my passwords? You can use online password strength testers, such as The Password Meter (**passwordmeter.com**) or Microsoft's test (**microsoft.com/protect/yourself/password/checker.mspx**), to

---

Connecting to Wireless Networks on the Road? Beware of "Evil Twins"!

When you are at the airport or coffee shop, you may need to connect to a wireless network and check your e-mail. You switch on your notebook, and the wireless network adapter finds a network called "free wifi" or "airport wireless." You connect, enter your credit card information to pay for your airtime, and start merrily surfing away. Three days later, your credit card company calls asking about the $2,400 big-screen TV you just bought at the local electronics store and the $3,200 of power tools charged at the home improvement store. You didn't make either of these purchases; you probably fell prey to an "evil twin" wireless hotspot.

Hackers know the areas where people are likely to seek access to wireless networks. They will often set up their own wireless networks in these areas with sound-alike names to lure unsuspecting Web surfers and get them to enter credit card information to gain access. Other times these "evil twins" offer free Internet access, and the hackers monitor traffic looking for sensitive information they can use.

So how can you protect yourself? Check with authorized personnel at places where you will be connecting to hotspots to determine the names of the legitimate hotspots. If you run across "free" access to a hotspot that isn't provided by a legitimate merchant, then you are better off not connecting at all because you can't be sure your information won't be used against you or that malicious files won't be downloaded to your computer.

Figure 15 | STRONG AND WEAK PASSWORD CANDIDATES

Strong Password	Reason
L8t2meGaNDalf351	Uses letters and numbers to come up with memorable phrase "Late to me" and adds it to a character name from *Lord of the Rings* plus a random number.
IwaLR8384GdY	First initials of first line of Green Day song *I Walk a Lonely Road* plus a random number and an abbreviation for Green Day.
P1zzA244WaterShiPDowN	Easily remembered word with mix of alphanumeric characters and upper- and lowercase letters, your locker number at your gym, plus the title of a book that you like (with upper- and lowercase letters).
S0da&ICB3N&J3RRY	Mix of numbers, symbols, and letters. Stands for soda and ice cream and the names of famous ice cream makers with the number 3 instead of the letter E.

Weak Password	Reason
Jsmith	Combination of first initial and last name.
4smithkids	Even though this has alphanumeric combination, it is too descriptive of a family.
Brown5512	Last name and last four digits of phone number are easily decoded.
123MainSt	A street address is an easily decoded password.

evaluate your passwords (see Figure 16). The Password Meter provides guidelines for good passwords and shows you how integrating various elements (such as symbols) affects the strength score for your password.

You should make sure you change your passwords on a regular basis (such as monthly or quarterly). Your school or your employer probably requires you to change your password regularly. This is also a good idea for your personal passwords. You should also not use the same password for every account that you have. Because remembering constantly changing strong passwords for numerous accounts can be

Figure 16

The Password Meter objectively evaluates your passwords.

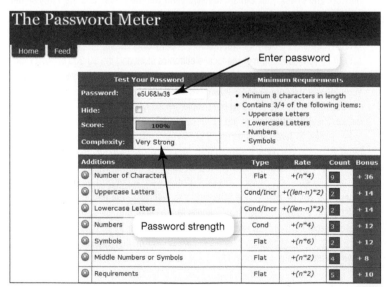

a challenge, you should use password-management tools, as described in the next section, to make the process easier to handle. If you have trouble thinking of secure passwords, there are many password generators available for free, such as Perfect Passwords (**grc.com/passwords.htm**) and the Bytes Interactive Password Generator (**goodpassword.com**).

Can I use a password to restrict access to my computer? Windows has built-in password protection for files as well as the entire desktop. If your computer is set up for multiple users with password protection, the Windows login screen requires you to enter a password to gain access to the desktop. You are also asked to enter a password hint to remind you in case you forget your password. The computer can be set to default back to the Welcome screen after it is idle for a set period of time. This forces a user to reenter a password to regain access to the computer. If someone attempts to log on to your computer without your password, that person won't be able to gain access. It is an especially good idea to use passwords on notebook computers or any computer that may be unattended for periods of time. Figure 17 shows the Control Panel screen used to set up a password on a user account.

There are two types of users in Windows: administrators and standard users. Setting up a password on a standard user account prevents other standard users from being able to access that user's files. However, users with administrator privileges can still see your files if you are a standard user. So be aware that your files may not be safe from all prying eyes!

Managing Your Passwords

How can I remember all of my complex passwords? Good security practices suggest that you have different passwords for different Web sites that you access and that you change your passwords frequently. The problem with well-constructed passwords is that they can be hard to remember. Fortunately, password-management tools are now widely available. This takes the worry out of forgetting passwords because the password-management software does the remembering for you.

Where can I obtain password-management software? Most current Internet security suites and Web browsers make it easy to keep track of passwords by providing password-management tools. For

example, to set up the password manager in Firefox, from the Tools menu, select Options, and then click the Security icon (the closed padlock) shown in Figure 18. In the Passwords section, check **Remember passwords for sites** to have Firefox remember passwords when you log onto Web sites. Check **Use a master password**, which causes a dialog box to appear, and enter a well-designed, secure password. The next time

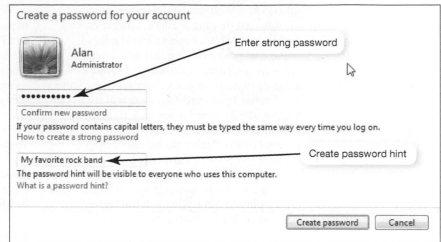

Create a password for your account

Alan
Administrator

•••••••••

Confirm new password

If your password contains capital letters, they must be typed the same way every time you log on.
How to create a strong password

My favorite rock band

The password hint will be visible to everyone who uses this computer.
What is a password hint?

Create password   Cancel

Enter strong password

Create password hint

Figure 17

Windows provides additional security for your files by locking unauthorized users out of your account.

>Click **Start**, click **Control Panel**, click **User Accounts** and **Family Safety**, click **UserAccounts**, and then click **Create a Password** for your account.

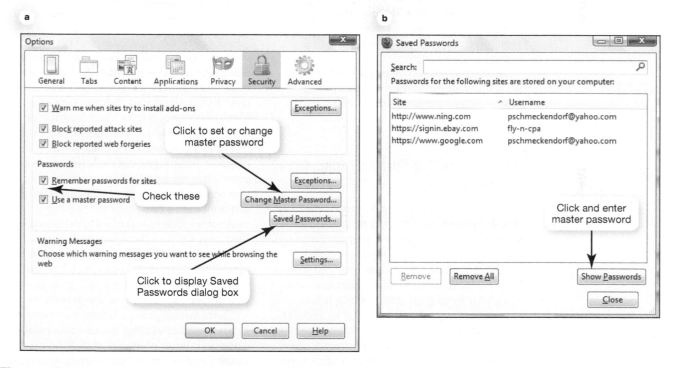

Figure 18

(a) The security tab in the Firefox browser options screen provides access to password-management tools. (b) The Firefox Saved Passwords dialog box displays all sites for which login information is saved.

>From the **Tools** menu, select **Options**. In the **Options** dialog box, click the **Show Passwords** button.

you go to a Web site that requires a login, Firefox will display a dialog box prompting you to have Firefox remember the login name and password for this site. Then, when you return to the site and select a login option, enter the master password and the Firefox Password Manager will fill in the login and password information for you.

You also can see a list of sites maintained by the Firefox Password Manager by clicking the Show Passwords button, which displays the Saved Passwords dialog box (see Figure 18). Passwords for each site are displayed after you click the Show Passwords button and enter the master password.

Even though you only need to remember the master password, you still need to make sure that it is a secure password (according to the rules we discussed earlier) and that you change it on a regular basis. Password managers are useful on the machine that you use on a regular basis. However, if you need to access your accounts from another computer (such as one at school), you will still need to know the individual passwords for each site you wish to access.

So start using secure passwords and let your browser (on your main computer) relieve you of the problem of trying to remember them all.

Anonymous Web Surfing: Hiding from Prying Eyes

Should I be concerned about surfing the Internet on shared or public computers? If you use shared computers in public places such as libraries, coffee shops, or college student unions, you should be concerned about a subsequent user of a computer spying on your surfing habits. You never know what nefarious tools have been installed by hackers on a public computer. When you browse the Internet, traces of your activity are left behind on that computer, often as temporary files. A wily hacker can glean sensitive information long after you have finished your latte and your surfing session.

What tools can I use to protect myself when using public computers? The current versions of Google Chrome, Firefox, and Internet Explorer include privacy tools that help you surf the Internet anonymously. Google Chrome's Incognito feature allows you to open a special version of the Google browser window. When surfing in this window, records of Web sites you visit and files you download do not appear in the Web browser's history files. Furthermore, any temporary files that were generated in that browsing session are deleted when you exit the Incognito window. The InPrivate Browsing feature of Internet Explorer and the Private Browsing feature of Firefox offer similar security features.

Portable privacy devices, such as the IronKey (**ironkey.com**) shown in Figure 19, provide an even higher level of surfing privacy. Simply plug the device into an available USB port on the machine on which you will be working. All sensitive Internet files, such as cookies, Internet history, and browser caches, will be stored on the privacy device, not on the computer you are using. Privacy devices such as these often come preloaded with software designed to shield your IP address from prying eyes, making it difficult (if not impossible) for hackers to tell where you are surfing on the Internet. These privacy devices also have password-management tools that store all of your login information and encrypt it so it will be safe if your privacy device falls into someone else's hands.

Another free practical solution is to take the Linux OS with you on a flash drive and avoid using the public computer's operating system. The interfaces of many Linux builds, such as Ubuntu (see Figure 20), look almost exactly like Windows and are easy to use.

There are several advantages to using a Linux-based operating system on a public computer. First, your risk of picking up viruses and other malicious programs is significantly reduced because booting a public computer from a flash drive completely eliminates any interaction with the public computer's operating system. This, in turn,

Figure 19

Portable privacy devices help to protect your privacy when you work on computers away from your home or office.

Figure 20

Ubuntu is a version of Linux that has a Windows-like interface and familiar browser tools like Firefox.

significantly reduces the chance that your flash drive will become infected by any malware running on the public computer.

Next, virus and hacking attacks against Linux are far less likely than attacks against Windows. Because Windows has more than 90 percent of the operating system market, people who write malware tend to target Windows systems. Finally, when you run software from your own storage medium (flash drive), you avoid reading and writing to the hard disk of the public computer. This significantly enhances your privacy because you don't leave traces of your activity behind.

Pendrivelinux.com (**pendrivelinux.com**) is an excellent resource that offers many different versions of Linux for download and includes step-by-step instructions on how to install them on your flash drive. If you are a Mac user, there is an option for you, too! The gOS version of Linux provides a close approximation of OS X, so you can feel right at home.

Biometric Authentication Devices

Besides passwords, how else can I restrict the use of my computer? A **biometric authentication device** is a device that reads a unique personal characteristic such as a fingerprint or the iris pattern in your eye and converts its pattern to a digital code. When you use the device, your pattern is read and compared to the one stored on the computer. Only users having an exact fingerprint or iris pattern match are allowed to access the computer.

Because no two people have the same biometric characteristics (fingerprints and iris patterns are unique), these devices provide a high level of security. They also eliminate the human error that can occur in password protection. You might forget your password, but you won't forget to bring your fingerprint to the computer! Some notebooks feature built-in fingerprint readers, and companies like SecuGen produce computer mice and keyboards (see Figure 21) that include built-in fingerprint readers. Other biometric devices, which include voice authentication and face pattern–recognition systems, are now widely offered in notebook computers.

Make sure to utilize some (or all) of these methods to keep your activities from prying eyes and to restrict access to your digital information.

Managing Online Annoyances

Surfing the Web, sending and receiving e-mail, and chatting online have become a common part of most of our lives. Unfortunately, the Web has become fertile ground

Figure 21

(a) The SecuGen OptiMouse Plus is a two-button mouse with a scroll wheel that includes a digital fingerprint reader. (b) The SecuGen Keyboard Plus features a fingerprint reader.

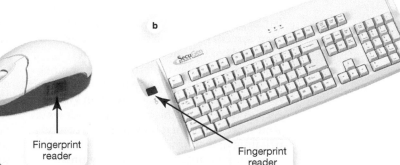

a

Fingerprint reader

b

Fingerprint reader

for people who want to advertise their products, track our Web browsing behaviors, or even con people into revealing personal information. In this section, we'll look at ways in which you can manage, if not avoid, these and other online headaches.

Malware, Adware, and Spyware

What is malware? **Malware** is software that has a malicious intent (hence the prefix *mal*). There are three primary forms of malware: adware, spyware, and viruses (which we have already discussed). Adware and spyware are not physically destructive like viruses and worms, which can destroy data. Known collectively as *grayware*, most are intrusive, annoying, or objectionable online programs that are downloaded to your computer when you install or use other online content such as a freeware program, game, or utility.

What is adware? **Adware** is software that displays sponsored advertisements in a section of your browser window or as a pop-up ad box. It is considered a legitimate (though sometimes annoying) means of generating revenue for those developers who do not charge for their software or information. Pop-up windows (small boxes that open up automatically on your screen) have been referred to as the billboards of the Internet because they appear and display advertisements or other promotional information when you install freeware programs or access certain Web sites. At one point, these pop-up windows were so common that they were incredibly irritating and annoying.

Some pop-ups, however, are legitimate and increase the functionality of the originating site. For example, your account balance may pop up on your bank's Web site. Fortunately, because Web browsers such as Firefox, Safari, and Internet Explorer have pop-up blockers built into their browsers, the occurrence of annoying pop-ups has been greatly reduced. You can access the pop-up blocker settings in your browser (see Figure 22) and add Web sites for which you will allow pop-ups. Whenever a pop-up is blocked, the browser displays an information bar at the top of the browser window or plays a sound to alert you. If you feel the pop-up is legitimate, you can then choose to accept it.

What is spyware? **Spyware** is an unwanted piggyback program that usually downloads with other software you want to install from the Internet. It runs in the background of your system. Without your knowledge, spyware transmits information about you, such as your Internet surfing habits, to the owner of the program so that the information can be used for marketing purposes. Many spyware programs use tracking cookies (small text files stored on your computer) to collect information, whereas others are disguised as benign programs that are really malicious programs (such as Trojan horses). One type of spyware program known as a **keystroke logger** monitors keystrokes with the intent of stealing passwords, login IDs, or credit card information.

Can I prevent spyware? Many Internet security suites now include antispyware software. However, you can also obtain stand-alone spyware removal software and run it on your computer to delete unwanted spyware. Because there are so many variants of spyware, your Internet security software may not detect all types that attempt to install themselves on your

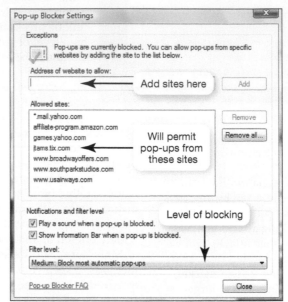

Figure 22

Internet Explorer's Pop-up Blocker Settings dialog box.

>Pop-up Blocker is found in the **Tools** menu on the **Internet Explorer** toolbar.

Think you aren't being closely watched by your employer? Think again! A survey of employers by the American Management Association and the ePolicy Institute revealed that, of the employers surveyed:

- 73 percent monitored e-mail messages
- 66 percent monitored Web surfing
- 48 percent monitored activities using video surveillance
- 45 percent monitored keystrokes and keyboard time
- 43 percent monitored computer files in some other fashion

There is a high probability that you are being monitored while you work and when you access the Internet via your employer's Internet connection (see Figure 23).

The two most frequently cited reasons for employee monitoring are to prevent theft and to measure productivity. Monitoring for theft isn't new, because monitoring cameras have been around for years, and productivity monitoring has been a consistent process for assembly line workers for decades. However, the Internet has led to a new type of productivity drain that is of concern to employers: **Cyberloafing**, or cyberslacking, means doing anything with a computer, while you are being paid to do your job, that is *not* an approved function of your job. Examples of cyberloafing activities are playing games, reading personal e-mail, checking sports scores, watching videos, and buying personal-use products on e-commerce sites. Estimates of business productivity losses due to cyberloafing top $50 billion annually.

Like most other Americans, you probably feel you have a right to privacy in the workplace. Unfortunately, the laws in the United States don't support a worker's right to privacy. Laws such as the 1986 Electronic Communications Privacy Act (ECPA), which prohibits unauthorized monitoring of electronic communications, have been interpreted by the courts in favor of employers. The bottom line is that employers who pay for equipment and software have the legal right to monitor their usage.

But just because an action is *legal* doesn't mean it is *ethical*. It is difficult to argue that an employer doesn't have the right to take measures to prevent theft and detect low productivity. The ethical issue here is whether or not the employees are made aware of monitoring policies. An ethical employer should treat employees with respect and dignity and inform employees of any monitoring. Employers have an ethical

responsibility (and a legal one as well, depending on the jurisdiction) not to place monitoring devices in sensitive locations such as bathrooms and dressing areas. However, in many states, the employer does not need to inform the employees in advance that they are being monitored. Conscientious employers include monitoring disclosures in published employee policies to avoid confusion and conflict.

Employers use a variety of software programs to monitor employee computer usage. Certain software packages keep track of every Web site you visit and the duration of your stay. Checking the baseball scores might take only three seconds and go unnoticed, but spending two hours updating your fantasy football team may be flagged. Keystroke loggers were originally used to monitor performance for people with input-intensive jobs like clerks and secretaries. Now these programs have the potential to be used to invade your privacy because they can record everything you type, even that nasty e-mail about the boss that you decided to delete!

Computer software can also be used to monitor the contents of your hard drive, so you don't want to collect 4,823 illegal MP3 files on your work computer. Some programs even track how long your computer is idle, which can give your manager a good idea of whether you were working or taking a three-hour lunch.

Since your employer might not tell you that your computer use is being monitored, you should assume that anything you do on your company-provided computer is subject to scrutiny. If you need to do personal work on your lunch hour or other breaks, you may be able to use your personal notebook computer to avoid the monitoring. Check with your employer to be sure you can connect personal computers to the corporate network or Internet connection. Note that courts in some jurisdictions have ruled that e-mails sent from third-party systems, such as Yahoo! and Gmail, are subject to monitoring if they are sent from employer-provided computer systems. Instant messaging is also subject to monitoring.

People who monitor employees have a duty to protect their right to privacy and not to disclose any information that they may inadvertently see during the course of monitoring. The acceptable computer use policies at most companies include guidelines for network administrators and other people who have high levels of access to sensitive information. When monitoring employees' work habits, management must ensure that compliance with the policies is tested periodically. Periodic reviews of procedures and compliance help ensure that established company policies are working as designed. An ethical employer strives to prevent misuse of personal data and accidental data loss. However, you can't always be certain that everyone who monitors you will behave ethically. Therefore, you need to think very carefully about exactly what personal tasks you are willing to risk engaging in on company computer systems.

So, do your employers have an ethical right to monitor your activities? Certainly, they have a right to ensure they are getting a fair day's work from you, just as you have an ethical obligation to provide a fair effort for a fair wage. However, employers should also be willing to respect the privacy rights of their employees and treat them as professionals, unless there is some indication of wrongdoing. Because employers may have a legal right to monitor you in the workplace, you should work under the assumption that everything you do on your work computer is subject to scrutiny and behave accordingly. Do your online shopping at home!

Figure 23
Big Brother might really be watching you at work.

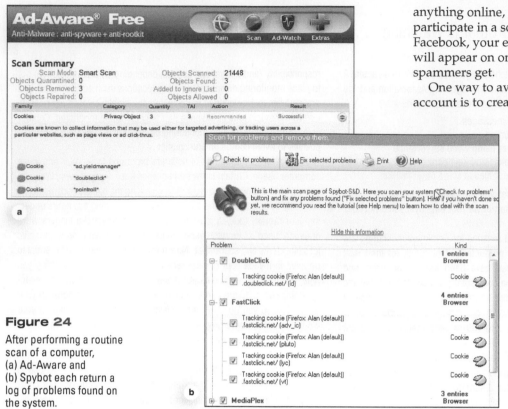

Figure 24

After performing a routine scan of a computer, (a) Ad-Aware and (b) Spybot each return a log of problems found on the system.

computer. Therefore, it is a good idea to install one or two additional stand-alone antispyware programs on your computer.

Because new spyware is created all the time, you should update and run your spyware removal software regularly. Windows comes with a program called Windows Defender, which scans your system for spyware and other potentially unwanted software. Malwarebytes Anti-Malware, Ad-Aware, and Spybot–Search & Destroy (all available from **download.com**) are other programs that are easy to install and update. Figure 24 shows an example of Ad-Aware and Spybot in action. They detect unwanted programs and allow you to delete the offending software easily.

Spam

How can I best avoid spam?
Companies that send out **spam**—unwanted or junk e-mail—find your e-mail address either from a list they purchase or with software that looks for e-mail addresses on the Internet. (Unsolicited instant messages are also a form of spam, called *spim*.) If you've used your e-mail address to purchase

anything online, open an online account, or participate in a social network such as Facebook, your e-mail address eventually will appear on one of the lists that spammers get.

One way to avoid spam in your primary account is to create a free Web-based e-mail address that you use only when you fill out forms or purchase items on the Web. For example, both Windows Live Mail and Yahoo! allow you to set up free e-mail accounts. If your free Web-based e-mail account is saturated with spam, then you can abandon that account with little inconvenience. It's much less convenient to abandon your primary e-mail address.

Another way to avoid spam is to filter it. A **spam filter** is an option you can select in your e-mail account that places known or suspected spam messages into a folder other than your inbox. Most Web-based e-mail services, such as Office Live Mail and Yahoo!, offer spam filters (see Figure 25). Files perceived to be spam are segregated in a special folder (often named "Spam" or "Junk Mail"). Microsoft Outlook also features a spam filter. Third-party programs that provide some control over spam include SPAMfighter and Cactus Spam Filter, both of which can be obtained at **download.com**.

How do spam filters work? Spam filters and filtering software can catch as much as 95 percent of spam by checking incoming e-mail subject headers and senders' addresses against databases of known spam. Spam filters also check your e-mail for frequently used spam patterns and keywords (such as "for free" and "over 21"). E-mail that the filter identifies as spam does not go into your inbox but rather to a folder set up for spam. Spam filters aren't perfect, and you should check the spam folder before deleting its contents because legitimate e-mail might end up there by mistake. Most programs provide you with a tool to reclassify e-mails that have been misidentified as spam.

Figure 25

In Yahoo! Mail, messages identified as spam are directed into a folder called "Spam" for review and deletion.

How else can I prevent spam?
There are several additional ways you can prevent spam.

1. Before registering on a Web site, read its privacy policy to see how it uses your e-mail address. Don't give the site permission to pass on your e-mail address to third parties.

2. Don't reply to spam to remove yourself from the spam list. By replying, you are confirming that your e-mail address is active. Instead of stopping spam, you may receive more.

3. Subscribe to an e-mail forwarding service such as Emailias (**emailias.com**) or Sneakemail.com (**sneakemail.com**). These services screen your e-mail messages, forwarding only those messages you designate as being okay to accept.

Cookies

What are cookies?   Cookies (also known as *tracking cookies*) are small text files that some Web sites automatically store on your computer's hard drive when you visit them. When you log on to a Web site that uses cookies, a cookie file assigns an ID number to your computer. The unique ID is intended to make your return visit to a Web site more efficient and better geared to your interests. The next time you log on to that site, the site marks your visit and keeps track of it in its database.

What do Web sites do with cookie information?   Cookies can provide Web sites with information about your browsing habits, such as the ads you've opened, the products you've looked at, and the time and duration of your visits. Companies use this information to determine the traffic flowing through their Web site and the effectiveness of their marketing strategy and placement on Web sites. By tracking such information, cookies enable companies to identify different users' preferences.

Can companies get my personal information when I visit their sites?   Cookies do not go through your hard drive in search of personal information such as passwords or financial data. The only personal information a cookie obtains is the information you supply when you fill out forms online.

Do privacy risks exist with cookies?   Some sites sell the personal information their cookies collect to Web advertisers who are building huge databases of consumer preferences and habits, collecting personal and business information such as phone numbers, credit reports, and the like. The main concern is that advertisers will use this information indiscriminately, thus infiltrating your privacy. And you may feel your privacy is being violated by tracking cookies that monitor where you go on a Web site.

Should I delete cookies from my hard drive?   Because cookies pose no security threat (it is virtually impossible to hide a virus or malicious software program in a cookie), take up little room on your hard drive, and offer you small conveniences on return visits to Web sites, there is no great reason to delete them. Deleting your cookie files could actually cause you the inconvenience of reentering data you have already entered into Web site forms. However, if you're uncomfortable with the accessibility of your personal information, you can periodically delete cookies or configure your browser to block certain types of cookies, as shown in Figure 26. Software such as

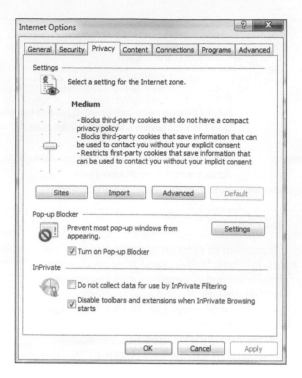

Figure 26

Tools are available, either through your browser (Internet Explorer is shown here) or as separate applications, to distinguish between cookies you want to keep and cookies you don't want on your system.

>On the Internet Explorer menu toolbar, click **Tools**, and then click **Internet Options**. The cookie settings are on the **Privacy** tab.

Cookie Pal (**kburra.com**) also can help you monitor cookies.

Protecting Yourself . . . from Yourself!

People are often too trusting or just plain careless when it comes to protecting private information about themselves or their digital data. When was the last time you created a copy of your digital data (such as the thousands of photographs you have stored on your hard drive)? The hard drive in your computer is likely to fail at some point, which may render all the data on it useless. What strategy do you have in place to protect your data from damage?

If you have a Facebook or Twitter account, you are probably constantly revealing information about your likes and dislikes, such as what movie you saw this weekend or the presents you received for your birthday. You might even be revealing information about where you live. Have you ever filled out an online form to enter a contest? Have you ever applied for a customer loyalty card at your local supermarket or electronics store? Think about how much information you voluntarily give up all the time in the course of running your digital

life. Con artists and scammers take advantage of people's tendency to reveal information freely to compromise their privacy and commit theft.

In this section, we discuss ways to keep your data safe from damage (either accidental or intentional) and to keep unscrupulous individuals from tricking you into revealing sensitive information.

Protecting Your Personal Information

If a complete stranger walked up to you on the street and asked you for your address and phone number, would you give it to them? Of course you wouldn't! But many people are much less careful when it comes to sharing sensitive information online. And often people inadvertently share information that they really only intended to share with their friends. With cybercrimes like identify theft rampant, you need to take steps to protect your personal information.

What information should I never share on Web sites? Your Social Security number, phone number, and street address are three key pieces of information that identity thieves need to steal an identity. This information should never be shared in a public area on any Web site.

Many sites, such as Facebook, ask for other potentially sensitive information when you sign up. This information might include your real name, e-mail address, birth date, zip code, and gender. After you register, social networking sites then encourage you to add profile details such as your school, your employer, your personal interests and hobbies, and who your friends are. Although it is fine to share this information with people you know, you need to be careful that your information isn't visible to everyone.

How can I tell who can see my information in a social network? Social networking sites, like Facebook, make privacy settings available in their account menus. If you have never changed your privacy settings in Facebook, you are probably sharing information more widely than you should. Since Facebook is designed to foster social interaction, the default privacy settings make it easy to search for people. Someone with nefarious intentions could glean quite a bit of information from your Facebook profile, including your contact information, which they might use to trick you into revealing other information that would lead to them stealing your identity.

How can I protect my information on Facebook? To begin, you need to change your privacy settings from some of the default options. On the upper right-hand side of the Facebook page, click Account and then click Privacy Settings. On the Privacy Settings page, select Profile Information to display the screen shown in Figure 27a. It's a good idea to set most of the options on this screen to Only Friends because, presumably, you are only friending people you trust.

The other screen you need to address is Contact Information Privacy Settings (see Figure 27b), which you can also reach from the Privacy Settings page. Restricting this information only to friends or to yourself is imperative. You don't want scammers contacting you via phone and trying to trick you into revealing sensitive information. So use discretion and keep your information as private as possible.

Backing Up Your Data

How might I damage the data on my computer? The data on your computer faces three major threats: unauthorized access, tampering, and destruction. As noted earlier, a hacker can gain access to your computer and steal or alter your data. However, a more likely scenario is that you will lose your data unintentionally. You may accidentally delete files. You may drop your notebook on the ground, causing the hard drive to break, resulting in complete data loss. A virus from an e-mail attachment you opened may destroy your original file. Your house or dorm may catch fire and destroy your computer. Because many of these possibilities are beyond your control, you should have a strategy for backing up your files, which is especially important if you are running a small business. (The backup strategy for small businesses is quite similar to the procedures recommended for individuals.)

What exactly is meant by "backing up data"? Backups are copies of files that you can use to replace the originals if they are lost or damaged. To be truly secure, backups must be stored away from where

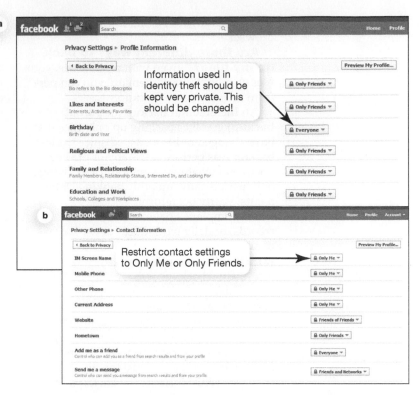

your computer is located. You wouldn't want a fire or a flood destroying the backups along with the original data. Removable storage media, such as external hard drives, DVDs, and flash drives have been popular choices for backing up files because they hold a lot of data and can be transported easily.

What types of files do I need to back up? Two types of files need backups—program files and data files.

A **program file** is used to install software and usually comes on CDs or DVDs or is downloaded from the Web. If any programs came preinstalled in your computer, then you may have received a CD or DVD that contains the original program. As long as you have the original media in a safe place, you shouldn't need to back up these files. If you have downloaded a program file from the Internet, however, you should make a copy of the program installation files on a removable storage device as a backup. If you didn't receive discs for installed programs with your computer, then see the next section for suggested strategies for backing up your entire computer.

A **data file** is a file you have created or purchased. Data files include such files as research papers, spreadsheets, music files, movies, contact lists, address books, e-mail

Figure 27

You should review the (a) Profile Information and (b) Contact Information privacy settings in Facebook to ensure you aren't sharing too much information.

archives, and your Favorites list from your browser.

Are there different ways to back up my files? Even with modest use, your files change. To back them up, you can perform an incremental backup.

An **incremental backup** (or **partial backup**) involves backing up only files that have changed or been created since the last backup was performed. Many of the key documents that you want to protect change only periodically: monthly banking statements, yearly tax returns, weekly employee payment records, or daily work documents. Using backup software that has an option for incremental backups will save a tremendous amount of time because backing up files that haven't changed is redundant.

An **image backup** (or **system backup**) means that all system, application, and data files are backed up, not just the files that changed. While incremental backups are more efficient, an image backup ensures you capture changes to application files, such as automatic software updates, that an incremental backup might not capture. The idea of imaging is to make an exact copy of the setup of your computer so that in the event of a total hard drive failure, you could copy the image to a new hard drive and have your computer configured exactly the way it was before the crash. This is a quick way to get up and running again.

How often should I back up my files? You should back up your data files frequently. How frequently depends on how much work you cannot afford to lose. You should always back up data files when you make changes to them, especially if those changes involve hours of work. It may not seem important to back up your history term paper file when you finish it, but do you really want to do all that work again if your computer crashes before you have a chance to turn in your paper?

Because your program and operating system files don't change as often as your data files, you can perform image backups on a less frequent basis. Most backup software can be configured to do backups automatically so you don't forget to perform them. You might consider scheduling backups of your data files on a daily basis and an image

backup of your entire system on a weekly basis.

To make backups easier, store all your data files in one folder on your hard drive. For example, in Windows and most other operating systems, on your hard drive you will find a folder called Documents. You can create subfolders (such as History Homework, Music Files, and so on) within the Documents folder. If you store all your data under one main folder on your hard drive, you simply configure your backup software to back up that folder and all subfolders beneath it.

Where do the backups of my files reside? This location is a decision that you need to make. You have three main choices:

> **"How often should I back up my files?"**

1. **Online sites.** In essence, online storage is like using the Internet as an alternative to a portable storage device (such as an external hard drive or flash drive). The beauty of online storage is that your data is available anywhere you are; you do not need to be at your computer or have to lug around your external hard drive to access the information. More important, because the information is stored online, it is in a secure, remote location, so data is much less vulnerable to all the potential disasters (such as a flood) that could harm data stored in your computer or external hard drive. If you are taking advantage of one of these free online storage services, selectivity is the key because of cost. Although you might have hundreds of gigabytes of data sitting on your computer, perhaps you only need to store several gigabytes online so that they are always available.

A convenient free storage option for Windows users is Windows Live SkyDrive (**skydrive.live.com**), which provides 25 GB of storage space. For non-Windows users or those needing even more storage space, check out ADrive (**adrive.com**) and its 50 GB of free storage! Fee-based plans at ADrive give users access to tools that allow them to schedule automatic backups of files and folders. However, image backups probably won't fit within the storage limits offered by free providers. For a fee, companies such as Iron Mountain (**backup.ironmountain.com**) and IBackup (**ibackup.com**) provide larger storage capacity.

If you store a backup of your entire system on the Internet, then you won't need to buy an additional hard drive for backups. This method also takes the worry out of finding a safe place to keep your backups because they're always stored in an area far away from your computer (on the backup company's server). However, the yearly fees can be expensive, so a cheaper option may be to buy an external hard drive.

2. **Local drives.** External hard drives are popular options for performing backups of data files and for complete image backups. Affordable external drives are available with capacities of 3 TB or more. These drives are usually connected to a single computer and often come with their own backup software (although you could still use the backup software included with your operating system). Although convenient and inexpensive, using external hard drives for backups still presents the dilemma of keeping the hard drive in a safe location. You need to keep the hard drive connected to your computer to perform scheduled backups, but for ultimate safety the hard drive should be stored in a location separate from the computer in case of catastrophic events, such as a fire. Therefore, using an external hard drive for backups is best done in conjunction with an online backup strategy for added safety.

3. **Network-attached storage devices and home servers.** Manufacturers such as HP, Seagate, and Buffalo Technology now make network-attached storage (NAS) devices and servers designed for home networks. The NAS devices are essentially large hard drives that are connected to a network of computers instead of one computer, and they can be used to back up multiple computers simultaneously. Home servers are not really servers like those found in client/server networks. Home servers act as high-capacity NAS devices for automatically backing up data and

sharing files. Both NAS devices and home servers are easy to configure and are very useful if you have multiple computers within a single household that need backing up.

How do I actually perform a file backup? Windows 7 includes the Backup and Restore utility, which provides a quick and easy way to schedule file backups, restore files from backups, or perform image (system) backups. You can access Backup and Restore from the Control Panel. Before starting this utility, make sure your external hard drive or NAS device is connected to your computer or network and is powered on.

When you start the Backup and Restore utility for the first time, no backups will have ever been configured. Select the Set up backup option to launch the Set up backup dialog box (see Figure 28a) and display a list of available backup devices. Select a device and click Next to proceed. On the next screen, you have the option to let Windows choose what to back up or to choose for

Figure 28

The Windows 7 Backup and Restore utility. (a) Select your backup destination. (b) Choose locations to back up. (c) Review your scheduled backups, restore files, and start wizards for system image and repair disc creation.

a
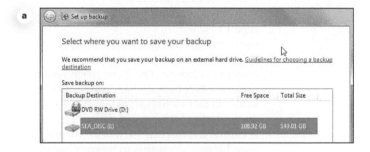

b
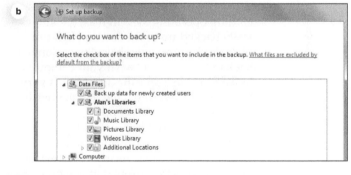

c

yourself what you want to back up. If you select the Let me choose option, the screen shown in Figure 28b displays. You can then click the appropriate check boxes to select the libraries you wish to back up. Click Next to proceed. On the following screen, you can review your settings and set up a schedule for the backups. When you click the Save settings and exit button, you are returned to the Back up or restore your files screen (see Figure 28c), which now shows the scheduled backup. You can also choose to restore backed-up files you have backed up from this screen.

From the Back up or restore your files screen, you also have two other options. If you click the Create a system image link, you will be walked through a series of steps to configure an image backup of your system. The Create a system repair disc link helps you create a DVD repair disc that can be used to boot your computer in case of a serious Windows error. This disc is also used when you need to restore your computer from an image backup, so it is a good idea to create the repair disc before you begin using your computer heavily.

"Should I back up files on my school's network?"

For Mac OS X users, backups are very easy to configure. The Time Machine feature (in Mac OS X Leopard and subsequent versions) detects when an external hard drive is connected to the computer or a NAS device is connected to your network. You are then asked if you want this to be your backup drive. If you answer yes, all of your files (including operating system files) are automatically backed up to the external drive or NAS device. You even have the option to go back in time and see what your computer looked like on a specific date. This is very handy for recovering a file that you wish you hadn't deleted.

No matter what backup strategy you choose, be sure to perform them on a regular basis because nearly everyone has need to access backup files at one time or another.

Should I back up my files that are stored on my school's network? Most likely, if you're allowed to store files on your school's network, these files are backed up on a regular basis. You should check with your school's network administrators to determine how often they're backed up and how you would go about requesting that files be restored from the backup media if they're damaged or deleted. But don't rely on these network backups to bail you out if your data files are lost or damaged. It may take days for the network administrators to get around to restoring your files. It is better to keep backups of your data files yourself (especially homework and project files) so that you can immediately restore them. Buy a large-capacity flash drive and carry it with you!

Social Engineering: Fooling the Unwary

What is social engineering? **Social engineering** is any technique that uses social skills to generate human interaction that entices individuals to reveal sensitive information. Social engineering often doesn't involve the use of a computer or face-to-face interaction. For example, telephone scams are a common form of social engineering because it is often easier to manipulate someone when you don't have to look at them.

How does social engineering work? Most social engineering schemes use a pretext to lure their victims. **Pretexting** involves creating a scenario that sounds legitimate enough that someone will trust you. For example, you might receive a phone call during which the caller says he is from the bank and that someone tried to use your account without authorization. The caller then tells you he needs to confirm a few personal details such as your birth date, Social Security number, bank account number, and whatever other information he can get out of you. The information he obtains can then be used to empty your bank account or commit some other form of fraud. Often pretexting is used to gain access to corporate computer networks. People will sometimes call random extensions in a large business, claiming to be from technical support. Eventually, the caller will find someone who has a problem and is happy that someone is willing to help. The scam artist will then elicit information such as

Computers in Society: Identity Theft—Is There More Than One of You Out There?

You've no doubt heard of identity theft. A thief steals your name, address, Social Security number, bank account and credit card information and runs up debts in your name. This leaves you holding the bag, and you're hounded by creditors collecting on the fraudulent debts. It sounds horrible—and it is. In fact, one of the authors of this textbook had his identity stolen and spent about 50 hours filing police reports, talking to credit agencies, closing bogus accounts, and convincing companies that the $25,000 of debt run up on six phony credit card accounts was done by an identity thief. Many victims of identity theft spend months (or even years) trying to repair their credit and eliminate fraudulent debts. Worse yet, if an identity thief uses your identity to obtain medical services at a hospital, you may be denied coverage at a later date because the thief's treatment has exceeded the limit of covered services on your policy.

Stories of identity thieves—such as the New York man accused of stealing more than 30,000 identities—abound in the media and should serve to make the public wary. However, many media pundits would have you believe that the only way your identity can be stolen is by a computer. This is simply not true. The Federal Trade Commission (**ftc.gov**) has identified other methods thieves use to obtain others' personal information. These include (1) stealing purses and wallets, in which people often keep unnecessary valuable personal information such as their ATM PIN codes; (2) stealing mail or looking through trash for bank statements and credit card bills, which provide valuable personal information; and (3) posing as bank or credit card company representatives and tricking people into revealing sensitive information over the phone.

Obviously, you're at risk from online attacks, too, such as phishing. Once identity thieves obtain your personal information, they can use it in many different ways. Identity thieves often request a change of address for your credit card bill or bank statement. By the time you realize that you aren't receiving your statements, the thieves have rung up bogus charges on your account or emptied your bank account. The thieves can open new credit card and bank accounts in your name. They then will write bad checks and not pay the credit card bills, which will ruin your credit rating.

Even worse, the identity thieves may counterfeit debit cards or checks for your legitimate accounts and empty them of funds. They might even take out a mortgage in your name and then disappear with the proceeds, leaving you with the debt.

Although foolproof protection methods don't exist, there are precautions that will help you minimize your risk. You should never reveal your password or your PIN code to anyone or place it in an easy-to-find location. Also, never reveal personal information unless you're sure that a legitimate reason exists for a business to know the information, and you can confirm you're actually dealing with a legitimate representative (don't fall for phishing schemes). If someone calls or e-mails asking you for personal information, decline and call the company with which you opened your account.

Obviously, you should create secure passwords for your online accounts. When shopping online, be wary of unfamiliar merchants that you can't contact through a mailing address or phone number, or businesses whose prices are too good to be true. These can be attempts to collect your personal information for use in fraudulent schemes.

If you have been the victim of identity theft, most states now allow you to freeze your credit history so that no new accounts can be opened until you lift the credit freeze. Even if you live in a state where you can't freeze your account, you can still place an extended fraud alert on your credit history for seven years, which also warns merchants that they should check with you (at your home address or phone number) before opening an account in your name.

Using common sense and keeping personal information in the hands of as few people as possible are the best defenses against identity theft. For additional tips on preventing identity theft or for procedures to follow if you are a victim, check out the Identity Theft Resource Center (**idtheftcenter.org**).

---

logins and passwords from the victim as part of the process for "solving the problem." The most common form of pretexting in cyberspace is phishing.

Phishing and Pharming

How are phishing schemes conducted? **Phishing** (pronounced "fishing") lures Internet users to reveal personal information such as credit card numbers, Social Security numbers, or other sensitive information that could lead to identity theft. The scammers send e-mail messages that look like they are from a legitimate business such as an online bank. The e-mail states that the recipient needs to update or confirm his or her account information. When the recipient clicks the provided link, he or she goes to a Web site. The site looks like a legitimate site but is really a fraudulent copy the scammer has created. Once the e-mail recipient confirms his or her personal information, the scammers capture it and can begin using it.

Is pharming a type of phishing scam? Pharming is much more insidious than phishing. Phishing requires a positive action by the person being scammed, such as going to a Web site mentioned in an e-mail and typing in your bank account information. **Pharming** is when malicious code is planted on your computer that alters your browser's ability to find Web addresses. Users are directed to bogus Web sites even when they enter the correct address of the real Web site or follow a bookmark that they previously had established for the Web site. So instead of ending up at your bank's Web site when you type in its address, you end up at a fake Web site that looks like your bank's site but is expressly set up for the purpose of gathering information.

How can I avoid being caught by phishing and pharming scams? You should never reply directly to any e-mail asking you for personal information. Never click on a link in an e-mail to go to a Web site. Instead, type the Web site address in the browser. Check with the company asking for the information and only give the information if you are certain it is needed.

Also, never give personal information over the Internet unless you know the site is secure. Look for the closed padlock, https, or a certification seal such as VeriSign to help reassure you that the site is secure. The latest versions of Firefox, Chrome, and Internet Explorer have phishing filters built in, so each time you access a Web site, the phishing filter checks for the site's legitimacy and warns you of possible Web forgeries. Finally, make sure you have Internet security software installed on your computer and that it is constantly being updated. Most Internet security packages can detect and prevent pharming attacks. The major Internet security packages—for example, McAfee and Norton (see Figure 29)—also offer phishing-protection tools. When you have the Norton Toolbar displayed in your browser, you are constantly informed about the legitimacy of the site you are visiting.

Another way to protect yourself is never to use your credit card number when you shop online. Although it sounds impossible, credit card providers such as Citibank are offering services such as "Virtual Account Numbers" for their customers. Before purchasing a product online, you visit an online site, where you are assigned a new virtual account number each time you visit. This number looks like a regular credit card number and is tied to your real credit card account. However, the virtual account number can be used only once. That means that if the number is stolen, it's no good to thieves. They can't use the virtual account number, because you've already used it.

Hoaxes

What is a hoax? A **hoax** is an attempt to make someone believe something that is untrue. Hoaxes target a large audience and are generally perpetrated as practical jokes, instruments of social change (which poke fun at an established norm in an effort to change it), or merely ways to waste people's valuable time. Although there are hoax Web sites such as Pacific Northwest Tree Octopus (**zapatopi.net/treeoctopus**), most cyberspace hoaxes are perpetrated by e-mail.

Why do people concoct e-mail hoaxes? As opposed to garnering financial rewards (like in a phishing fraud), the motives of e-mail hoax creators can be more complex. Many people start an e-mail hoax just for the challenge of seeing if their "brainchild" can be spread globally. Other hoaxes start as innocent practical jokes between friends that take on lives of their own via the fast communication available on the Internet. Many hoaxes become so well known that they are accepted by society as true events even though they are false. Once this happens to a hoax, it becomes known as an **urban legend**. An example is the phony story about the man who woke up in a bathtub full of ice water and found he had had his kidney stolen. Hoaxes may be compared to acts of real-world vandalism like graffiti. Graffiti artists "make their mark" on the world, physically; hoaxers may consider they are making a similar mark when a bogus e-mail they have created becomes widespread.

Sometimes hoaxes are based on misinformation or are a way to vent frustration. An e-mail hoax that reappears every time there is a spike in gasoline prices is the Gas Boycott (Gas War) hoax. To boost the scheme's credibility, the e-mail touts it as

Figure 29

Not sure whether you are on the Amazon Web site or a cleverly disguised phishing site? Norton Site Safety reassures you that all is well.

having been invented by reputable business-people. The e-mail explains how boycotting certain gasoline companies will drive the price of gasoline down and urges recipients of the e-mail to join the fight. The originator of this hoax was probably frustrated by high gas prices and, armed with a poor understanding of economics, distributed this brainstorm. Unfortunately, this tactic can have no effect on gasoline prices because it only shifts demand for gasoline from certain oil companies to other sources. Because it does not reduce the overall demand for gasoline, the price of gas will not decline. Did you receive this e-mail and think it sounded like a plausible idea? How many people did you forward it to?

How can I tell if an e-mail is a hoax? Sometimes it is difficult to separate fact from fiction. Many hoax e-mails are well written and crafted in such a way that they sound very real. Before using the Forward button and sending an e-mail to all your friends, check it out at one of the many Web sites that keep track of and expose e-mail hoaxes. Check sites such as Snopes (**snopes.com**), Hoax-Slayer (**hoax-slayer.com**, shown in Figure 30), or TruthOrFiction.com (**truthorfiction.com**). These sites are searchable, so you can enter a few keywords from an e-mail you suspect may be a hoax and quickly find similar e-mails and explanations of whether they are true or false. Checking out e-mails before forwarding them on to friends, family, and co-workers will save other people's time and help end the spread of these time wasters.

Protecting Your Physical Computing Assets

Your computer isn't useful to you if it is damaged. Therefore, it's essential to select and ensure a safe environment for it. This includes protecting it from environmental factors, power surges, power outages, and theft.

Environmental Factors

Why is the environment critical to the operation of my computer equipment? Computers are delicate devices

and can be damaged by the adverse effects of abuse or a poor environment. Sudden movements (such as a fall) can damage your notebook computer or mobile device's internal components. You should make sure that your computer sits on a flat, level surface, and, if it is a notebook, carry it in a padded case to protect it. If you do drop your computer, have it professionally tested by a computer repair facility to check for any hidden damage.

Electronic components do not like excessive heat or excessive cold. Unfortunately, computers generate a lot of heat, which is why they have fans to cool their internal components. Make sure that you place your desktop computer where the fan's input vents (usually found on the rear of the system unit) are unblocked so that air can flow inside. Chill mats that contain cooling fans and sit underneath notebook computers are useful accessories for dissipating heat. And don't leave computing devices in a car during especially hot or cold weather because components can be damaged by extreme temperatures. Naturally, a fan drawing air into a computer also draws in dust and other particles, which can wreak havoc on your system. Therefore, keep the room in which your computer is located as clean as possible. Even in a clean room, the fan ducts can become packed with dust, so vacuum it periodically to keep a clear airflow into your computer. Finally, because food crumbs and liquid can damage keyboards and other computer components, consume food and beverages away from your computer.

Figure 30

Sites like Hoax-Slayer help you research potential hoaxes.

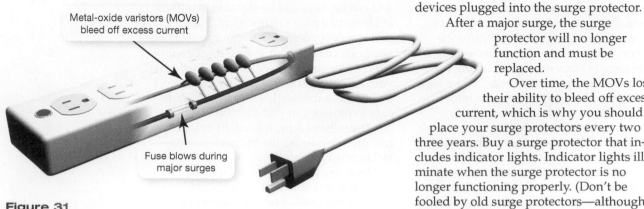

Metal-oxide varistors (MOVs) bleed off excess current

Fuse blows during major surges

Figure 31

Anatomy of a surge protector.

Power Surges

What is a power surge? Power surges occur when electrical current is supplied in excess of normal voltage (120 volts in the United States). Old or faulty wiring, downed power lines, malfunctions at electric company substations, and lightning strikes can all cause power surges. A **surge protector** is a device that protects your computer against power surges (see Figure 31). To use a surge protector, you simply plug your electrical devices into the outlets of the surge protector, which in turn plugs into the wall.

How do surge protectors work? Surge protectors contain two components that are used to protect the equipment that is connected to them. Metal-oxide varistors (MOVs) bleed off excess current during minor surges and feed it to the ground wire, where it harmlessly dissipates. The MOVs can do this while still allowing normal current to pass through the devices plugged into the surge protector. Because the ground wire is critical to this process, it is important to plug the surge protector into a grounded (typically, three-prong) power outlet.

During major surges that overwhelm the MOVs, a fuse inside the surge protector blows, which stops the flow of current to all devices plugged into the surge protector. After a major surge, the surge protector will no longer function and must be replaced.

Over time, the MOVs lose their ability to bleed off excess current, which is why you should replace your surge protectors every two to three years. Buy a surge protector that includes indicator lights. Indicator lights illuminate when the surge protector is no longer functioning properly. (Don't be fooled by old surge protectors—although they can still function as multiple-outlet power strips, they deliver power to your equipment without protecting it.) A power surge could ruin your computer and other devices if you don't protect them. At $20 to $40, a quality surge protector is an excellent investment.

Besides my computer, what other devices need to be connected to a surge protector? All electronic devices in the home that have solid state components, such as TVs, stereos, printers, and phones, should be connected to a surge protector. Printers and other computer peripherals all require protection. However, it can be inconvenient to use individual surge protectors on everything. A more practical method is to install a **whole-house surge protector** (see Figure 32). Whole-house surge protectors function like other surge protectors, but they protect *all* electrical devices in the house. Typically, you will need an electrician to install a whole-house surge protector, which will cost $200 to $300 (installed).

Is my equipment 100 percent safe when plugged into a surge protector? Surge protectors won't necessarily guard against all surges. Lightning strikes can generate such high voltages that they can overwhelm a surge protector. As tedious as it sounds, unplugging

Surge protector

Figure 32

A whole-house surge protector usually is installed at the breaker panel or near the electric meter.

computers and peripherals during an electrical storm is the only way to achieve absolute protection.

How can I prevent my computers from losing power during a power outage? Computers can develop software glitches caused by a loss of power if not shut down properly. Mission-critical computers such as Web servers often are protected by an **uninterruptible power supply (UPS)**, as shown in Figure 33, which is a device that contains surge protection equipment and a large battery. When power is interrupted (such as during a blackout), the UPS continues to send power to the attached computer from its battery. Depending on the battery capacity, you have between about 20 minutes and 3 hours to save your work and shut down your computer properly.

Figure 33

A UPS device should not be mistaken for a fat surge protector!

Deterring Theft

Because they are portable, notebooks are easy targets for thieves. Even though they are not considered portable, desktop computers are also subject to theft. Three approaches to deterring computer theft include alarming them, locking them down, or installing devices that alert you (or destroy data) when the computer is stolen.

Alarms

What type of alarm can I install on my notebook computer? To prevent your notebook from being stolen, you can attach a motion alarm to it (see Figure 34).

SOUND BYTE Surge Protectors

In this Sound Byte, you'll learn about the major features of surge protectors and how they work. You'll also learn about the key factors you need to consider before buying a surge protector, and you'll see how easy it is to install one.

When you leave your notebook, you use a small device called a *key fob activator* or punch in a code to activate the alarm. If your notebook is moved while the alarm is activated, it emits a wailing 100-decibel sound. The fact that the alarm is visible acts as an additional theft deterrent, just like a "Beware of Dog" sign in a front yard.

Locks and Surrounds

How can I lock up a notebook computer? Chaining a notebook to your work surface can be another effective way to prevent theft. As shown in Figure 35, a special locking mechanism is attached to the notebook (some notebooks are even manufactured with locking ports), and a hardened steel cable is connected to the locking mechanism. The other end of the cable is looped around something large and heavy, such as a desk. The cable lock requires the use of a key or combination to free the notebook. You should consider taking a cable lock with you when traveling to help deter theft from hotel rooms.

Software Alerts

How can my computer alert me when it is stolen? You've probably heard of LoJack, the theft-tracking device used in cars. Car owners install a LoJack transmitter somewhere in their vehicle. If the vehicle is stolen, police activate the transmitter and use its signal to locate the car. Similar

Figure 34

A notebook alarm sends out an ear-piercing sound if your notebook is moved before you deactivate the alarm.

Alarm

Figure 35

Cable locks are an effective deterrent to theft.

systems now exist for computers. Tracking software such as Computrace LoJack for Laptops (**absolute.com**), PC PhoneHome, and Mac PhoneHome (**pcphonehome.com**) enables the computer to alert authorities to the computer's location if it is stolen. This software can be installed in either notebook or desktop computers.

To enable your computer to help with its own recovery, install the tracking software on your hard drive. The software contacts a server at the software manufacturer's Web site each time you connect to the Internet. If your computer is stolen, you notify the software manufacturer. The software manufacturer instructs your computer to transmit tracking information (such as an IP address)

that will assist authorities in locating and retrieving the stolen computer.

What if the thieves find the tracking software and delete it? The files and directories holding the software are not visible to thieves looking for such software, so they probably won't know the software is there. Furthermore, the tracking software is written in such a way that even if the thieves tried to reformat the hard drive, it would detect the reformat and hide the software code in a safe place in memory or on the hard drive. (Some sectors of a hard drive are not rewritten during most reformattings.) That way, it can reinstall itself after the reformatting is completed.

Are there ways to protect data contained on mobile devices? Smartphones can be vulnerable to unauthorized access if they are left unattended or are stolen. Although some devices offer basic protection features (such as password protection), sensitive business information often requires an additional level of protection. Security software such as TealLock from TealPoint Software (**tealpoint.com**) offers additional protection features such as data encryption and protection against attempts to break into a device through "brute force" attacks (running a program to guess all possible passwords). Most programs feature optional data self-destruct modes (sometimes known as **bomb software**) that destroy data on both internal memory and external data cards if repeated attempts are made to crack passwords.

Figure 36 | COMPUTER SECURITY CHECKLIST

	Yes	No
Virus and Spyware Protection		
Is antivirus and antispyware software installed on all your computers?		
Is the antivirus and antispyware software configured to update itself automatically and regularly?		
Is the software set to scan your computer on a regular basis (at least weekly) for viruses and spyware?		
Firewall		
Do all your computers have firewall software installed and activated before connecting to the Internet?		
Is your router also able to function as a hardware firewall?		
Have you tested your firewall security by using the free software available at **grc.com**?		
Wireless Security		
Have you changed the default password for your router?		
Have you changed the name (SSID) of your network and turned off SSID broadcasting?		
Have you enabled WPA or WEP encryption for your network?		
Software Updates		
Have you configured your operating systems (Windows, OS X) to install new software patches and updates automatically?		
Is other software installed on your computer (such as Microsoft Office) configured for automatic updates?		
Is the Web browser you are using the latest version?		

How can I ensure that I've covered all aspects of protecting my computer? The checklist in Figure 36 is a guide to ensure you didn't miss any critical aspects of security. If you've addressed all of these issues, then you can feel reasonably confident that your Internet access will be secure and free from problems.

Taking a few precautions regarding your data security can provide huge benefits such as peace of mind and the avoidance of time spent correcting problems. So enjoy your computing experiences, but do so safely.

1. From which types of viruses do I need to protect my computer?

A computer virus is a program that attaches itself to another program and attempts to spread to other computers when files are exchanged. Computer viruses can be grouped into five categories: (1) boot-sector viruses, (2) logic bombs and time bombs, (3) worms, (4) scripts and macros, and (5) encryption viruses. Once run, they perform their malicious duties in the background and are often invisible to the user.

2. What can I do to protect my computer from viruses?

The best defense against viruses is to install antivirus software. You should update the software on a regular basis and configure it to examine all e-mail attachments for viruses. You should periodically run a complete virus scan on your computer to ensure that no viruses have made it onto your hard drive.

3. How can hackers attack my computing devices, and what harm can they cause?

A hacker is defined as anyone who breaks into a computer system unlawfully. Hackers can use software to break into almost any computer connected to the Internet (unless proper precautions are taken). Once hackers gain access to a computer, they can potentially (1) steal personal or other important information, (2) damage and destroy data, or (3) use the computer to attack other computers.

4. What is a firewall, and how does it keep my computer safe from hackers?

Firewalls are software programs or hardware devices designed to keep computers safe from hackers. By using a personal firewall, you can close open logical ports to invaders and potentially make your computer invisible to other computers on the Internet.

5. How do I create secure passwords and manage all of my passwords?

Secure passwords contain a mixture of upper- and lowercase letters, numbers, and symbols, and are at least 14 characters long. Passwords should not contain words that are in the dictionary or easy-to-guess personal information (like your pet's name). Online password checkers can be used to evaluate the strength of your passwords. Utilities built into Web browsers and Internet security software can be used to manage your passwords and alleviate the need to remember numerous complex passwords.

6. How can I surf the Internet anonymously and use biometric authentication devices to protect my data?

The current versions of the popular browsers include tools (such as Chrome's Incognito feature) that hide your surfing activities by not recording Web sites that you visit, or files that you download, in your browser's history files. Biometric authentication devices use a physical attribute (such as a fingerprint) that is not easily duplicated to control access to data files or computing devices. Some notebooks today feature fingerprint readers and facial recognition software to control access.

7. How do I manage online annoyances such as spyware and spam?

The Web is filled with annoyances such as spam, pop-ups, cookies, spyware, and scams such as phishing that make surfing the Web frustrating and sometimes dangerous. Software tools help to prevent or reduce spam, adware, and spyware, while exercising caution can prevent serious harm caused by phishing, pharming, and other Internet scams and hoaxes.

summary

8. **What data do I need to back up, and what are the best methods for doing so?**

Data files created by you (such as Word and Excel files) or purchased by you (such as music files) need to be backed up in case they are inadvertently deleted or damaged. Application software (such as Microsoft Office) may need to be reinstalled if files are damaged, so backups (usually the DVDs or CDs the application came on) must be maintained. Web sites such as Adrive and Skydrive are great for backing up individual files. External hard drives are popular choices for holding image backups of your entire system. Windows 7 and OS X contain solid backup tools that help automate backup tasks.

9. **What is social engineering, and how do I avoid falling prey to phishing and hoaxes?**

Social engineering schemes use human interaction, deception, and trickery to fool people into revealing sensitive information such as credit card numbers and passwords. Phishing schemes usually involve e-mails that direct the unwary to a Web site that appears to be legitimate (such as a bank site) but is specifically designed to capture personal information for committing fraud. To avoid phishing scams, you should never reply directly to any e-mail asking you for personal information, and never click on a link in an e-mail to go to a Web site. You can research topics you believe to be hoaxes at sites such as Snopes (**snopes.com**).

10. **How do I protect my physical computing assets from environmental hazards, power surges, and theft?**

Computing devices should be kept in clean environments free from dust and other particulates and should not be exposed to extreme temperatures (either hot or cold). You should protect all electronic devices from power surges by hooking them up through surge protectors, which will protect them from most electrical surges that could damage the devices. Notebook computers can be protected from theft either by attaching alarms to them or by installing software that will help recover the computer, if stolen, by reporting the computer's whereabouts when it is connected to the Internet.

key terms

adware

antivirus software

backdoor program

backup

biometric authentication device

black-hat hacker

bomb software

boot-sector virus

botnet

cookie

cybercrime

cybercriminal

cyberloafing

data file

denial-of-service (DoS) attack

distributed denial-of-service
(DDoS) attack

drive-by download

dynamic addressing

e-mail virus

encryption virus

firewall

hacker

hoax

identity theft

image backup (system backup)

incremental backup (partial backup)

inoculation

Internet protocol address (IP address)

keystroke logger

logic bomb

logical port

logical port blocking

macro virus

malware

master boot record

multipartite virus

network address translation (NAT)

packet

packet filtering

packet sniffer

personal firewall

pharming

phishing

polymorphic virus

pretexting

program file

quarantining

script

script kiddy

social engineering

spam

spam filter

spyware

static addressing

stealth virus

surge protector

time bomb

Trojan horse

uninterruptible power supply
(UPS)

urban legend

virus

virus signature

white-hat hacker

whole-house surge protector

worm

zombie

Word Bank

- adware
- antivirus software
- backup(s)
- distributed denial-of-service (DDoS)
- firewall

- hacker(s)
- identity theft
- keystroke logger(s)
- logical port(s)
- phishing

- social engineering
- spyware
- surge protector
- virus
- zombie(s)

Instructions: Fill in the blanks using the words from the Word Bank above.

Emily learned a lot about computer security in her computer literacy class. She already knew it was important to exercise caution when using the Internet because she had been the victim of (1) _____, which destroyed her credit rating. A(n) (2) _____ had obtained her credit card information by posing as an employee of her bank, using a method known as (3) _____. In her class, Emily learned that hackers could install (4) _____, a type of software that will capture everything she types, to steal her personal information. And one of Emily's classmates received a (5) _____ e-mail that directed her to a fake Web site that looked like her bank's Web site and resulted in her bank account information being stolen. The computers in the lab at school had just been cleaned of (6) _____ software that was displaying annoying pop-up advertisements. The computer technician who fixed this problem indicated that (7) _____ software, which was monitoring computer user activity, was often inadvertently installed on lab computers by students downloading files.

Emily found out that her router could be configured as a(n) (8) _____ to repel malicious hacking mischief. Turning off the unused (9) _____ would repel most attacks on her home network. With this protection, it was unlikely that a hacker would turn her PC into a(n) (10) _____ to launch (11) _____ attacks. However, after the scare with the Conficker (12) _____, Emily was careful to warn her family not to open files from untrusted sources. She also made sure all of the computers in her home had (13) _____ installed to protect them from viruses. For extra security, Emily installed an external hard drive so that she could create (14) _____ of her data files, and she replaced her power strip with a(n) (15) _____ to make sure power spikes didn't ruin her computer after all of the other precautions she'd taken.

While attending college, you are working at a company that manufactures industrial adhesives. Recently, the company computers have been behaving strangely and running slowly. Your investigation revealed that although antivirus software was initially installed on the company computers, the subscriptions have lapsed and the software is out of date. It also appears that no antispyware software was ever deployed. Your boss heard that you are taking a computer course and has asked you to run a seminar to educate management about the potential problems and solutions.

Instructions: Using the preceding scenario, draft an antivirus and antispyware plan for the company using as many of the keywords from the chapter as you can. Be sure that the company managers, who are unfamiliar with many computer terms, can understand the report.

Securing Your System: Protecting Your Digital Data and Devices

Instructions: Answer the multiple-choice and true–false questions below for more practice with key terms and concepts from this chapter.

Multiple Choice

1. Computer viruses that hide in memory to escape detection are known as
   a. logic bombs.
   b. Trojan horses.
   c. stealth viruses.
   d. multipartite viruses.

2. Viruses that that feature a series of commands hidden on a web site are called
   a. boot-sector viruses.
   b. script viruses.
   c. polymorphic viruses.
   d. time bombs.

3. Antivirus software segregates infected files to prevent further spread in a process known as
   a. inoculation. c. disinfection.
   b. quarantine. d. eradication.

4. Hackers without sophisticated computer knowledge who use tools developed by others to break into systems are called
   a. black-hat hackers.
   b. script kiddies.
   c. amateur hackers.
   d. white-hat hackers.

5. Which are programs that pretend to be a useful program but do something malicious on your computer?
   a. Trojan horses
   b. Backdoor programs
   c. Zombies
   d. Spyware

6. Large groups of software programs that run automatically on many computers at the same time often to perpetrate DoS attacks are known as
   a. Trojan horses.
   b. backdoor programs.
   c. zombie webs.
   d. botnets.

7. When hackers use many zombie computers to launch an attack on another computer or Web site, the attack is known as a
   a. zombie infestation.
   b. distributed denial-of-service attack.
   c. phishing attack.
   d. pharming plague.

8. Which are the virtual pathways into a computer that firewalls close?
   a. Packet gateways
   b. IP addresses
   c. Logical ports
   d. Data paths

9. Programs that download to your computer, usually without your knowledge, for the purpose of collecting information, is a type of cyberannoyance known as
   a. pharmware.
   b. adware.
   c. spyware.
   d. bloatware.

10. A backup of the entire contents of your hard drive is knows as
    a. a system backup.
    b. an incremental backup.
    c. an image backup.
    d. an incremental backup.

True–False

___F___ 1. An incremental backup back ups all files on your computer in a specified location.
___T___ 2. Even a properly installed surge protector may fail to protect a computer from all power surges.
___T___ 3. Phishing is a form of social engineering.
___F___ 4. When malicious code is planted on your computer that interferes with your browser's ability to find Web addresses, it is known as *phishing*.
___T___ 5. If a password includes numbers, symbols, and upper- and lowercase letters, it is considered to be a strong password.

making the
transition to...
next semester

making the
transition to...
next semester

1. Backup Procedures

After reading this chapter, you know you should have a good backup strategy in place for your key data. Consider the following and prepare answers in an appropriate format as directed by your instructor.

a. How often do you back up critical data files such as homework files? What type of device do you use for backing up files? Where do you store the backups to ensure they won't be destroyed if a major disaster (such as a fire) destroys your computer? Do you use online sites for file backups?

b. List the applications (such as Microsoft Office) that are currently installed on your computer. Where is the media (DVDs) for your application software stored? For any software you purchased in an Internet download, have you burned a copy of the installation files to DVD in case you need to reinstall the software?

c. Have you ever made an image backup of your entire system? If so, what software do you use for image backups, and where are the image backups stored? If not, research image backup software on the Internet and find an appropriate package to use. Will you need to purchase an additional backup device to hold your image backup or does your current device have room for an image backup? If you need a new device, find one on the Internet that is appropriate. What is the total cost of the software and hardware you will need to implement your image backup strategy?

2. Connecting Your Computer to Public Networks

In the course of your education, you are constantly connecting your notebook to various wireless public networks such as those in the school library and neighborhood coffee shop. As you know from reading this chapter, you are more vulnerable to hackers when connected to a wireless network in a public place. Conduct research on the Internet about surfing at public hot spots and prepare a list of sensible precautions for you and your classmates to take when surfing on an open network.

3. Botnet Awareness

Botnets are serious computer infestations that affect large numbers of computers at one time. Still, many students are unaware of this threat even as botnets strike college campuses. Using the Internet, research botnets and prepare a short flyer for your fellow students that explains the threats posed by botnets and software that can be used to detect botnets.

4. Internet Security Suites

Full-featured Internet security suites offer comprehensive protection for your computer. But how do you know which suite meets your needs? Research the features of three Internet security suites such as Norton Internet Security, AVG Internet Security, Kaspersky Internet Security, Trend Micro Internet Security, or McAfee Internet Security. Prepare a document for your instructor comparing the features and prices of each security suite for a home with four computers. Explain which security suite you would choose for your home and why you would choose it.

Securing Your System: Protecting Your Digital Data and Devices

1. File Backup Strategies

Your employer was recently the victim of a break-in, and all three dozen of its computers were stolen. Your company lost invaluable data because there was no comprehensive backup strategy in place for its computers. Your boss has asked you to prepare a report outlining a new file backup plan for the company. While preparing your report, consider the following:

a. How often should computer data be backed up? Should full backups or incremental backups be performed? Are image backups necessary?

b. Eighteen employees have notebook computers that they take off company premises. How will backups for notebooks be handled?

c. Research companies that provide online backup solutions for businesses. Which one provides the most cost effective solution for backing up three dozen computers? Can backups be performed automatically as employees change data files?

2. Securing Customer Data

Many corporations are collecting vast amounts of sensitive data (such as credit card numbers, birth dates, etc.) about their customers. Assume you are working for a business that accepts orders for merchandise through a Web site. Answer the following questions:

a. What types of information should you collect from your customers? What information couldn't you justify collecting from your customers using a valid business reason (i.e., Social Security number)?

b. Your company would like to send e-mails to customers on their birthdays, offering them a special discount on merchandise purchased within one week of their birthday. How would you explain to customers why you are collecting their birth dates, and what measures would you need to take to keep this data secure?

c. How would you ensure that information shared with third parties (such as delivery companies) is kept secure?

d. If your computer system was compromised and customer data was stolen, what would you say to customers regarding the loss of their personal data? What steps would you recommend your customers take to prevent identity theft due to your losing control of their data?

3. Is Your Computer Vulnerable?

Visit Gibson Research (**grc.com**) and run the company's ShieldsUP and LeakTest programs on your personal computer.

a. Did your computer get a clean report? If not, what potential vulnerabilities did the testing programs detect? If ports were shown as being vulnerable, research what these ports do and explain what steps you will take to protect them.

b. A properly configured firewall protects your computer from port vulnerabilities. Use the Internet to research firewall products and find three free firewall products. Which one appears to provide the best protection?

c. Besides adding a firewall to your system, what other measures should you take to protect your system from exploitation by hackers?

4. Computer Security Careers

Computer security professionals are among the highest paid employees in information technology organizations. Using employment sites such as **Monster.com**, **computerjobs.com**, and **dice.com**, research computer security jobs available in the state where your school is located (try searching "computer security"). Select three entry-level computer security jobs from different employers and prepare a document comparing the following: What are the educational requirements for computer security jobs? What job skills are required? How much prior work experience are firms looking for? Are programming skills required? With cloud computing becoming more popular, how will that affect the outlook for computer security jobs?

Securing Your System: Protecting Your Digital Data and Devices

Instructions: Albert Einstein used *Gedankenexperiments*, or critical thinking questions, to develop his theory of relativity. Some ideas are best understood by experimenting with them in our own minds. The following critical thinking questions are designed to demand your full attention but require only a comfortable chair—no technology.

1. **Protecting Your Home Network**

   Many people have networks in their homes. Consider the network installed in your home (or in a friend's home if you don't have a network).
   a. Is your network set up to provide adequate protection against hackers? If not, what would you need to do to make it secure?
   b. Are the computers on your home network protected against viruses and malware? What software do you use for protection and how often is it updated? Have you ever had problems from a virus or spyware infestation? If so, how did you resolve the problem?

2. **Password Protection**

   You know from reading this chapter that secure passwords are essential to protecting your digital information. Consider the following:
   a. How many online accounts do you have that have passwords? List them. Are the passwords for these accounts secure, based on the suggestions proposed in this chapter? Do you change your passwords on a regular basis?
   b. How do you keep track of all of your passwords? Do you use password-management software? If so, what product are you using? How often do you change your master password? If you don't use password-management software, what methodology do you use for remembering and tracking your passwords?

3. **Shouldn't Protection Be Included?**

   The Uniform Commercial Code, which governs business in every state except Louisiana, covers the implied warranty of merchantability. This warranty's basic premise is that a company selling goods guarantees that their products will do what they are designed to do (i.e., a car will transport you from place to place) and that there are no significant defects in the product. But computers are routinely sold with only trial versions of antimalware software.
   a. Does the failure of OS manufacturers to include antimalware tools constitute a breach of the implied warranty of merchantability? Why or why not? Microsoft does have an antimalware product (Security Essentials), but it requires a separate download. Should Microsoft be required to include Security Essentials as part of the Windows product?
   b. Computer hardware manufacturers don't make OS software, but they sell computers that would be unusable without an OS. What responsibility do they have in regard to providing antimalware protection to their customers?

4. **Restricting Information to Keep You Safe**

   Many countries, such as China, have laws that control the content of the Internet and restrict their citizens' access to information. The United States, with the exception of specific areas such as cyberbullying and pornography, does not currently take steps to restrict its citizens' access to the Internet. Unfortunately, this freedom of information does carry some cost because some information on the Web can be potentially dangerous to the general public.
   a. Do you think the U.S. government should censor information on the Web, such as instructions for making weapons, to protect the general public? Why or why not? If you think there should be some censorship, do you think such a law would violate the First Amendment right to free speech? Explain your answer.
   b. Would you be willing to live with a lower level of information access to increase your sense of well being? What topics do you feel would make you feel more secure if they were censored?

Securing Your System: Protecting Your Digital Data and Devices

Protecting Your Local Real Estate Office

Problem

Computer networks with high-speed connections to the Internet are common in most businesses today. However, along with easy access to computing devices and the Web comes the danger of theft of digital assets.

Task

A recent graduate of your school has opened a 15-person real estate office in a neighboring town. He approached your instructor for help in ensuring that his computers are adequately protected from viruses, malware, and hackers. Because he is currently low on funds, he is hoping that there may be free software available that can adequately shield his company from harm.

Process

Break the class into three teams. Each team will be responsible for investigating one of the following issues:

1. **Firewalls**. Research free firewall software and locate at least three software options that can be deployed at the business. Be sure to concentrate on software that is easy to configure and requires little or no user interaction to be effective.
2. **Antivirus software**. Research alternatives that can be used to protect the computers in the office from virus infection. Find at least three alternatives and support your recommendations with reviews (from publications such as *PC Magazine* or *Consumer Reports*) that evaluate the free packages and compare them to commercial solutions.
3. **Antimalware software**. Research free packages that will offer protection from malware. Locate at least three alternatives and determine whether the recommended software can be updated automatically. (Many free versions require manual updates.) Most companies that provide free malware protection also offer commercial packages (for a fee) that provide automatic updates. You may need to recommend that the company purchase software to ensure that a minimum of employee intervention is needed to keep the software up to date.

Present your findings to your class and discuss the pros and cons of free and commercial software. Provide your instructor with a report suitable for eventual presentation to the owner of the real estate office.

Conclusion

With the proliferation of viruses and malware, it is essential to protect business (and home) computers and networks from destruction and disruption. Free alternatives might work, but you should ensure that you have done adequate research to determine the best possible protection solution for your particular situation.

In this exercise, you will research and then role-play a complicated ethical situation. The role you play may or may not match your own personal beliefs, but your research and use of logic will enable you to represent whichever view is assigned. An arbitrator will watch and comment on both sides of the arguments, and together the team will agree on an ethical solution.

Topic: Content Control (Censorship) to Protect Children

Many parents use Web filtering software (also known as content-control software) to protect their children from objectionable content on the Internet. However, the software is also widely used in libraries, schools, and other public places where people other than parents are making decisions about what information to restricted. In 2000, the U.S. federal government began requiring libraries to use content filtering software as a condition to receiving federal funds under the provisions of the Children's Internet Protection Act (CIPA). Libraries that don't receive federal funds still do not have to install filtering software unless their state (like Virginia in 2007) passes laws requiring them to do so to receive state funding. Upon installation of the software, it is up to the library administrators to decide what content is restricted (as guided by the provisions of laws such as CIPA). Therefore, content restriction can vary widely from library to library.

Research Areas to Consider

• United States Supreme Court case *United States v. American Library Association* (2003)

• Content-filtering software and First Amendment rights

• Violating children's free speech rights

• Children's Internet Protection Act (CIPA)

Process

Divide the class into teams.

1. Research the areas cited above and devise a scenario in which parents have complained about their child not being able to access a certain Web site needed for school research.
2. Team members should write a summary that provides background information for their character—for example, parent, library administrator, and arbitrator—and details their character's behaviors to set the stage for the role-playing event. Then, team members should create an outline to use during the role-playing event.
3. Team members should arrange a mutually convenient time to meet for the exchange, using the chat room feature of MyITLab, the discussion board feature of Blackboard, or meeting in person.
4. Team members should present their case to the class or submit a PowerPoint presentation for review by the rest of the class, along with the summary and resolution they developed.

Conclusion

As technology becomes ever more prevalent and integrated into our lives, more and more ethical dilemmas will present themselves. Being able to understand and evaluate both sides of the argument, while responding in a personally or socially ethical manner, will be an important skill.

Securing Your System: Protecting Your Digital Data and Devices

glossary

adware A program that downloads on your computer when you install a freeware program, game, or utility. Generally, adware enables sponsored advertisements to appear in a section of your browser window or as a pop-up ad box.

antivirus software Software that is specifically designed to detect viruses and protect a computer and files from harm.

backdoor program A program that enables a hacker to take complete control of a computer without the legitimate user's knowledge or permission.

backup A backup is a copy of computer files that you can use to replace the originals if they are lost or damaged.

biometric authentication device A device that uses some unique characteristic of human biology to identify authorized users.

black-hat hacker A hacker who uses his knowledge to destroy information or for illegal gain.

bomb software Software that destroys data on a computing device if someone continually tries to access information by guessing the password.

boot-sector virus A virus that replicates itself into the master boot record of a flash drive or hard drive.

botnet A large group of software applications (called *robots* or *bots*) that runs without user intervention on a large number of computers.

cookie A small text file that some Web sites automatically store on a client computer's hard drive when a user visits the site.

cybercrime Any criminal action perpetrated primarily through the use of a computer.

cybercriminal An individual who uses computers, networks, and the Internet to perpetrate crime.

cyberloafing Doing anything with a computer that is unrelated to a job (such as playing video games), while one is supposed to be working. Also called *cyberslacking*.

data file File that contains stored data.

denial of service (DoS) attack An attack that occurs when legitimate users are denied access to a computer system because a hacker is repeatedly making requests of that computer system that tie up its resources and deny legitimate users access.

distributed denial of service (DDoS) attack An automated attack that is launched from more than one zombie computer at the same time.

drive-by download The use of malicious software to attack your computer by downloading harmful programs onto your computer, without your knowledge, while you are surfing a Web site.

dynamic addressing The process of assigning Internet Protocol (IP) addresses when users log on using their In-

ternet service provider (ISP). The computer is assigned an address from an available pool of IP addresses.

e-mail virus A virus transmitted by e-mail that often uses the address book in the victim's e-mail system to distribute itself.

encryption virus A malicious program that searches for common data files and compresses them into a file using a complex encryption key, thereby rendering the files unusable.

firewall A software program or hardware device designed to prevent unauthorized access to computers or networks.

hacker Anyone who unlawfully breaks into a computer system (whether an individual computer or a network).

hoax An e-mail message or Web site that contains information that is untrue, and is published with the purpose of deceiving others.

identity theft The process by which someone uses personal information about someone else (such as the victim's name, address, and Social Security number) to assume the victim's identity for the purpose of defrauding others.

image backup (system backup) A copy of an entire computer system, created for restoration purposes.

incremental backup (partial backup) A type of backup that only backs up files that have changed since the last time those files were backed up.

inoculation A process used by antivirus software; compares old and current qualities of files to detect viral activity.

Internet Protocol address (IP address) The means by which all computers connected to the Internet identify each other. It consists of a unique set of four numbers separated by dots such as 123.45.178.91.

keystroke logger A type of spyware program that monitors keystrokes with the intent of stealing passwords, login IDs, or credit card information.

logic bomb A computer virus that runs when a certain set of conditions is met, such as when specific dates are keyed off the computer's internal clock.

logical port A virtual communications gateway or path that enables a computer to organize requests for information (such as Web page downloads and e-mail routing) from other networks or computers.

logical port blocking A condition in which a firewall is configured to ignore all incoming packets that request access to a certain port so that no unwanted requests will get through to the computer.

macro virus A virus that is distributed by hiding it inside a macro.

malware Software that is intended to render a system temporarily or permanently useless or to penetrate a computer system completely for purposes of information gathering. Examples include spyware, viruses, worms, and Trojan horses.

glossary

master boot record A small program that runs whenever a computer boots up.

multipartite virus Literally meaning "multipart" virus; a type of computer virus that attempts to infect both the boot sector and executable files at the same time.

network address translation (NAT) A process that firewalls use to assign internal Internet Protocol (IP) addresses on a network.

packet A small segment of data that is bundled for sending over transmission media. Each packet contains the address of the computer or peripheral device to which it is being sent.

packet filtering A feature found in firewalls that filters out unwanted data packets sent to specific logical ports.

packet sniffer A program that looks at (sniffs) each data packet as it travels on the Internet.

personal firewall A firewall specifically designed for home networks.

pharming Planting malicious code on a computer that alters the browser's ability to find Web addresses and directs users to bogus Web sites.

phishing The process of sending e-mail messages to lure Internet users into revealing personal information such as credit card or Social Security numbers or other sensitive information that could lead to identity theft.

polymorphic virus A virus that changes its virus signature (the binary pattern that makes the virus identifiable) every time it infects a new file. This makes it more difficult for antivirus programs to detect the virus.

pretexting The act of creating an invented scenario (the pretext) to convince someone to divulge information.

program file A file that is used in the running of software programs and does not store data.

quarantining The placement (by antivirus software) of a computer virus in a secure area on the hard drive so that it won't spread infection to other files.

script A list of commands (mini-programs or macros) that can be executed on a computer without user interaction.

script kiddy An amateur hacker who lacks sophisticated computer skills. These individuals are typically teenagers, who don't create programs used to hack into computer systems but instead use tools created by skilled hackers that enable unskilled novices to wreak the same havoc as professional hackers.

social engineering Any technique that uses social skills to generate human interaction for the purpose of enticing individuals to reveal sensitive information.

spam Unwanted or junk e-mail.

spam filter An option you can select in your e-mail account that places known or suspected spam messages into a folder other than your inbox.

spyware An unwanted piggyback program that downloads with the software you want to install from the Internet and then runs in the background of your system.

static addressing A means of assigning an Internet Protocol (IP) address that never changes and is most likely assigned manually by a network administrator.

stealth virus A virus that temporarily erases its code from the files where it resides and hides in the active memory of the computer.

surge protector A device that protects computers and other electronic devices from power surges.

time bomb A virus that is triggered by the passage of time or on a certain date.

Trojan horse A computer program that appears to be something useful or desirable (such as a game or a screen saver), but at the same time does something malicious in the background without the user's knowledge.

uninterruptible power supply (UPS) A device designed to power a computer from large batteries for a brief period during a loss of electrical power.

urban legend A hoax that becomes so well known that it is accepted by society as true even though it is false. Also known as an *urban myth*.

virus A computer program that attaches itself to another computer program (known as the host program) and attempts to spread itself to other computers when files are exchanged.

virus signature A portion of the virus code that is unique to a particular computer virus and makes it identifiable by antivirus software.

white-hat hacker A hacker who breaks into systems just for the challenge of it (and who doesn't wish to steal or wreak havoc on the systems). Such hackers tout themselves as experts who are performing a needed service for society by helping companies realize the vulnerabilities that exist in their systems.

whole-house surge protector A surge protector that is installed on (or near) the breaker panel of a home and protects all electronic devices in the home from power surges.

worm A program that attempts to travel between systems through network connections to spread infections. Worms can run independently of host file execution and are active in spreading themselves.

zombie A computer that is controlled by a hacker who uses it to launch attacks on other computer systems.

credits

Chapter opener	Robert F. Balazik\Shutterstock	Figure 8	Kevin Siers. © 2000 The Charlotte Observer. KING FEATURES SYNDICATE
Figure 1	Mauro Bighin\Shutterstock		

Securing Your System: Protecting Your Digital Data and Devices

Index

Page references followed by "f" indicate illustrated figures or photographs; followed by "t" indicates a table.